Learning HBase

Learn the fundamentals of HBase administration and development with the help of real-time scenarios

Shashwat Shriparv

BIRMINGHAM - MUMBAI

Learning HBase

First published: November 2014

Production reference: 1181114

Published by Packt Publishing Ltd.
Livery Place
35 Livery Street
Birmingham B3 2PB, UK.

ISBN 978-1-78398-594-4

www.packtpub.com

Credits

Author
Shashwat Shriparv

Reviewers
Ashutosh Bijoor
Chhavi Gangwal
Henry Garner
Nitin Pawar
Jing Song
Arun Vasudevan

Commissioning Editor
Akram Hussain

Acquisition Editor
Kevin Colaco

Content Development Editor
Prachi Bisht

Technical Editor
Pankaj Kadam

Copy Editors
Janbal Dharmaraj
Sayanee Mukherjee

Project Coordinator
Sageer Parkar

Proofreaders
Bridget Braund
Maria Gould
Lucy Rowland

Indexer
Tejal Soni

Graphics
Ronak Dhruv

Production Coordinator
Aparna Bhagat

Cover Work
Aparna Bhagat

About the Author

Shashwat Shriparv was born in Muzaffarpur, Bihar. He did his schooling from Muzaffarpur and Shillong, Meghalaya. He received his BCA degree from IGNOU, Delhi and his MCA degree from Cochin University of Science and Technology, Kerala (C-DAC Trivandrum).

He was introduced to Big Data technologies in early 2010 when he was asked to perform a proof of concept (POC) on Big Data technologies in storing and processing logs. He was also given another project, where he was required to store huge binary files with variable headers and process them. At this time, he started configuring, setting up, and testing Hadoop HBase clusters and writing sample code for them. After performing a successful POC, he initiated serious development using Java REST and SOAP web services, building a system to store and process logs to Hadoop using web services, and then storing these logs in HBase using homemade schema and reading data using HBase APIs and HBase-Hive mapped queries. Shashwat successfully implemented the project, and then moved on to work on huge binary files of size 1 to 3 TB, processing the header and storing metadata to HBase and files on HDFS.

Shashwat started his career as a software developer at C-DAC Cyber Forensics, Trivandrum, building mobile-related software for forensics analysis. Then, he moved to Genilok Computer Solutions, where he worked on cluster computing, HPC technologies, and web technologies. After this, he moved to Bangalore from Trivandrum and joined PointCross, where he started working with Big Data technologies, developing software using Java, web services, and platform as Big Data. He worked on many projects revolving around Big Data technologies, such as Hadoop, HBase, Hive, Pig, Sqoop, Flume, and so on at PointCross. From here, he moved to HCL Infosystems Ltd. to work on the UIDAI project, which is one of the most prestigious projects in India, providing a unique identification number to every resident of India. Here, he worked on technologies such as HBase, Hive, Hadoop, Pig, and Linux, scripting, managing HBase Hadoop clusters, writing scripts, automating tasks and processes, and building dashboards for monitoring clusters.

Acknowledgments

First, I would like to thank a few people from Packt Publishing: Kevin for encouraging me to write this book, Prachi for assisting and guiding me throughout the writing process, Pankaj for helping me out in technical editing, and all other contributors to this book.

I would like to thank all the developers, contributors, and forums of Hadoop, HBase, and Big Data technologies for giving the industry such awesome technologies and contributing to it continuously. Thanks to Lars and Noll for their contribution towards HBase and Hadoop, respectively.

I would like to thank some people who helped me to learn from life, including teachers at my college—Roshani ma'am (Principal), Namboothari sir, Santosh sir, Manjush ma'am, Hudlin Leo ma'am, and my seniors Jitesh sir, Nilanchal sir, Vaidhath sir, Jwala sir, Ashutosh sir, Anzar sir, Kishor sir, and all my friends in Batch 6. I dedicate this book to my friend, Nikhil, who is not in this world now. Special thanks to Ratnakar Mishra and Chandan Jha for always being with me and believing in me. Thanks also go out to Vineet, Shashi bhai, Shailesh, Rajeev, Pintu, Darshna, Priya, Amit, Manzar, Sunil, Ashok bhai, Pradeep, Arshad, Sujith, Vinay, Rachana, Ashwathi, Rinku, Pheona, Lizbeth, Arun, Kalesh, Chitra, Fatima, Rajesh, Jasmin, and all my friends from C-DAC Trivendrum college. I thank all my juniors, seniors, and friends in college. Thanks to all my colleagues at C-DAC Cyber Forensic: Sateesh sir, my project manager; Anwer Reyaz. J, an enthusiast who is always encouraging; Bibin bhai sahab; Ramani sir; Potty sir; Bhadran sir; Thomas sir; Satish sir; Nabeel sir; Balan sir; Abhin sir; and others. I would also like to thank Mani sir; Raja sir; my friends and teammates: Maruthi Kiran, Chethan, Alok, Tariq, Sujatha, Bhagya, and Mukesh; Sri Gopal sir, my team leader; and all my other colleagues from PointCross. I thank Ramesh Krishnan sir, Manoj sir, Vinod sir, Nand Kishor sir, and my teammates Varun bhai sahab, Preeti Gupta, Kuldeep bhai sahab, and all my colleagues at HCL Infosystems Ltd. and UIDAI. I would also like to thank Satish sir; Sudipta sir; my manager, Atul sir; Pradeep; Nikhil; Mohit; Brijesh; Kranth; Ashish Chopara; Sudhir; and all my colleagues at Cognilytics, Inc.

Currently, he is working with Cognilytics, Inc. on Big Data technologies, HANA, and other high-performance technologies.

You can find out more about him at https://github.com/shriparv and http://helpmetocode.blogspot.com. You can connect with him on LinkedIn at http://www.linkedin.com/pub/shashwat-shriparv/19/214/2a9. You can also e-mail him at dwivedishashwat@gmail.com.

Shashwat has worked as a reviewer on the book *Pig Design Pattern*, *Pradeep Pasupuleti*, *Packt Publishing*. He also contributed to his college magazine, *InfinityTech*, as an editor.

Last but not the least, I would like to thank papa, Dr. Rameshwar Dwivedi; mummy, Smt. Rewa Dwivedi; bhai, Vishwas Priambud; sister-in-law, Ragini Dwivedi; sweet sister, Bhumika; brother-in-law, Chandramauli Dwivedi; and new members of my family, Vasu and Atmana.

If I missed any names, it does not mean that I am not thankful to them, they all are in my heart and I am thankful to everyone who has come in my life and left their mark. Also, thanking is not in any order.

About the Reviewers

Ashutosh Bijoor (Ash) is Chief Technology Officer at Accion Labs India Private Limited. He has over 20 years of experience in the technology industry with customers ranging from start-ups to large multinationals in a wide range of industries, including high tech, engineering, software, insurance, banking, chemicals, pharmaceuticals, healthcare, media, and entertainment. He is experienced in leading and managing cross-functional teams through an entire product development life cycle.

Ashutosh is skilled in emerging technologies, software architectures, framework design, and agile process definition. He has implemented enterprise solutions as well as commercial products in domains such as Big Data, business intelligence, graphics and image processing, sound and video processing, and advanced text search and analytics.

His e-mail ID is `ashutosh.bijoor@accionlabs.com`. You can also visit his website at `http://bijoor.me`.

Chhavi Gangwal is currently associated with Impetus Infotech (India) Pvt. Ltd. as a technical lead. With over 7 years of experience in the IT industry, she has worked on various dimensions of social media and the Web and witnessed the rise of Big Data first hand.

Presently, Chhavi is leading the development of Kundera, a JPA 2.0-compliant object-datastore mapping library for NoSQL data stores. She is also actively involved in the product management and development of multitude of Big Data tools. Apart from a working knowledge of several NoSQL data stores, Java, PHP, and different JavaScript frameworks, her passion lies in product designing and learning the latest technologies. Connect with Chhavi on `https://www.linkedin.com/profile/view?id=58308893`.

Nitin Pawar started his career as a release engineer with Veritas Systems, and so, the quality of software systems is always the main goal in his approach towards work. He has been lucky to work in multiple work profiles at companies such as Yahoo! for almost 5 years, where he learned a lot about the Hadoop ecosystem. After this, he worked with start-ups in analytics and Big Data domains, helping them design backend analytics infrastructures and platforms.

He enjoys solving problems and helping others facing technical issues. Reviewing this book gave him a better understanding of the HBase system, and he hopes that the readers will like it too.

He has also reviewed the book *Securing Hadoop*, *Sudheesh Narayanan*, and a video, *Building Hadoop Clusters [Video]*, *Sean Mikha*, both by Packt Publishing.

Jing Song has been working in the software industry as an engineer for more than 14 years since she graduated school. She enjoys solving problems and learning about new technologies in the Computer Science domain. Her interests and experiences lie across multiple tiers such as web-frontend GUI to middleware, middleware to backend SQL RDBMS, and NoSQL data storage. In the last 5 years, she has mainly focused on enterprise application performance and cloud computing areas. Jing currently works for Apple as a tech lead, leading various Java applications from design to implementation and performance tuning.

Arun Vasudevan is a technical lead at Accion Labs India Private Limited. He specializes in Business Analytics and Visualization and has worked on solutions in various industry verticals, including insurance, telecom, and retail. He specializes in developing applications on Big Data technologies, including Hadoop stack, Cloud technologies, and NoSQL databases. He also has expertise on cloud infrastructure setup and management using OpenStack and AWS APIs.

Arun is skilled in Java J2EE, JavaScript, relational databases, NoSQL technologies, and visualization using custom-built JavaScript visualization tools such as D3JS. Arun manages a team that delivers business analytics and visualization solutions.

His e-mail address is `arun.vasudevan@accionlabs.com`. You can also visit his LinkedIn account at `https://www.linkedin.com/profile/view?id=40201159`.

www.PacktPub.com

Support files, eBooks, discount offers, and more

For support files and downloads related to your book, please visit www.PacktPub.com.

Did you know that Packt offers eBook versions of every book published, with PDF and ePub files available? You can upgrade to the eBook version at www.PacktPub.com and as a print book customer, you are entitled to a discount on the eBook copy. Get in touch with us at service@packtpub.com for more details.

At www.PacktPub.com, you can also read a collection of free technical articles, sign up for a range of free newsletters and receive exclusive discounts and offers on Packt books and eBooks.

https://www2.packtpub.com/books/subscription/packtlib

Do you need instant solutions to your IT questions? PacktLib is Packt's online digital book library. Here, you can search, access, and read Packt's entire library of books.

Why subscribe?

- Fully searchable across every book published by Packt
- Copy and paste, print, and bookmark content
- On demand and accessible via a web browser

Free access for Packt account holders

If you have an account with Packt at www.PacktPub.com, you can use this to access PacktLib today and view 9 entirely free books. Simply use your login credentials for immediate access.

I would like to thank god for giving me this opportunity.
I dedicate this book to baba, dadi, nana, and nani.

Table of Contents

Preface

This book will provide a top-down approach to learning HBase, which will be useful for both novices and experts. You will start learning configuration, code to maintenance, and troubleshooting—a kind of all-in-one HBase knowledge bank. This will be a step-by-step guide, which will help you work on HBase. The book will include day-to-day activities using HBase administration, and the implementation of Hadoop, plus HBase cluster setup from ground approach. The book will cover a complete list of use cases and explanations to implement HBase as an effective Big Data tool. It will also help you understand the layout and structure of HBase. There are lots of books available on the market on HBase, but they lack something in them; some of them focuses more on configuration and some on coding, but this book will provide a kind of start-to-end approach, which will be useful for a person with zero knowledge in HBase to the person proficient in HBase. This book is a complete guide to HBase administration and development with real-time scenarios and an operation guide.

This book will provide an understanding of what HBase is like, where it came from, who all are involved, why should we consider using it, why people are using it, when to use it, and how to use it. This book will give overall information about the HBase ecosystem. It's more like an HBase-confusion-buster book, a book to read and implement in real life. The book has in-depth theory and practical examples on HBase features. This theoretical and practical approach clears doubts on Hadoop and HBase. It provides complete guidance on configuration/management/troubleshooting of HBase clusters and their operations. The book is targeted at administration and development aspects of HBase; administration with troubleshooting, setup, and development with client and server APIs. This book also enables you to design schema, code in Java, and write shell scripts to work with HBase.

What this book covers

Chapter 1, Understanding the HBase Ecosystem, introduces HBase in detail, and discusses its features, its evolution, and its architecture. We will compare HBase with traditional databases and look at add-on features and the various underlying components, and its uses in the industry.

Chapter 2, Let's Begin with HBase, deals with the HBase components in detail, their internal architecture, communication between different components, how it provides scalability, as well as the HBase reading and writing cycle process, HBase housekeeping tasks, region-related operations, the different components needed for a HBase cluster configuration, and some basic OS tuning.

Chapter 3, Let's Start Building It, lets us proceed ahead with building an HBase cluster. In this chapter, you will find information on the various components and the places we can get it from. We will start configuring the cluster and consider all the parameters and optimization tweaks while building the Hadoop and HBase cluster. One section in the chapter will focus on the various component-level and OS-level parameters for an optimized cluster.

Chapter 4, Optimizing the HBase/Hadoop Cluster, teaches us to optimize the HBase cluster according to the production environment and running cluster troubleshooting tasks. We will look at optimization on hardware, OS, software, and network parameters. This chapter will also teach us how we can optimize Hadoop for a better HBase.

Chapter 5, The Storage, Structure Layout, and Data Model of HBase, discusses HBase's data model and its various data model operations for fetching and writing data in HBase tables. We will also consider some use cases in order to design schema in HBase.

Chapter 6, HBase Cluster Maintenance and Troubleshooting, covers all the aspects of HBase cluster management, operation, and maintenance. Once a cluster is built and in operation, we need to look after it, continuously tune it up, and troubleshoot in order to have a healthy HBase cluster. We will also study the commands available with HBase and Hadoop shell.

Chapter 7, Scripting in HBase, explains an automation process using HBase and shell scripts. We will learn to write scripts as an administrator or developer to automate various data-model-related tasks. We will also read about various backup and restore options available in HBase and how to perform them.

Chapter 8, Coding HBase in Java, teaches Java coding in HBase. We will start with basic Java coding in HBase and learn about Java APIs available for client requests. You will also learn to build a basic client in Java, which can be used to contact an HBase cluster for various operations using Java code.

Chapter 9, Advance Coding in Java for HBase, focuses more on Java coding in HBase. It is a more detailed learning about all the different kind of APIs, classes, methods, and interfaces available in Java for HBase. You will also see the different kind of web services or thrift services, which you can use to ease up the coding and using the inbuilt service and not implementing the entire architecture code in Java. This chapter has a section that includes a discussion of some special features of HBase and some open source projects available, which can be used in coordination with HBase for a production cluster and a project.

Chapter 10, HBase Use Cases, discusses the use cases in the industry, which are being used with HBase as their underlying technology.

What you need for this book

The following are the prerequisites you must have before starting with this book:

- Any flavor of Linux (Ubuntu, Red Hat, Debian, CentOS, Fedora, openSUSE, or any other Linux flavor)
- Oracle Java v1.6 or higher

You can go for any one of the following sets.

If you prefer Apache:

- Apache Hadoop
- Apache HBase
- ZooKeeper

If you prefer Cloudera:

- Cloudera Hadoop
- Cloudera HBase
- Cloudera ZooKeeper

Who this book is for

If you are an administrator or developer who wants to enter the world of Big Data and BigTable and would like to learn about HBase, this is the book for you. This book starts with the basic theory and has a practical approach to make it suitable for all readers.

Conventions

In this book, you will find a number of styles of text that distinguish between different kinds of information. Here are some examples of these styles, and an explanation of their meaning.

Code words in text, database table names, folder names, filenames, file extensions, pathnames, dummy URLs, user input, and Twitter handles are shown as follows: "This includes information about the location of the .META. table."

A block of code is set as follows:

```
Configuration conf = HBaseConfiguration.create();
HTable table = new HTable(conf, "logtable");
Scan scan = new Scan();
scan.setMaxVersions(2);
ResultScanner result = table.getScanner(scan);
for (Result result: scanner) {
    System.out.println("Rows which were scanned : " +
      Bytes.toString(result.getRow()));
}
```

Any command-line input or output is written as follows:

```
sudo yum clean all;
sudo yum install hadoop-hdfs-namenode
sudo yum install hadoop-hdfs-secondarynamenode
sudo yum install hadoop-0.20-mapreduce-tasktrackerhadoop-hdfs-
datanode
sudo yum install hbase
```

New terms and **important words** are shown in bold. Words that you see on the screen, in menus or dialog boxes for example, appear in the text like this: "In the **Network Connections** window, click on **Edit...** and enter the information accordingly."

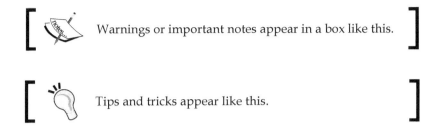

Warnings or important notes appear in a box like this.

Tips and tricks appear like this.

Reader feedback

Feedback from our readers is always welcome. Let us know what you think about this book—what you liked or may have disliked. Reader feedback is important for us to develop titles that you really get the most out of.

To send us general feedback, simply send an e-mail to feedback@packtpub.com, and mention the book title via the subject of your message.

If there is a topic that you have expertise in and you are interested in either writing or contributing to a book, see our author guide on www.packtpub.com/authors.

Customer support

Now that you are the proud owner of a Packt book, we have a number of things to help you to get the most from your purchase.

Downloading the example code

You can download the example code files for all Packt books you have purchased from your account at http://www.packtpub.com. If you purchased this book elsewhere, you can visit http://www.packtpub.com/support and register to have the files e-mailed directly to you.

Errata

Although we have taken every care to ensure the accuracy of our content, mistakes do happen. If you find a mistake in one of our books—maybe a mistake in the text or the code—we would be grateful if you would report this to us. By doing so, you can save other readers from frustration and help us improve subsequent versions of this book. If you find any errata, please report them by visiting http://www.packtpub.com/submit-errata, selecting your book, clicking on the **errata submission form** link, and entering the details of your errata. Once your errata are verified, your submission will be accepted and the errata will be uploaded on our website, or added to any list of existing errata, under the Errata section of that title. Any existing errata can be viewed by selecting your title from http://www.packtpub.com/support.

Piracy

Piracy of copyright material on the Internet is an ongoing problem across all media. At Packt, we take the protection of our copyright and licenses very seriously. If you come across any illegal copies of our works, in any form, on the Internet, please provide us with the location address or website name immediately so that we can pursue a remedy.

Please contact us at copyright@packtpub.com with a link to the suspected pirated material.

We appreciate your help in protecting our authors, and our ability to bring you valuable content.

Questions

You can contact us at questions@packtpub.com if you are having a problem with any aspect of the book, and we will do our best to address it.

1
Understanding the HBase Ecosystem

HBase is a horizontally scalable, distributed, open source, and a sorted map database. It runs on top of Hadoop file system that is **Hadoop Distributed File System (HDFS)**. HBase is a NoSQL nonrelational database that doesn't always require a predefined schema. It can be seen as a scaling flexible, multidimensional spreadsheet where any structure of data is fit with on-the-fly addition of new column fields, and fined column structure before data can be inserted or queried. In other words, **HBase** is a column-based database that runs on top of Hadoop distributed file system and supports features such as linear scalability (scale out), automatic failover, automatic sharding, and more flexible schema.

HBase is modeled on Google BigTable. It was inspired by Google BigTable, which is compressed, high-performance, proprietary data store built on the Google file system. HBase was a developed as a Hadoop subproject to support storage of structural data, which can take advantage of most distributed files systems (typically, the Hadoop Distributed File System known as HDFS).

The following table contains key information about HBase and its features:

Features	Description
Developed by	Apache
Written in	Java
Type	Column oriented
License	Apache License
Lacking features of relational databases	SQL support, relations, primary, foreign, and unique key constraints, normalization

Features	Description
Website	`http://hbase.apache.org`
Distributions	Apache, Cloudera
Download link	`http://mirrors.advancedhosters.com/apache/hbase/`
Mailing lists	<ul><li>The user list: `user-subscribe@hbase.apache.org`</li><li>The developer list: `dev-subscribe@hbase.apache.org`</li></ul>
Blog	`http://blogs.apache.org/hbase/`

HBase layout on top of Hadoop

The following figure represents the layout information of HBase on top of Hadoop:

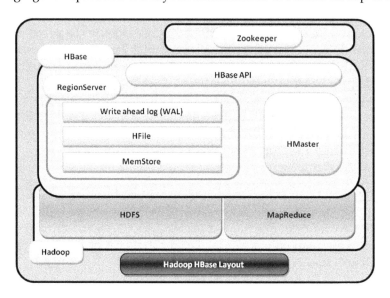

There is more than one ZooKeeper in the setup, which provides high availability of master status; a RegionServer may contain multiple rations. The RegionServers run on the machines where DataNodes run. There can be as many RegionServers as DataNodes. RegionServers can have multiple HRegions; one HRegion can have one HLog and multiple HFiles with its associate's MemStore.

HBase can be seen as a master-slave database where the master is called HMaster, which is responsible for coordination between client application and HRegionServer. It is also responsible for monitoring and recording metadata changes and management. Slaves are called HRegionServers, which serve the actual tables in form of regions. These regions are the basic building blocks of the HBase tables, which contain distribution of tables. So, HMaster and RegionServer work in coordination to serve the HBase tables and HBase cluster.

Usually, HMaster is co-hosted with Hadoop NameNode daemon process on a server and communicates to DataNode daemon for reading and writing data on HDFS. The RegionServer runs or is co-hosted on the Hadoop DataNodes.

Comparing architectural differences between RDBMs and HBase

Let's list the major differences between relational databases and HBase:

Relational databases	HBase
Uses tables as databases	Uses regions as databases
File systems supported are FAT, NTFS, and EXT	File system supported is HDFS
The technique used to store logs is commit logs	The technique used to store logs is **Write-Ahead Logs (WAL)**
The reference system used is coordinate system	The reference system used is ZooKeeper
Uses the primary key	Uses the row key
Partitioning is supported	Sharding is supported
Use of rows, columns, and cells	Use of rows, column families, columns, and cells

HBase features

Let's see the major features of HBase that make it one of the most useful databases for the current and future industry:

- **Automatic failover and load balancing**: HBase runs on top of HDFS, which is internally distributed and automatically recovered using multiple block allocation and replications. It works with multiple HMasters and region servers. This failover is also facilitated using HBase and RegionServer replication.

- **Automatic sharding**: An HBase table is made up of regions that are hosted by RegionServers and these regions are distributed throughout the RegionServers on different DataNodes. HBase provides automatic and manual splitting of these regions to smaller subregions, once it reaches a threshold size to reduce I/O time and overhead.

- **Hadoop/HDFS integration**: It's important to note that HBase can run on top of other file systems as well. While HDFS is the most common choice as it supports data distribution and high availability using distributed Hadoop, for which we just need to set some configuration parameters and enable HBase to communicate to Hadoop, an out-of-the-box underlying distribution is provided by HDFS.

- **Real-time, random big data access**: HBase uses **log-structured merge-tree (LSM-tree)** as data storage architecture internally, which merges smaller files to larger files periodically to reduce disk seeks.

- **MapReduce**: HBase has a built-in support of Hadoop MapReduce framework for fast and parallel processing of data stored in HBase.

 You can search for the package `org.apache.hadoop.hbase.mapreduce` for more details.

- **Java API for client access**: HBase has a solid Java API support (client/server) for easy development and programming.

- **Thrift and a RESTful web service**: HBase not only provides a thrift and RESTful gateway but also web service gateways for integrating and accessing HBase besides Java code (HBase Java APIs) for accessing and working with HBase.

- **Support for exporting metrics via the Hadoop metrics subsystem**: HBase provides **Java Management Extensions (JMX)** and exporting matrix for monitoring purposes with tools such as Ganglia and Nagios.

- **Distributed**: HBase works when used with HDFS. It provides coordination with Hadoop so that distribution of tables, high availability, and consistency is supported by it.

- **Linear scalability (scale out)**: Scaling of HBase is not scale up but scale out, which means that we don't need to make servers more powerful but we add more machines to its cluster. We can add more nodes to the cluster on the fly. As soon as a new RegionServer node is up, the cluster can begin rebalancing, start the RegionServer on the new node, and it is scaled up, it is as simple as that.

- **Column oriented**: HBase stores each column separately in contrast with most of the relational databases, which uses stores or are row-based storage. So in HBase, columns are stored contiguously and not the rows. More about row- and column-oriented databases will follow.

- **HBase shell support**: HBase provides a command-line tool to interact with HBase and perform simple operations such as creating tables, adding data, and scanning data. This also provides full-fledged command-line tool using which we can interact with HBase and perform operations such as creating table, adding data, removing data, and a few other administrative commands.

- **Sparse, multidimensional, sorted map database**: HBase is a sparse, multidimensional, sorted map-based database, which supports multiple versions of the same record.

- **Snapshot support**: HBase supports taking snapshots of metadata for getting the previous or correct state form of data.

HBase in the Hadoop ecosystem

Let's see where HBase sits in the Hadoop ecosystem. In the Hadoop ecosystem, HBase provides a persistent, structured, schema-based data store. The following figure illustrates the Hadoop ecosystem:

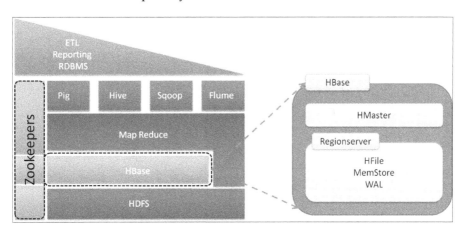

HBase can work as a separate entity on the local file system (which is not really effective as no distribution is provided) as well as in coordination with Hadoop as a separate but connected entity. As we know, Hadoop provides two services, a distributed files system (HDFS) for storage and a MapReduce framework for processing in a parallel mode. When there was a need to store structured data (data in the form of tables, rows and columns), which most of the programmers are already familiar with, the programmers were finding it difficult to process the data that was stored on HDFS as an unstructured flat file format. This led to the evolution of HBase, which provided a way to store data in a structural way.

Consider that we have got a CSV file stored on HDFS and we need to query from it. We would need to write a Java code for this, which wouldn't be a good option. It would be better if we could specify the data key and fetch the data from that file. So, what we can do here is create a schema or table with the same structure of CSV file to store the data of the CSV file in the HBase table and query using HBase APIs, or HBase shell using key.

Data representation in HBase

Let's look into the representation of rows and columns in HBase table:

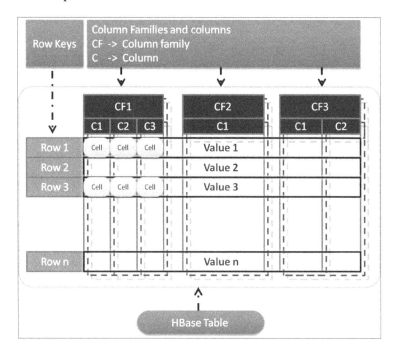

An HBase table is divided into rows, column families, columns, and cells. Row keys are unique keys to identify a row, column families are groups of columns, columns are fields of the table, and the cell contains the actual value or the data.

So, we have been through the introduction of HBase; now, let's see what Hadoop and its components are in brief. It is assumed here that you are already familiar with Hadoop; if not, following a brief introduction about Hadoop will help you to understand it.

Hadoop

Hadoop is an underlying technology of HBase, providing high availability, fault tolerance, and distribution. It is an Apache-sponsored, free, open source, Java-based programming framework which supports large dataset storage. It provides distributed file system and MapReduce, which is a distributed programming framework. It provides a scalable, reliable, distributed storage and development environment. Hadoop makes it possible to run applications on a system with tens to tens of thousands of nodes. The underlying distributed file system provides large-scale storage, rapid data access. It has the following submodules:

- **Hadoop Common**: This is the core component that supports the other Hadoop modules. It is like the master components facilitating communication and coordination between different Hadoop modules.

- **Hadoop distributed file system**: This is the underlying distributed file system, which is abstracted on the top of the local file system that provides high throughput of read and write operations of data on Hadoop.

- **Hadoop YARN**: This is the new framework that is shipped with newer releases of Hadoop. It provides job scheduling and job and resource management.

- **Hadoop MapReduce**: This is the Hadoop-based processing system that provides parallel processing of large data and datasets.

Other Hadoop subprojects are HBase, Hive, Ambari, Avro, Cassandra (Cassandra isn't a Hadoop subproject, it's a related project; they solve similar problems in different ways), Mahout, Pig, Spark, ZooKeeper (ZooKeeper isn't a Hadoop subproject. It's a dependency shared by many distributed systems), and so on. All of these have different usability and the combination of all these subprojects forms the Hadoop ecosystem.

Core daemons of Hadoop

The following are the core daemons of Hadoop:

- **NameNode**: This stores and manages all metadata about the data present on the cluster, so it is the single point of contact to Hadoop. In the new release of Hadoop, we have an option of more than one NameNode for high availability.
- **JobTracker**: This runs on the NameNode and performs the MapReduce of the jobs submitted to the cluster.
- **SecondaryNameNode**: This maintains the backup of metadata present on the NameNode, and also records the file system changes.
- **DataNode**: This will contain the actual data.
- **TaskTracker**: This will perform tasks on the local data assigned by the JobTracker.

The preceding are the daemons in the case of Hadoop v1 or earlier. In newer versions of Hadoop, we have ResourceManager instead of JobTracker, the node manager instead of TaskTrackers, and the YARN framework instead of a simple MapReduce framework. The following is the comparison between daemons in Hadoop 1 and Hadoop 2:

Hadoop 1	Hadoop 2
HDFS	
• NameNode • Secondary NameNode • DataNode	• NameNode (more than one active/standby) • Checkpoint node • DataNode
Processing	
• MapReduce v1 • JobTracker • TaskTracker	• YARN (MRv2) • ResourceManager • NodeManager • Application Master

Comparing HBase with Hadoop

As we now know what HBase and what Hadoop are, let's have a comparison between HDFS and HBase for better understanding:

Hadoop/HDFS	HBase
This provide file system for distributed storage	This provides tabular column-oriented data storage
This is optimized for storage of huge-sized files with no random read/write of these files	This is optimized for tabular data with random read/write facility
This uses flat files	This uses key-value pairs of data
The data model is not flexible	Provides a flexible data model
This uses file system and processing framework	This uses tabular storage with built-in Hadoop MapReduce support
This is mostly optimized for write-once read-many	This is optimized for both read/write many

Comparing functional differences between RDBMs and HBase

Lately, we are hearing about NoSQL databases such as HBase, so let's just understand what actually HBase has and lacks in comparison to conventional relational databases that have existed for so long now. The following table differentiates it well:

Relational database	HBase
This supports scale up. In other words, when more disk and memory processing power is needed, we need to upgrade it to a more powerful server.	This supports scale out. In other words, when more disk and memory processing power is needed, we need not upgrade the server. However, we need to add new servers to the cluster.

Relational database	HBase
This uses SQL queries for reading records from tables.	This uses APIs and MapReduce for accessing data from HBase tables.
This is row oriented, that is, each row is a contiguous unit of page.	This is column oriented, that is, each column is a contiguous unit of page.
The amount of data depends on configuration of server.	The amount of data does not depend on the particular machine but the number of machines.
It's Schema is more restrictive.	Its schema is flexible and less restrictive.
This has ACID support.	There is no built-in support for HBase.
This is suited for structured data.	This is suited to both structured and nonstructural data.
Conventional relational database is mostly centralized.	This is always distributed.
This mostly guarantees transaction integrity.	There is no transaction guaranty in HBase.
This supports JOINs.	This does not support JOINs.
This supports referential integrity.	There is no in-built support for referential integrity.

So with these differences, both have their own usability and use cases. When we have a small amount of data that can be accommodated in RDBMS without performance lagging, we can go with RDBMS.

When we need more **Online Transaction Processing (OLTP)** and the transaction type of processing, RDBMS is easy to go. When we have a huge amount of data (in terabytes and petabytes), we should look towards HBase, which is always better for aggregation on columns and faster processing.

We have gone through the word, column-oriented database, in the previous introduction; now let's discuss the difference between the column-oriented databases and the row-oriented databases, which are the traditional relational databases.

These column-oriented database systems have been shown to perform more than an order of magnitude, better than traditional row-oriented database systems on analytical workloads found in data warehouse systems, decision system, and business intelligence applications. These are more I/O-efficient for write-once read-many queries.

Logical view of row-oriented databases

The following figure shows how data is represented in relational databases:

Record Id	Name	Address	Telephone	Note
1	Aa	Aa Address	Aa Telephone	Aa Note
2	Bb	Bb Address	Bb Telephone	Bb Note
3	Cc	Cc Address	Cc Telephone	Cc Note
4	Dd	Dd Address	Dd Telephone	Dd Note
5	Ee	Ee Address	Ee Telephone	Ee Note

Logical view of column-oriented databases

The following figure shows how logically we can represent NoSQL/column-oriented databases such as HBase:

Record Id	Name	Address	Telephone	Note
1	Aa	Aa Address	Aa Telephone	Aa Note
2	Bb	Bb Address	Bb Telephone	Bb Note
3	Cc	Cc Address	Cc Telephone	Cc Note
4	Dd	Dd Address	Dd Telephone	Dd Note
5	Ee	Ee Address	Ee Telephone	Ee Note

Row-oriented data stores store rows in a contiguous unit on the page, and the number of rows are packed into a page. They are much faster for small numbers of rows and slow for aggregation. On the contrary, column-oriented data stores columns in a contiguous unit on the page, columns may extend up to millions of entries, so they run for many pages. These are much faster for aggregation and analytics. The root of column-oriented database systems can be traced to the 1970 when transposed file first appeared. Column-oriented data stores are better for compression than row-oriented data stores. The following is the comparison between these two:

Row-oriented data stores	Column-oriented data stores
These are efficient for addition/modification of records	These are efficient for reading data
They read pages containing entire rows	They read only needed columns

Row-oriented data stores	Column-oriented data stores
These are best for OLTP	These are not so optimized for OLTP yet
This serializes all the values in a row together, then the value in the next row, and so on	This serializes all the value of columns together and so on
Row data are stored in contiguous pages in memory or on disk	Columns are stored in pages in memory or on disk

Suppose the records of a table are stored in the pages of memory. When they need to be accessed, these pages are brought to the primary memory, if they are not already present in the memory.

If one row occupies a page and we need all specific column such as `salary` or `rate of interest` from all the rows for some kind of analytics, each page containing the columns has to be brought in the memory; so this page in page out will result in a lot of I/O, which may result in prolonged processing time.

In column-oriented databases, each column will be stored in pages. If we need to fetch a specific column, there will be less I/O as only the pages that contain the specified column needed to be brought in the main memory and read, and we need not bring and read all the pages containing rows/records henceforth into the memory. So the kind of queries where we need to just fetch specific columns and not whole record(s) or sets is served best in column-oriented database, which is useful for analytics wherein we can fetch some columns and do some mathematical operations such as sum and average.

Pros and cons of column-oriented databases

The following are pros of column-oriented database:

- This has built-in support for efficient and data compression.
- This supports fast data retrieval.
- Administration and configuration is simplified. It can be scaled out and hence is very easy to expand.
- This is good for high performance on aggregation queries (such as COUNT, SUM, AVG, MIN, and MAX).
- This is efficient for partitioning as it provides features of automatic sharding mechanism to distribute bigger regions to smaller ones.

The following are cons of column-oriented database:

- Queries with JOINs and data from many tables are not optimized.
- It records and deletes lot of updates and has to make frequent compaction and splits too. This reduces its storage efficiency.
- Partitioning or indexing schemes can be difficult to design as a relational concept is not implicit.

About the internal storage architecture of HBase

The following figure shows the principle algorithm and data structure HBase works on, that is, LSM-tree, and the way of merging, and precedes the explanation:

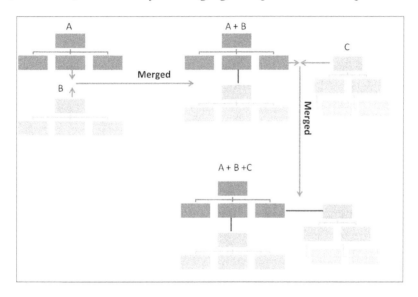

HBase stores file using LSM-tree, which maintains data in two separate parts that are optimized for underlying storage. This type of data structure depends on two structures, a current and smaller one in memory and a bigger one on the persistent disk, and once the part in memory becomes bigger than a certain limit, it is merged with the bigger structure that is stored on the disk using a merge sort algorithm and a new in-memory tree is created for newer insert requests. It transforms random data access into sequential data access, which improves read performance, and merging is a background process, which does not affect the foreground processing.

Getting started with HBase

We will discuss this section in a bit questionnaire manner, and will come to understand HBase with the help of scenarios and conditions.

When it started

The following figure shows the flow of HBase: birth, growth, and current status:

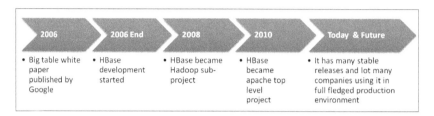

It all started in 2006 when a company called Powerset (later acquired by Microsoft) was looking forward to building a natural language search engine. The person responsible for the development was Jim Kellerman and there were also many other contributors. It was modeled around the Google BigTable white paper that came out in 2006, which was running on **Google File System (GFS)**.

It started with a TAR file with a random bunch of Java files with initial HBase code. It was first added to the `contrib` directory of Hadoop as a small subcomponent of Hadoop and with the dedicated effort for filling up gaps; it has slowly and steadily grown into a full-fledged project. It was first added with Hadoop 0.1.0 and as it become more and more feature rich and stable, it was promoted to Hadoop subproject and then slowly with more and more development and contribution from the HBase user and developer group, it has became one of the top-level projects at Apache.

The following figure shows HBase versions from the beginning till now:

Let's have a look at the year-by-year evolution of HBase's important features:

- **2006**: The idea of HBase started with the white paper of Google BigTable

- **2007**: Data compression on the per column family was made available, addition and deletion of column families online was added, script to start/stop HBase cluster was added, MapReduce connecter was added, HBase shell support was added, support of row and column filter was added, algorithm to distribute region was evenly added, first rest interface was added, and hosted the first HBase meetup

- **2008**: HBase 0.1.0 to 0.18.1, HBase moved to new SVN, HBase added as a contribution to Hadoop, HBase become Hadoop subproject, first separate release became available, and Ruby shell added

- **2009**: HBase 0.19.0 to 0.20.*, improvement in writing and scanning, batching of writing and scanning, block compression, HTable interface to REST, addition of binary comparator, addition of regular expression filters, and many more

- **2010 till date**: HBase 0.89.* - 0.94.*, support for HDFS durability, improvement in import flow, support for MurmurHash3, addition of daemon threads for NameNode and DataNode to indicate the VM or kernel-caused pause in application log, tags support for key value, running MapReduce over snapshot files, introduction of transparent encryption of HBase on disk data, addition of per key-value security, offline rebuilding `.META.` from file system data, snapshot support, and many more

For more information, just visit `https://issues.apache.org/jira/browse/HBASE` and explore more detailed explanations and more lists of improvements and the addition of new features.

- **0.96 to 1.0 and Future**: HBase Version 1 and higher, add utility for adorning HTTP context, fully high availability with Hadoop HA, rolling upgrades, improved failure detection and recovery, cell-level access security, inline cell tagging, quota and grouping, reverse scan, rolling upgrade, and it will be more useful for analytics purposes and helpful for data scientists

While we wait for new features in v1.0; we can always visit `http://hbase.apache.org` for the latest releases and features.

Here is the link from where we can download HBase versions:

`http://apache.mirrors.tds.net/hbase/stable`

Let's now discuss HBase and Hadoop compatibility and the features they provide together.

Prior to Hadoop v1.0, when DataNode used to crash, HBase Write-Ahead Log — the logfiles that maintain the read/write operation before the final writing is done to the MemStore — would be lost and hence the data too. This version of Hadoop integrated append branch into the main core, which increased the durability for HBase. Hadoop v1.0 has also implemented the facility of disk failure, making RegionServer more robust.

Hadoop v2.0 has integrated high availability of NameNode, which also enables HBase to be more reliable and robust by enabling the multiple HMaster instances. Now with this version of HBase, upgrading has become easy because it is made independent of HDFS upgrades. Let's see in the following table how recent versions of Hadoop have enhanced HBase on the basis of performance, availability, and features:

Criteria	Hadoop v1.0	Hadoop v2.0	Hadoop v2.x
Features	Durability using `hflush()`	• `hsync()` • snapshot • hard linking (https://issues.apache.org/jira/browse/HDFS-3370) • HBase-aware block placement	
Performance	Short-circuit read	• Native CRC • Datanodekeepalive	• Direct write API (HBase provides the utility classes and the ImportTSV tool itself to write directly into HFile. Then, using the `IncrementalLoadHFile`, these files are loaded into the regions managed by RS. Once these two steps are over, client can read the data normally) • Zero copy API (in this operation, the CPU does not copy data from one memory area to another. This is used to save on processing power and memory when sending files over a network) • Direct codec API (used at server side for writing cells to WAL as well as for sending edits as part of the distributed-splitting process)

Miscellaneous features in newer HBase are HBase isolation and allocation, online-automated repair of table integrity and region consistency problems, dynamic configuration changes, reverse scanning (stop row to start row), and many other features; users can visit `https://issues.apache.org/jira/browse/HBASE` for features and advancement of each HBase release.

HBase components and functionalities

Here let's discuss various components of HBase and their components recursively:

- ZooKeeper
- HMaster
- RegionServer
- Client
- Catalog tables

ZooKeeper

ZooKeeper is a high-performance, centralized, multicoordination service system for distributed application, which provides a distributed synchronization and group service to HBase.

It enables the users and developer to focus on the application logic and not on the coordination with the cluster, for which it provides some API that can be used by the developers to use and implement coordination task such as master server, and managing application and cluster communication system.

In HBase, ZooKeeper is used to elect a cluster master in order to keep track of available and online servers, and to keep the metadata of the cluster. ZooKeeper APIs provide:

- Consistency, ordering, and durability
- Synchronization
- Concurrency for a distributed clustered system

The following figure shows ZooKeeper:

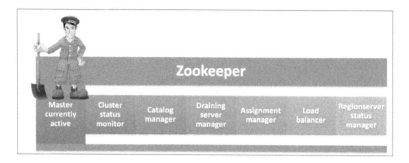

It was developed at Yahoo Research. And the reason behind the name ZooKeeper is that in Hadoop system, projects are based on animal names, and in discussion regarding naming this technology, this name emerged as it manages the availability and coordination between different components of a distributed system.

ZooKeeper not only simplifies the development but also sits on the top distributed system as an abstraction layer to facilitate the better reachability to the components of the system. The following figure shows the request and response flow:

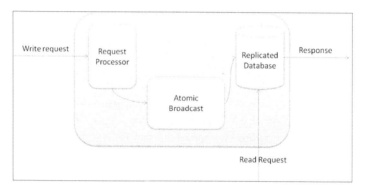

Let's consider a scenario wherein we have a few people who want to fill 10 rooms with some items. One instance would be where we will show how they find their way to the room to keep the items. Some of the rooms will be locked, which will lead the people to move on to other rooms. The other instance would be where we can allocate some representatives with information about the rooms, condition of rooms, and state of rooms (open, closed, fit for storing, not fit, and so on). We can then send them with items to those representatives for the information. The representative will guide the person towards the right room, which is available for storage of items, and the person can directly move to the specified room and store the item. This will not only ease the communication and the storage process but also reduce the overhead from the process. The same technique can be applied in the case of the ZooKeepers.

ZooKeeper maintains a tree with ZooKeeper data internally called a znode. This can be of two types:

1. Ephemeral, which is good for applications that need to understand whether a specific distributed resource is available or not.

2. The persistent one will be stored till a client does not delete it explicitly and it stores some data of the application too.

Why an odd number of ZooKeepers?

ZooKeepers are based on a majority principle; it requires that we have a quorum of servers to be up, where quorum is `ceil(n/2)`, for a cluster of three nodes ensemble means two nodes must be up and running at any point of time, and for five node ensemble, a minimum three nodes must be up. It's also important for election purpose for the ZooKeeper master. We will discuss more options of configuration and coding of ZooKeeper in later chapters.

HMaster

HMaster is the component of the HBase cluster that can be thought of as NameNode in the case of Hadoop cluster; likewise, it acts as a master for RegionServers running on different machines. It is responsible for monitoring all RegionServers in an HBase cluster and also provides an interface to all HBase metadata for the client operations. It also handles RegionServer failover, and region splits.

There may be more than one instance of HMaster in an HBase cluster that provides **High Availability (HA)**. So, if we have more than one master, only one master is active at a time; at the start up time, all the masters compete to become the active master in the cluster and whichever wins becomes the active master of the cluster. Meanwhile, all other master instances remain passive till the active master crashes, shuts down, or loses a lease from the ZooKeeper.

In short, it is a coordination component in an HBase cluster, which also manages and enables us to perform an administrative task on the cluster.

Let's now discuss the flow of starting up the HMaster process:

1. Block (do not serve requests) until it becomes active HMaster.

2. Finish initialization.

3. Enter loop until stopped.

4. Do cleansing when it is stopped.

HMaster exports some of the following interfaces that are metadata-based methods to enable us to interact with HBase:

Related to	Facilities
HBase tables	Creating table, deleting table, enabling/disabling table, and modifying table
HBase column families	Adding columns, modifying columns, and removing columns
HBase table regions	Moving regions, assigning regions, and unassign regions

In HBase, there is a table called .META. (table name on file system), which keeps all information about regions that is referred by HMaster for information about the data. By default, HMaster runs on port number 60000 and its HTTP Web UI is available on port 60010, which can always be changed according to our need.

HMaster functionalities can be summarized as follows:

- Monitors RegionServers
- Handles RegionServers failover
- Handles metadata changes
- Assignment/unassignment of regions
- Interfaces all metadata changes
- Performs reload balancing in idle time
- It publishes its location to client using ZooKeeper
- HMaster Web UI provides all information about HBase cluster (table, regions, RegionServers and so on)

If a master node goes down

If master goes down, in this scenario, the cluster may continue working normally as clients talk directly to RegionServers. So, cluster may still function steadily. The HBase catalog table (.META. and -ROOT-) exists as HBase tables and it's not stored in master resistant memory. However, as master performs critical functions such as RegionServers' failovers and region splits, these functions may be hampered and if not taken care will create a huge setback to the overall cluster functioning, so the master must be started as soon as possible.

So now, Hadoop is HA enabled and thus HBase can always be made HA using multiple HMasters for better availability and robustness, so we can now consider having multiple HMaster.

RegionServer

RegionServers are responsible for holding the actual raw HBase data. Recall that in a Hadoop cluster, a NameNode manages the metadata and a DataNode holds the raw data. Likewise, in HBase, an HBase master holds the metadata and RegionServer's store. These are the servers that hold the HBase data, as we may already know that in Hadoop cluster, NameNode manages the metadata and DataNode holds the actual data. Likewise, in HBase cluster, RegionServers store the raw actual data. As you might guess, a RegionServer is run or is hosted on top of a DataNode, which utilizes the underlying DataNodes at underlying file system, that is, HDFS.

The following figure shows the architecture of RegionServer:

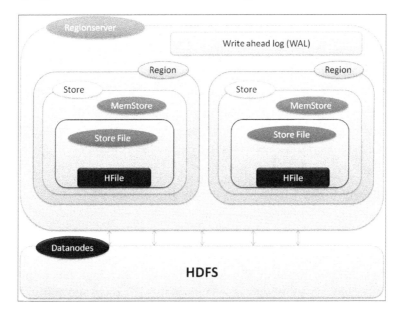

RegionServer performs the following tasks:

- Serving regions(tables) assigned to it
- Handling client read/write requests
- Flushing cache to HDFS
- Maintaining HLogs
- Performing compactions
- Responsible for handling region splits

Components of a RegionServer

The following are the components of RegionServers

- **Write-Ahead logs**: This is also called edit. When data is read/modified to HBase, it's not directly written in the disk rather it is kept in memory for some time (threshold, which we can configure based on size and time). Keeping this data in memory may result in a loss of data if the machine goes down abruptly. So to solve this, the data is first written in an intermediate file, which is called Write-Ahead logfile and then in memory. So in the case of system failure, data can be reconstructed using this logfile.

- **HFile**: These are the actual files where the raw data is stored physically on the disk. This is the actual store file.

- **Store**: Here the HFile is stored. It corresponds to a column family for a table in HBase.

- **MemStore**: This component is in memory data store; this resides in the main memory and records the current data operation. So, when data is stored in WAL, RegionServers stores key-value in memory store.

- **Region**: These are the splits of HBase table; the table is divided into regions based on the key and are hosted by RegionServers. There may be different regions in a RegionServer.

We will discuss more about these components in the next chapter.

Client

Client is responsible for finding the RegionServer, which is hosting the particular row (data). It is done by querying the catalog tables. Once region is found, the client directly contacts RegionServers and performs the data operation. Once this information is fetched, it is cached by the client for further fast retrieval. The client can be written in Java or any other language using external APIs.

Catalog tables

There are two tables that maintain the information about all RegionServers and regions. This is a kind of metadata for the HBase cluster. The following are the two catalog tables that exist in HBase:

- `-ROOT-`: This includes information about the location of `.META.` table
- `.META.`: This table holds all regions and their locations

At the beginning of the start up process, the `.mMeta` location is set to root from where the actual metadata of tables are read and read/write continues. So, whenever a client wants to connect to HBase and read or write into table, these two tables are referred and information is returned to client for direct read and write to the RegionServers and the regions of the specific table.

Who is using HBase and why?

The following is a list of just a few companies that use HBase in production. There are many companies who are using HBase, so we will list a few and not all.

- **Adobe**: They have an HBase cluster of 30 nodes and are ready to expand it. They use HBase in several areas from social services to structured data and processing for internal use.

- **Facebook**: They use it for messaging infrastructure.

- **Twitter**: They use it for a number of applications including people search, which relies on HBase internally for data generation, and also their operations team uses HBase as a time series database for cluster-wide monitoring/performance data.

- **Infolinks**: They use it for process advertisement selection and user events for our in-text advertising network.

- **StumbleUpon**: They use it with MapReduce data source to overcome traditional query speed limits in MySQL.

- **Trend Micro**: They use it as cloud-based storage.

- **Yahoo!**: They are use HBase to store document fingerprint for detecting near-duplicates. They have a cluster of a few nodes that run HDFS, MapReduce, and HBase. The table contains millions of rows; we use this for querying duplicated documents with real-time traffic.

- **Ancestry.com**: This company uses it for DNA analysis.

- **UIDAI**: This is an Indian government project; they use HBase for storing resident details.

- **Apache**: They use it for maintaining wiki.

- **Mozilla**: They are moving Socorro project to HBase.

- **eBay**: They use HBase for indexing site inventory.

 And we can keep listing, but we will stop it here and for further information, please visit `http://wiki.apache.org/hadoop/Hbase/PoweredBy`.

When should we think of using HBase?

Using HBase is not the solution to all problems; however, it can solve a lot of problems efficiently. The first thing is that we should think about the amount of data; if we have a few million rows and a few read and writes, then we can avoid using it. However, think of billions of columns and thousands of read/write data operations in a short interval, we can surely think of using HBase.

Let's consider an example, Facebook uses HBase for its real-time messaging infrastructure and we can think of how many messages or rows of data Facebook will be receiving per second. Considering that amount of data and I/O, we can currently think of using HBase. The following list details a few scenarios when we can consider using HBase:

- If data needs to have a dynamic or variable schema
- If a number of columns contain more null values (blank columns)
- When we have a huge number of dynamic rows
- If our data contains a variable number of columns
- If we need to maintain versions of data
- If high scalability is needed
- If we need in-built compression on records
- If a high volume of I/O is needed

There are many other cases where we can use HBase and it can be beneficial, which is discussed in later chapters.

When not to use HBase

Let's now discuss some points when we don't compulsorily have to use HBase just because everyone else is using it:

- When data is not in large amounts (in TBs and more)
- When JOINs and relational DB features are needed
- Don't go with the belief "every one is using it"
- If RDBMS fits your requirements, use RDBMS

Understanding some open source HBase tools

The following is the list of some HBase tools that are available in the development world:

- **hbaseexplorer**: This tool provides UI for HBase; using this tool, we can perform the following operations:
    - ° Data visualization
    - ° Table creation, deletion, and cloning
    - ° Table statistics
    - ° Scans

 For reference, go to `http://sourceforge.net/projects/hbaseexplorer/`.

- **Toad for Cloud Databases**: This is the tool to connect to HBase and perform various functions.

 For reference, go to `http://www.toadworld.com/products/toad-for-cloud-databases/default.aspx`.

- **HareDB HBase Client**: This is an HBase client, which can be used more easily with its user-friendly interface, which makes it a GUI tool for HBase (including PIG and high speed Hive Query)

 For reference, go to `http://sourceforge.net/projects/haredbhbaseclie/`.

- **hrider**: The hrider is a UI application that provides an easier way to view or manipulate the data saved in the HBase.

 For reference, go to `https://github.com/NiceSystems/hrider`.

- **Hannibal**: This is a tool for Apache HBase region monitoring.

 For reference, go to `https://github.com/sentric/hannibal`.

- **Performance Monitoring & Alerting (SPM)**: SPM is a proactive performance monitoring, anomaly detection, and alerting solution available in the Cloud (SaaS) as well as own premise. SPM can monitor Solr, Elasticsearch, Hadoop, HBase, ZooKeeper, Kafka, Storm, Redis, JVM, system metrics, custom metrics, and more.

 For reference, go to `http://sematext.com/spm/`.

- **Phoenix**: This tool is a SQL skin over HBase, delivered as a client-embedded JDBC driver, powering the HBase use cases at Salesforce.com. Phoenix targets low-latency queries (milliseconds), as opposed to batch operation via MapReduce.

 For reference, go to `https://github.com/forcedotcom/phoenix` and `http://phoenix.apache.org/`.

- **Impala**: Cloudera Impala is a parallel processing SQL query engine, which runs in Apache Hadoop. The Apache-licensed, open source Impala project combines modern, scalable, parallel database technology with the power of Hadoop. Users can directly query data stored in HDFS and Apache HBase without requiring data movement or transformation.

 For reference, go to `http://www.cloudera.com/content/cloudera-content/cloudera-docs/Impala/latest/Cloudera-Impala-Version-and-Download-Information/Cloudera-Impala-Version-and-Download-Information.html`.

The Hadoop-HBase version compatibility table

As there are compatibility issues in almost all systems; likewise, HBase also has compatibility issues with Hadoop versions, which means all versions of HBase can't be used use on top of all Hadoop versions. The following is the version compatibility of Hadoop-HBase that should be kept in mind while configuring HBase on Hadoop (credit: Apache):

Hadoop versions	HBase 0.92.x	HBase 0.94.x	HBase 0.96.0	HBase 0.98.0
Hadoop 0.20.205	Supported	Not supported	Not supported	Not supported
Hadoop 0.22.x	Supported	Not supported	Not supported	Not supported
Hadoop 1.0.0-1.0.2	Supported	Supported	Not supported	Not supported
Hadoop 1.0.3+	Supported	Supported	Supported	Not supported
Hadoop 1.1.x	Not tested enough	Supported	Supported	Not supported
Hadoop 0.23.x	Not supported	Supported	Not tested enough	Not supported
Hadoop 2.0.x-alpha	Not supported	Not tested enough	Not supported	Not supported
Hadoop 2.1.0-beta	Not supported	Not tested enough	Supported	Not supported
Hadoop 2.2.0	Not supported	Not tested enough	Supported	Supported
Hadoop 2.x	Not supported	Not tested enough	Supported	Supported

We can always visit `https://hbase.apache.org` for more updated version compatibility between HBase and Hadoop.

Applications of HBase

The applications of HBase are as follows:

- **Medical**: HBase is used in the medical field for storing genome sequences and running MapReduce on it, storing the disease history of people or an area, and many others.

- **Sports**: HBase is used in the sports field for storing match histories for better analytics and prediction.

- **Web**: HBase is used to store user history and preferences for better customer targeting.

- **Oil and petroleum**: HBase is used in the oil and petroleum industry to store exploration data for analysis and predict probable places where oil can be found.

- **e-commerce**: HBase is used for recording and storing logs about customer search history, and to perform analytics and then target advertisement for better business.

- **Other fields**: HBase can be used in many other fields where it's needed to store petabytes of data and run analysis on it, for which traditional systems may take months. We will discuss more about use cases and industry usability in further chapters.

HBase pros and cons

Let's now briefly discuss HBase pros and cons.

The following are some advantages of HBase:

- Great for analytics in association with Hadoop MapReduce
- It can handle very large volumes of data
- Supports scaling out in coordination with Hadoop file system even on commodity hardware
- Fault tolerance
- License free
- Very flexible on schema design/no fixed schema
- Can be integrated with Hive for SQL-like queries, which is better for DBAs who are more familiar with SQL queries
- Auto-sharding
- Auto failover
- Simple client interface
- Row-level atomicity, that is, the PUT operation will either write or fail

The following are some missing aspects:

- Single point of failure (when only one HMaster is used)
- No transaction support
- JOINs are handled in MapReduce layer rather than the database itself
- Indexed and sorted only on key, but RDBMS can be indexed on some arbitrary field
- No built-in authentication or permissions

So overall, we can say if we are in a position to neglect these cons, we can go with HBase which provides many other benefits that are not there in RDBMS. We can see that it's still an evolving technology with Hadoop and with time, it will become more mature and rich, which will make it one of the best tools for analytical database and distributed fault tolerant database. It is an open source Apache project where users and developers can contribute and add more and more features.

Hadoop HBase and a combination of some other Hadoop subproject can do wonders in the data analysis field; using these technologies, the data can be a hidden treasure, which were stored somewhere uselessly as a dump and now they can be very beneficial for understanding various prospects of a specific industry.

Summary

So in this chapter, we discussed the introductory aspects of HBase and related projects. We have also discussed HBase's components and their place in the HBase ecosystem. This chapter then provided a brief historical context for HBase and we have related it with some common uses of HBase in the industry.

In the next chapter, we will begin with HBase, understanding the different considerations and prerequisites for getting started with HBase. We will also discuss some of the concerns a new user might face during their first encounter with HBase.

2
Let's Begin with HBase

In the previous chapter, we learned in depth about HBase and its ecosystem. In this chapter, we will discuss HBase and its components in a bit more detail. This chapter will guide you through understanding the prerequisites and assumptions that one has to make when one starts using HBase. It will also focus on the requirements to configure HBase cluster and the parameters that you need to keep in mind to have a healthy and helpful HBase. You will also get to know HBase components and their deployment considerations. Let's take a look at the topics that we are going to discuss in this chapter:

- HFile
- HBase region
- Scalability
- Reading and writing cycle
- Write-Ahead Logs
- MemStore
- Some HBase housekeeping concepts
- Region operations
- Capacity planning
- List of available HBase distributions
- Prerequisites for HBase

Understanding HBase components in detail

To understand the components of HBase, let's start from the bottom, from HFile to RegionServers, and then progress towards the master. There can be one to *n* RegionServers, one to *n* DataNodes, and one to *n* ZooKeeper nodes. Refer to the following figure:

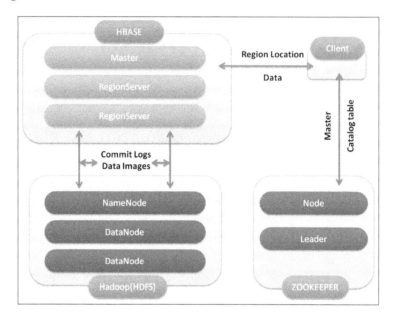

HFile

HFile is designed after Google SSTable, which is a reinterpretation of Google's implementation based on their *Bigtable* paper. It was implemented after HBase v0.20.0; earlier, an alternate file format, that is, MapFile was being temporarily used. An HFile internally consists of HFile blocks that are its building blocks.

Go through the links https://hbase.apache.org/book/apes03.html and https://issues.apache.org/jira/browse/HBASE-3857, and also go through the PDF files present on the previous link for an actual file representation of HFile on the disk.

Region

Regions are the basic blocks of RegionServers that provide distribution, availability, and storage for columns and column families on an HBase cluster. The overall structure goes like this:

HBase table	Table representation in HBase
Region	Region that constitutes the HBase table
Store	Store is per column family for every region, for each HBase table
MemStore	This exists for each region of the table and for each store
Store file	This exists for each region of the table and each MemStore
Block	This is the basic building block of store files

On HDFS, the structure looks like in the following figure:

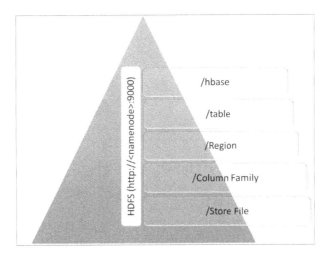

In the preceding figure, /hbase refers to the HBase directory on HDFS, /table is inside the /hbase directory, and so on. Once we have an HBase running cluster, we can navigate on HDFS to see the storage structure of the HBase directory. We can visit the Web UI of Hadoop NameNode and the /hbase directory that is created when we configure and start the daemon processes, such as HMaster RegionServers. The /hbase directory's name depends on what we assign for the hbase.rootdir setting in the HBase configuration. By navigating to the path, we can understand the logical storage of the HBase root directory on top of HDFS; the following diagram shows how the **Write-Ahead Log (WAL)** structure is stored on HDFS.

HLogs are the files that save all edit logs to HStore files. These are HBase WALs. Internally, it performs logfile rolling. There is one HLog file per RegionServer, and write-ahead (writing changes to a logfile and then performing the actual write) is performed on this logfile for every region on a particular RegionServer. This HLog file consists of multiple on-disk files. The following diagram shows the structure of HLog files on HDFS. In this figure, `/.logs` stands for the `./logs` directory inside the HBase directory on HDFS.

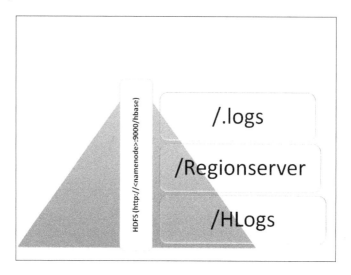

Scalability – understanding the scale up and scale out processes

In the previous chapter, we learned about the HBase scale out process; let's see what it means and how it's done. Let's discuss scale out and scale up, and which is better for what. In the case of HBase, it scales out and does not scale up, which is provided by the underlying HDFS file system and Hadoop, which is a distributed system and can scale out on the fly with just an addition of new machines, whenever it's needed. In HBase, we can always add a new Hadoop DataNode; on DataNodes, we can host many RegionServers for higher scalability. Refer to the following figure:

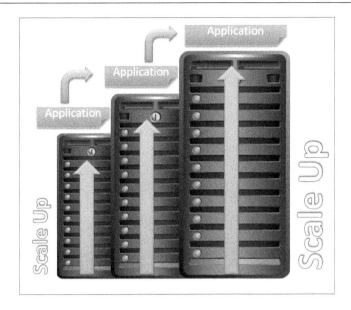

Scale in

You must be aware of the fact that the traditional scaling of the system, application, and database depends on the capacity of the system on which they are hosted. This is called vertical scaling, where an application is migrated to a more powerful machine with more memory, processing power, and storage. In this type of scaling, there are limited powerful servers; a server cannot keep on growing in order of processing power, or even memory-wise, as there is always a limit to it at any given point in time. There might be only a specific processor, a server, or an OS available, which might support a specific amount of memory at one time, and which can't grow beyond this limit. So, these types of systems are not very scale friendly. This process of scaling vertically is really heavy on finance.

In this type of system, there is always a more powerful, centralized machine that is responsible for handling all the operations. With the increase in data size or the processing power requirement, the system struggles, and it is at that time that we need to upgrade the system to a better configuration. Some problems of scale up or vertically scaled systems are as follows:

- Data migration and software and hardware upgradation
- Application reconfiguration
- Reconfiguration overhead

Some benefits of scale up systems are: less and one-time configuration till upgrade, less power, less cooling system, less space, and a centralized system.

Scale out

On the contrary, scale out or scale horizontally means virtually adding processing power, memory, and storage to the system. Here, servers are not replaced with a more powerful server, but a new machine is added to the system when there is a need for more storage, processing power, and main memory. Here, in this system, multiple machines work virtually as a single system to provide large-scale processing power. Let's discuss why we should choose the scale out-based system. Refer to the following figure for better understanding:

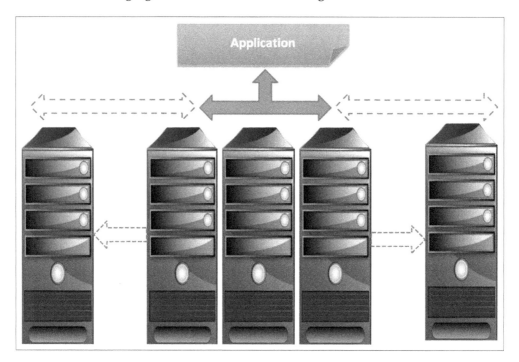

A scale out-based system enables us to have a redundant and high availability system. It is cost effective, which means that there is no need to invest in high-end machines, no application migration overhead, and servers can be located in many locations. It is suitable for massive parallel computing, where a number of machines take up the workload evenly. The following figure shows the HBase scaling method:

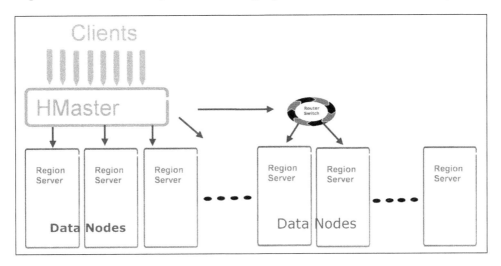

In HBase, we can add new RegionServers on the fly; for this, new DataNodes are added, the RegionServer daemon is started on these DataNodes, and scalability is obtained. In short, we first add a number to the cluster, and then start the DataNode and RegionServer daemons on the newly added node.

Let's talk about HBase communication between daemons (nodes). The different daemons and the HBase nodes communicate with each other using **Remote Procedure Call** (**RPC**), which enables the HBase components to make calls to in-built functions. It also enables each component to behave towards these calls as if they were local. This in turn enables the procedures or subroutines to be executed to a different address space, such as another computer system. This kind of intercommunication prevents the rewriting of the server architecture code.

The following figure shows the RPC flow:

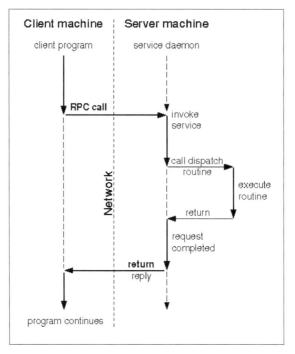

In HBase, `HBaseRPC` is the class that facilitates HBase to use RPC among the components. It is based on the Java dynamic proxy pattern. It uses an `invoker` class that implements InvocationHandler to intercept client-side method calls, and then it marshalls the method name and argument through HBaseClient. The communication between client and server using RPC works as follows:

1. The client contacts ZooKeeper to find who the active HMaster is and what the location of the root RegionServer is.

2. Then, the client communicates RegionServer using HRegionInterface to read/write the table.

3. Client applications talk to HMaster using HMasterInterface in order to dynamically create a table, add a column family, and for other operations.

4. Then, HMaster communicates to RegionServers using HRegionInterface to open, close, move, split, or flush the region.

5. Active HMaster data and the root RegionServer location are cached into ZooKeepers by HMaster.

6. RegionServer then reads the data from ZooKeeper to get information about log-splitting tasks, which is updated to fetch a task report status.

7. RegionServer then communicates with HMaster using HMasterRegionInterface to convey information such as the loading of RegionServer, errors with RegionServer, and the start up process of RegionServers.

   Sometimes, RegionServer also communicates with the root region or the meta region, with the help of HRegionInterface, to check the current status of a region or to create a new daughter region while region splitting.

8. This communication is repeated with a tick time interval or a threshold time interval to keep everything updated.

Reading and writing cycle

Now, let's see how the read-and-write operation takes place in HBase diagrammatically:

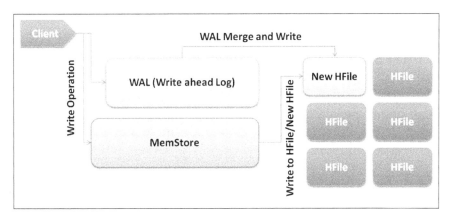

Let's discuss and understand how the read-and-write operation takes place in and from HBase tables. In HBase, the client does not write data to HFile directly; it is first written to WAL and then to HBase MemStore, which is shared by an HStore in the main memory and then flushed to HFile later. Refer to the following figure:

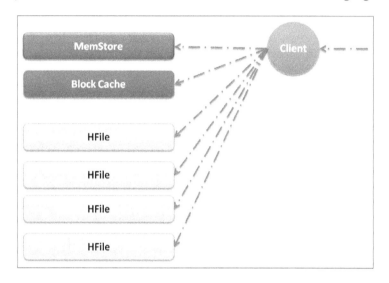

Write-Ahead Logs

Write-Ahead Logs facilitate the data reliability and reside on HDFS; each RegionServer hosts a single WAL. In the case of a RegionServer crash where MemStore is not flushed, WAL is used to restore the data to a new RegionServer. So, only once data is written successfully to WAL and MemStore, the write operation is said to be successful.

MemStore

MemStore acts as an in-memory write buffer with a default size of 64 MB. Once data in MemStore reaches the threshold (which is by default 40 percent of the heap size or 64 MB), it is flushed to a new HFile on HDFS for persistence. The 64 MB HFile is not related to block size here; Hadoop internally manages block allocation and storage. HBase does not play a role in the underlying mechanism of block replication or dividing HFiles into blocks. Each column family might have many HFiles, but the HFile will only belong to a specific column family.

Now, let's take a look at the process flow of reading from HBase. The reading process starts when the client initiates a read request; the client gets the RegionServer and region information, and it communicates this to the acquired RegionServer. At the acquired RegionServer, the client first tries to read from MemStore; if hit, the read activity completes; if it's a miss, it navigates to block cache. Finally, it reaches out to HFile to read the required row of data. If there is a missing record, the corresponding HFile is loaded into the memory that contains the required row of data. So, MemStore and block cache provide real-time access to data for performance purposes, and HFile provides persistent, on-demand data.

Block cache follows the **least recently used** (**LRU**) algorithm. Every RegionServer has a single block cache that keeps the most frequently accessed data from HFile in the main memory, which results in reducing the disk seek for data access time.

HBase housekeeping

As data is being added to HBase, it writes an immutable file to store. Each store is made up of column families, and regions consist of these row-key ordered files as it's immutable. So, there will be more files rather than one on the fly. Due to many files, the I/O will be slower, and hence lag in reading and writing, resulting in slower operation. To overcome these types of problems, HBase uses the compaction methodology; let's look into it now. Refer to the following figure for a better understanding:

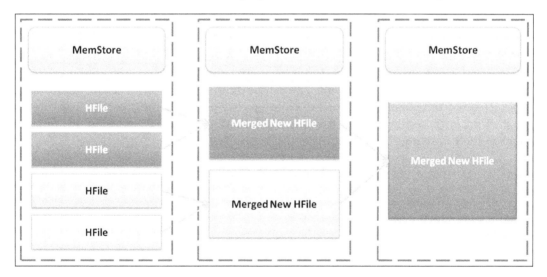

Compaction

As the name suggests, compaction makes files more compact and, hence, efficient to read up files. When new data is written to HBase, HFile is generated and the number of HFiles might increase the I/O overhead. So, to minimize this, the HFiles are merged to one HFile periodically. As MemStore gets filled, a new HFile is created. If these files are not merged in time, there will be a huge overhead on the system. Compaction is nothing but the merging of two or more HFiles using the N-way merge sort algorithms, since HFiles are already in a sorted order. Once files are merged, the new file is loaded and the older file is discarded or deleted.

There are different types of compactions; let's look at them now.

Minor compaction

Minor compaction takes place on multiple HFiles in HStore. In this type of compaction, a number of adjacent HFiles are picked up, merged, and rewritten into a larger single HFile. When this is done, the deleted or expired files are not removed, they are still present in the resulting HFile. Files to be merged in minor compaction are chosen heuristically. Minor compaction affects the HBase performance and, therefore, there is a limit on the number of files to be merged; by default, it is 10.

Major compaction

Major compaction folds all the HFiles together to form a single HFile. In this type of compaction, the deleted and expired records are discarded, and the active and non-deleted files are kept. Generally, it is manually triggered on large clusters. Major compaction is not a region merge, but it happens with HStore. In this, all the HFiles of a column family are merged. This compaction can also be triggered on an entire table. This is a time-consuming process and an expensive operation; it also affects the performance, so it must be triggered when there are fewer requests to the cluster. Refer to the following figure:

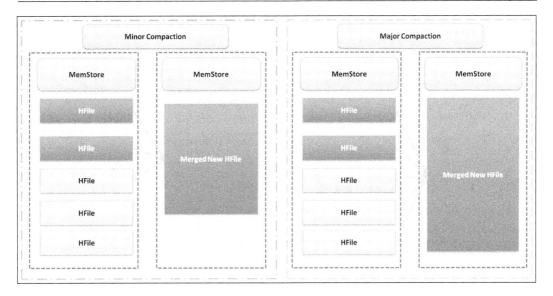

Region split

Region split is done by RegionServers. In a RegionServer, once a region becomes overloaded or exceeds the threshold value of 256 MB, it is spliced into new regions. The flow of region splitting is shown in the following figure:

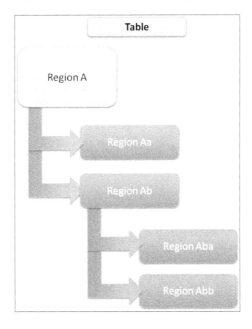

The following is the flow of region splitting, as illustrated in the preceding figure:

1. The region to be split is made offline by RegionServer.
2. A region is spliced into two regions.
3. The newer daughter region information is updated in the `.META.` table.
4. The new daughter region formed is opened and made available.
5. The region split information is passed to HMaster for an update.

Region assignment

This is one of the main tasks of HMaster. Let's see how it works:

1. HBase HMaster calls AssignmentManager for region assignment.
2. AssignmentManager looks into the current region assignment scenario in the `.META.` table. If the region assignment is correct and valid, it keeps the region; if region assignment is invalid or incorrect, `LoadBalancerFactory` creates DefaultLoadBalancer.
3. Then, DefaultLoadBalancer assigns a new region to RegionServer.
4. The whole assignment process is updated into the `.META.` table.
5. Once this is done successfully, the assigned region is opened and made available by the corresponding RegionServer.

Region merge

As new regions are created on a region-size threshold, and since this might result in greater number of regions, it might bring high cost on memory, I/O, and throughput performance. When the RegionServer number threshold is at its maximum (usually, 100 per RegionServer), region merge is initiated by RegionServer. This process flows as follows:

1. The client initiates the process for region merge and sends an RPC region merge request to HMaster.
2. HMaster moves regions together to RegionServer and sends requests for a region merge operation.
3. RegionServer makes regions offline to be merged, and regions are merged.
4. The metadata of regions that are merged are deleted from the `.META.` table, and the new merged region's metadata is updated/added to the `.META.` table.
5. The resulting region is then made online and available for reading, and HMaster is updated for the region information.

RegionServer failovers

When RegionServer fails, the region on the server goes offline and is not available for read or write. Once this happens, and HMaster detects it, the assignment of regions will be made invalid. The region assignment to another RegionServer will be initiated, and it will follow the same steps we discussed in the region assignment process.

All other information on regions and operations on them will be discussed in *Chapter 6*, *HBase Cluster Maintenance and Troubleshooting*.

The HBase delete request

When HBase receives a delete request for some data, it does not delete it immediately. The data that needs to be deleted is marked as a tombstone using the tombstone marker. It is a predicate deletion, which is a feature supported by LSM-trees on which HBase is based. This is done because HFile is immutable, and deletion of this is not available inside HFile on HDFS. One of the major compactions takes place when the marked record or data is discarded, and a new HFile is created without the marked data.

The reading and writing cycle

The following figure shows us how the overall reading and writing is done in HBase:

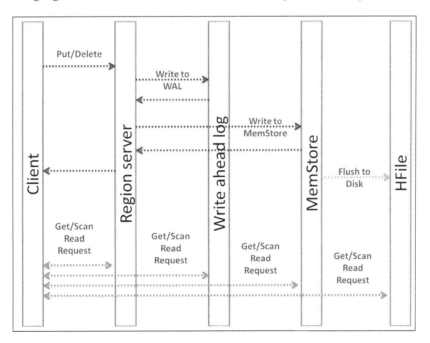

As we can see in the preceding figure, whenever a write request is sent, it is first written to WAL and then to MemStore, and when MemStore and WAL reach the threshold, it is flushed to the disk file for persistence. Also, when client needs to read some data, it queries the `.META.` table and then contacts the specific RegionServer; if data is found, it is returned to client, else the read activity continues from WAL to MemStore, and then to HFile, to read data where it is found.

List of available HBase distributions

Let's see the list of HBase distributions that we can use. While building up the HBase cluster, we need to keep in mind that if we use the distribution of a specific vendor, we must use the Hadoop distribution of the same vendor. This is required for compatibility and ease of configuration.

Some major distributions of Hadoop/HBase are as follows:

- Apache (`http://hbase.apache.org/`)
- Cloudera (`http://www.cloudera.com`)
- Hortonworks (`http://hortonworks.com`)
- MapR (`http://www.mapr.com`)

There are also many other distributions that are still evolving.

Prerequisites and capacity planning for HBase

When we start configuring the HBase cluster, we always need to keep some considerations in mind. First things first, before configuring HBase, our Hadoop cluster must be up and running well.

Here, we will discuss various parameters from OS to network and from disk to processing and memory considerations. We will discuss some prerequisites for HBase and various factors that affect the cluster functioning. If our Hadoop is healthy, HBase will be healthy too, so we have to consider a good, healthy, and smoothly running Hadoop cluster on top of which we can have a full-fledged, healthy, and smoothly running HBase cluster.

In this section, we will discuss the considerations for a Hadoop as well as an HBase cluster. Then, in the following chapters, we will discuss the full-fledged, step-by-step cluster configuration using the top-down method to configure a Hadoop cluster, and then an HBase cluster, running in different modes that are standalone, pseudo-distributed, and fully distributed clusters of Apache and Cloudera distributions.

HBase uses a local hostname to report its IP address, so the cluster network and its machines must be forward and backward (reverse) DNS resolvable. Let's now discuss forward and backward (reverse) DNS resolution in brief. Take a look at the following figure:

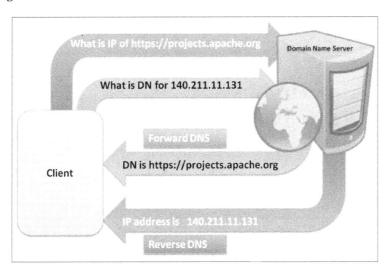

The forward DNS resolution

The forward DNS resolution uses the domain name to find the IP address of a machine in the network. This is also known as a Domain Name System, where a domain name server finds out or tells the equivalent IP address.

The reverse DNS resolution

The reverse DNS resolution uses an IP address to find out the hostname of a machine. This is important in configuration, as both resolutions are important and each machine in the cluster must be able to communicate with other machines using the hostname and the IP address.

Every machine must be accessible using the hostname as well as the IP address for proper functioning of the HBase cluster.

The following figure shows the basic prerequisites for configuring an HBase cluster:

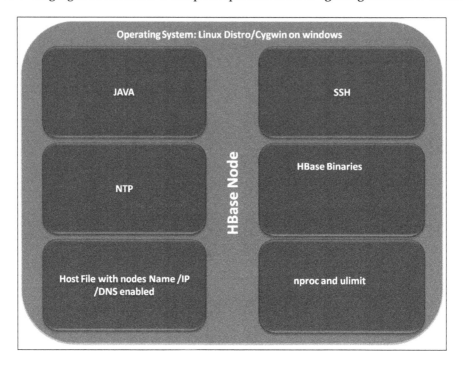

We will need a Linux distribution for a full-fledged production cluster. If we need support, we can go with the enterprise or paid versions of Linux, such as the Red Hat Enterprise edition, Debian-based distros with enterprise support. If we don't want to invest initially, we can go with free versions of these distros, such as CentOS, Ubuntu, or any other Linux distro. HBase clusters can be configured on Mac too, and there is another option to build testing and evaluation.

An HBase cluster can be configured on Windows too, which is not good for production. However, people who just want to test and evaluate it, and are not in a position to switch to Linux directly, can opt for this option. For this, we will need to install Cygwin (a software package that enables us to run native apps on Windows) on Windows and configure HBase cluster on it.

Java

We need to have Java installed on our system. This is one of the basic requirements as all the daemon processes run under JVM. We will discuss installing Java on various platforms such as Ubuntu, Red Hat distributions, and some other Linux distributions in the following chapters, where we will build up a cluster step-by-step. We must install Sun Java 6 (formally, Oracle Java) or a later version.

We can go for RPM versions of Red Hat distros and archive (tar) files for other distros.

In fact, Java is a must for Hadoop configuration, and we can configure HBase on top of Hadoop once Hadoop is running fine. The following is what Apache says about Java for Hadoop/HBase:

> *Hadoop requires Java 7 or a late version of Java 6. It is built and tested on both OpenJDK and Oracle (HotSpot)'s JDK/JRE.*

 You can find more details on Java requirements at `http://wiki.apache.org/hadoop/HadoopJavaVersions`.

SSH

We can configure SSH for easy server-to-host communication. If our cluster is inside a secure network, we can configure a passwordless SSH. This is not compulsory, but if configured, we can use all HBase scripts, such as `start-hbase.sh` and others, if a passwordless SSH is configured.

SSH is cryptographic for secure communication between machines on a network, remote, remote execution, and other secure networks between two networked computers. It connects via an insecure network, a server and a client running, and programs. We will discuss configuring SSH on various platforms in the upcoming chapters.

The following figure shows how nodes communicate using the SSH (SSH is used only for configuration purposes, and HBase does not use it to communicate between its daemons) protocol:

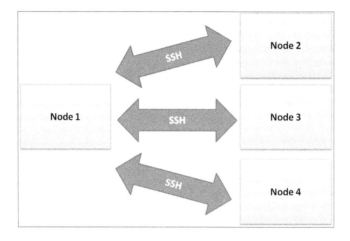

Domain Name Server

HBase uses a local hostname to report its IP address. Related to this, we can have a host file-based DNS, or we need to set up a Domain Name Server to resolve the machines in a clustered network for production servers.

The primary network interface is used by HBase for communication, so we need to configure a hostname for our primary interface.

The following are the simple steps which we can use to verify correct DNS configurations to avoid issues related to DNS with HBase configuration and operation:

1. Set a hostname for each machine in the cluster.
2. Check if forward and reverse domains are the resolving means with which you can access nodes using both an IP and a hostname.
3. Use a DNS verification tool to verify the correctness.

The following diagram shows where and how we need to change the DNS settings:

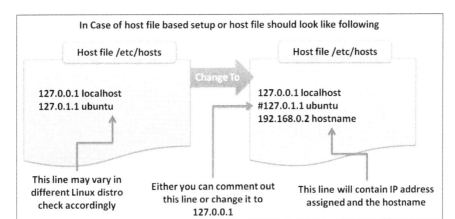

To be on the safe side, try to have both the host file- and DNS-based resolution policies. If DNS fails sometimes, the operation is not disrupted and nodes might communicate with each other even in the case of a DNS failure. Everything depends on the two important parameters, namely, the host file-based resolution and the DNS-based resolution policy. You can always change this parameter in the `hbase-site.xml` file to override the setting that is in `hbase-default.xml`, according to any network interface. You need to use one of the following files:

- `hbase.master.dns.interface`
- `hbase.regionserver.dns.interface`

If we configure our settings related to DNS, and the host resolution is accurate from the beginning, we can avoid a lot of issues that come up with RegionServers, ZooKeepers, and other components.

We can use the following commands in Linux to verify the settings for correctness and reachability, and once we are confident that the DNS-related settings are all correct, recheck, verify, and then move forward:

```
dig, nslookup, ping
```

The loopback IP must be set to 127.0.0.1 instead of 127.0.1.1 for the localhost.

Using Network Time Protocol to keep your node on time

The Network Time Protocol is a networking time protocol that keeps the machine time updated. In an HBase cluster, all machines must have a synchronized time. This service might be available; we need to enable it. If it is not available, we can always install it using a package manager available on the Linux distros we are using. Take a look at the following diagram:

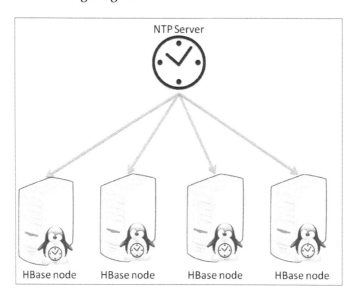

The preceding diagram shows how an NTP server functions with HBase. We will see how to install this service at the configuration stage.

OS-level changes and tuning up OS for HBase

HBase tends to open a lot of files in operation, so we need an OS tune up and changes for better performance and trouble-free operations. Two parameters that we need to change in Linux distros are as follows:

- **Nproc**: Number of processes active at a time under a user
- **Ulimit**: Number of open files at a time under a specific user

To set `nproc` and `ulimit` values, we need to change it in the `limits.conf` file found in Linux. To check the content of this file, we need to execute the `ulimit -a` command. The following screenshot shows the existing and needed setting changes related to the OS level:

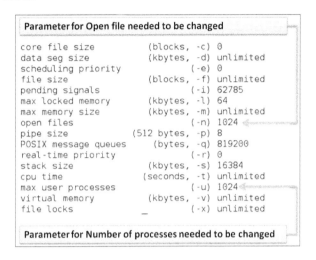

```
  Parameter for Open file needed to be changed

core file size          (blocks, -c) 0
data seg size           (kbytes, -d) unlimited
scheduling priority           (-e) 0
file size               (blocks, -f) unlimited
pending signals               (-i) 62785
max locked memory       (kbytes, -l) 64
max memory size         (kbytes, -m) unlimited
open files                    (-n) 1024
pipe size           (512 bytes, -p) 8
POSIX message queues     (bytes, -q) 819200
real-time priority            (-r) 0
stack size              (kbytes, -s) 16384
cpu time              (seconds, -t) unlimited
max user processes            (-u) 1024
virtual memory          (kbytes, -v) unlimited
file locks              _     (-x) unlimited

  Parameter for Number of processes needed to be changed
```

To find this file, navigate to the `/etc/security` directory (`/etc/launchd.conf` on OS X) that can be opened and modified in any text editor. The file can be changed from a command line too. For a permanent effect, we need to change it into a `limit.conf` file and save it to make it persistent.

In a newly installed system, the value for `open files` is usually `1024`, which is not enough for setup as HBase opens a lot of files during read/write operations and processing, and it also starts a lot of new processes and subprocesses while running. Not properly configuring these parameters might result in a lot of runtime errors such as `java.io.IOException` (too many open files), `OutOfMemoryException`, and others; all the frequent exceptions will be discussed in the *Troubleshooting the most frequent HBase errors and their explanation* section of *Chapter 6, HBase Cluster Maintenance and Troubleshooting*. These parameters are not universal but can be set according to the existing system configuration. This also depends on the amount of heap memory available. On a node with good configuration, we can set the range between 24 K and 65 K, or more if required. However, there is a limit that depends on the system resources; changing these values incorrectly might break down the system.

There are two types of limits; they are hard limit and soft limit:

- Soft limits are the currently enforced limits
- Hard limits mark the maximum value that cannot be exceeded by setting a soft limit

So, we need to have the same value for both the hard and soft limits. However, soft limits will always be less than or equal to the hard limit. To change the hard limit, we need root access to the system, but the soft limit can be changed by the process. The hard limit is set by processes with superuser privileges, and it cannot be exceeded by processes running with lower privileges.

Once HBase and Hadoop starts functioning, it initiates the opening of more files or starts more processes that reach the OS limit. So, if we don't set it properly, the OS tends to kill this process, or due to the restriction, we will not be able to create a new required process or open a new file to read or write, which will cause runtime exception and affect the cluster. In fact, it might break down an HBase daemon or node. After changing the value, we need to reboot the system.

Summary

In this chapter, we discussed components of HBase and its subcomponents. We also discussed various initial configurations related to the network, OS, and so on, which are good to configure at the beginning for better operation and performance of an HBase cluster. As per the system requirements, we can say that we will have a Hadoop cluster running, where NameNode will have more memory to hold metadata, average processing power, and storage. These are not really required by NameNode because it serves requests, and all the other operations such as read/write and processing take place at the slave nodes. For the slave nodes, we need to have more memory in memory files—more dedicated storage defines the storage capacity of a node, and hence the cluster, and it also means a high processing time because the real processing takes place on these machines.

We also discussed the prerequisites and basic requirements before building up. In the next chapter, we will start building the cluster, and will discuss advance and configuration parameters. We will start building the Hadoop and HBase clusters and also learn how to build a live cluster that can run in different modes.

3
Let's Start Building It

This chapter will guide users to get started and have a complete configured cluster. It will also show the ways in which they can verify and test the cluster. We will download and install various components such as Java, and will see configurations related to Hadoop/HBase such as DNS configuration. Then, we will discuss the installation and configuration of Hadoop, HBase, and other components such as ZooKeeper, and we will go through various files involved in the configuration process. We will also learn to configure Apache Hadoop/HBase and Cloudera Hadoop. We have a small section in this chapter that will help you configure Hadoop on Windows.

In this chapter, we will cover the following topics:

- Installing and configuring SSH
- Installing and configuring NTP
- Configuring Apache Hadoop
- Configuring Apache HBase
- Installing and configuring ZooKeeper
- Installing Cloudera Hadoop and HBase

Downloading Java on Ubuntu

The following are the links from where we can download the required files:

- **Java**:http://www.oracle.com/technetwork/java/javase/downloads/index.html
- **Apache Hadoop**: http://www.apache.org/dyn/closer.cgi/hadoop/common/
- **Apache HBase**: http://apache.mirrors.hoobly.com/hbase/

- **Cloudera**: The following are the different versions you can opt for:
  - **CDH4**: `http://www.cloudera.com/content/cloudera-content/cloudera-docs/CDH4/latest/CDH-Version-and-Packaging-Information/cdhvd_topic_7.html`
  - **CDH5**: `http://www.cloudera.com/content/support/en/documentation.html`

First, we need to know whether our installed OS is 64 bit or 32 bit; we can check this using the `uname -a` command.

If you use a 32-bit OS, the output will be as follows:

```
Linux infinity 3.5.0-17-generic #28-Ubuntu SMP Tue Oct 9 19:31:23 UTC
2012 i686 i686 i386 GNU/Linux

I686 denotes 32 bit
```

If you use a 64-bit OS, the output will be as follows:

```
Linux infinity 3.5.0-17-generic #28-Ubuntu SMP Tue Oct 9 19:31:23 UTC
2012 x86_64x86_64x86_64 GNU/Linux

Here x86_64* will denote 64-bit
```

Alternatively, you can use the `file /sbin/init` command to check the version of OS.

The 32-bit OS will give the following output:

```
/sbin/init: ELF 32-bit LSB shared object, Intel 80386, version 1
(SYSV), dynamically linked (uses shared libs), for GNU/Linux 2.6.24,
BuildID[sha1]=0xa0c5c22661e7197bbb64908bafd674ec2e782bb6, stripped
```

The 64-bit OS will give the following output:

```
/sbin/init: ELF 64-bit LSB shared object, x86-64, version 1 (SYSV),
dynamically linked (uses shared libs), for GNU/Linux 2.6.24,
BuildID[sha1]=0xa0c5c22661e7197bbb64908bafd674ec2e782bb6, stripped
```

Java installation can always be verified issuing the `java -version` command. By default, it displays the version of installed Java; if Java is not installed, this command will show the output as not found. It is advisable that we remove OpenJDK and install Oracle JDK.

After we get information about the version of OS, we can download the equivalent Java version, either 64 bit or 32 bit, from the link mentioned earlier.

It is suggested that we use a 64-bit OS for Hadoop and other ecosystem components.

We will consider 64-bit OS and JDK 8. You can always go with lower or higher versions of Java, but it must be 1.6 or above. Now, let's see the installing process of JDK on Ubuntu and CentOS.

The following are the installation steps of Java on Ubuntu using GUI (we configure it on Ubuntu here):

1. To download the latest version of Java, visit `http://www.oracle.com/technetwork/java/javase/downloads/index.html`. You will be directed to the web page, which is similar to the one shown in the following screenshot:

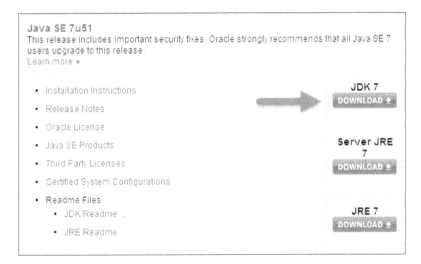

Otherwise, you can use the following link to download the version of Java, the one I am using, JDK 8:

`http://www.oracle.com/technetwork/java/javase/downloads/jdk8-downloads-2133151.html`

2. Once JDK is downloaded, we can proceed to install and configure it. Though we downloaded Java using a GUI, we'll proceed to configure it using a command line.

Now, let's start installing Java. We will use the downloaded `jdk-7u45-linux-x64.tar.gz` file.

[Note that the filename varies according to which downloaded version of Java you are using.]

3. Enter the following command to remove OpenJDK from the system. It's up to us whether we leave OpenJDK or remove it; if there is any component on the machine that requires OpenJDK, we can leave it as it is, or remove it using the following command.

```
sudo apt-get purge openjdk*
```

4. Create a directory for Java installation, using the following command:

```
sudo mkdir -p /usr/local/Java
```

5. Copy the downloaded compressed TAR file to the /usr/local/java directory:

```
sudo cp -r jdk-7u45-linux-x64.tar.gz /usr/local/java
```

6. Change the current directory to the Java directory we created in the previous step:

```
cd /usr/local/java
```

7. Extract the compressed file to /usr/local/java:

```
sudo tar -xvzfjdk-7u45-linux-x64.tar.gz
```

8. List out the extracted file using the ls command; it will display JDK or another name, according to the downloaded file.

9. Rename the JDK file to jdk, as follows:

```
mv jdk-7u45-linux-x64 jdk
```

10. Create the Java_Home environment variable to point to the JRE installation directory:

```
JAVA_HOME=/usr/local/java/jdk
```

11. Add the path of the Java home directory to the PATH variable of the system:

```
PATH=$PATH:$HOME/bin:$JAVA_HOME/bin
```

12. Add JRE_HOME to the variable:

```
JRE_HOME=/usr/local/java/jdk/jre
```

13. Add the path of the JRE directory to the system path:

```
PATH=$PATH:$HOME/bin:$JRE_HOME/bin
```

14. Add the runtime Java home:

```
export JAVA_HOME
```

15. Add the runtime JRE home:

```
export JRE_HOME
```

16. Update the entire path with Java and JRE:

```
export PATH
```

17. To make these variables permanent and global, we can add commands from step 10 to 16 in the `/etc/profile` or `.bashrc` file for the current user. If we execute these commands on a command line, the variables will be set as temporary variables, and once the system is restarted, they will be lost. So, it is always recommended that these commands be added to the specified file for consistency.

18. Now, the following command lines will make a Ubuntu system aware of where Java is installed and set it as the Java alternative. This will enable us to talk to Java by just typing in `Java`, `javac`, or `javws`.

The following command will set an alternate Java available on the system:

```
sudo update-alternatives --install "/usr/bin/java" "java"
"/usr/local/java/jdk/jre/bin/java" 1
```

The following command will set the `javac` path:

```
sudo update-alternatives --install "/usr/bin/javac" "javac"
"/usr/local/java/jdk/bin/javac" 1
```

The following command will set the `javaws` path:

```
sudo update-alternatives --install "/usr/bin/javaws" "javaws"
"/usr/local/java/jdk/jre/bin/javaws" 1
```

The following lines make Java (that we are configuring) the default for the system:

```
sudo update-alternatives --set java /
usr/local/java/jdk/jre/bin/java
```

The following command will set the Java runtime environment for the system:

```
sudo update-alternatives --set javac
/usr/local/java/jdk/bin/javac
```

The following command will set the Java compiler for the system:

```
sudo update-alternatives --set javaws
/usr/local/java/jdk/bin/javaws
```

The following command will set Java Web Start for the system:

```
sudo update-alternatives --set javaws
/usr/local/java/jdk/jre/bin/javaws
```

The following command will reload the variable set in the `profile` file:

```
/etc/profile
```

The following command will check whether Java is installed properly:

```
java -version
```

If the installation is a success, it should give the installed Java version as the output. Once you get the correct Java version as the output, you have successfully installed Java.

Just like the way we installed Java in the preceding steps, we can install Java on CentOS, Red Hat, or Debian, but if needed, we can install Java using the `.rpm` package on CentOS/Red Hat, which is a bit easier and cleaner to install. Let's see this too:

1. Download the `.rpm` package of JDK from the following link:

   ```
   http://www.oracle.com/technetwork/java/javase/downloads/jdk8-
   downloads-2133151.html
   ```

2. Once downloaded, we can execute the following commands to install it:

   If you are on Debian, the following command is used to log in to root for installation:

   ```
   sudo -
   ```

   If you are on Red Hat, the following command is used to log in to root for installation:

   ```
   sudo su -
   ```

   Now, type in the filename of the `.rpm` package you downloaded:

   ```
   rpm -Uvhjdk-8-linux-x64.rpm
   ```

   Set a Java alternative using the following command:

   ```
   alternatives --install /usr/bin/java java
   /opt/jdk1.6.0_37/jre/bin/java 20000
   ```

   The following command will output a list of available Java versions; here, we can select the default Java version that we installed:

   ```
   alternatives --config Java
   ```

3. Then, type in `Java -version` to verify the successful installation of Java.

After the successful installation of Java, we can move forward to configure and install SSH in Ubuntu and Red Hat distros. We already discussed what SSH is in the previous chapter, now let's see how to install and configure it to make the Hadoop/HBase nodes communicate with each other. We will set a passwordless SSH so that the scripts are shipped with Hadoop and HBase.

It is not compulsory to set up SSH as these processes can run and communicate with each other as they can communicate using HTTP or RPC with SSH when the daemon process is started. However, we will install SSH such as `start-all.sh`, `start-dfs.sh`, `start-mapred.sh`, and `start-HBase.sh` as it helps us to administrate daemons easily from a single node. We will also install scripts that come with Hadoop/HBase and we will need a passwordless setup to communicate with all machines in the cluster and start or stop processes from a single point, that is, from the NameNode or HMaster node. So, let's set up SSH now.

Considering host configurations

Host and DNS configurations play a very import role in communication among the components of Hadoop and HBase. So, we need to have the host domain name forward and backward resolvable. This section will cover the different methods to consider for host configurations.

Host file based

First, we set a hostname for the machine; we change the hostname of the node by changing it into a hostname file, which is found in the `/etc/` directory. We can use a command or edit the hostname file.

Command based

The following command sets the new hostname for the system, but if we want to make it persistent, we need to open the `hostname` file from the `/etc/` directory and change it in the file:

```
sudo hostname <name we need to give for the system>
```

Have a look at the following example:

```
sudo hostname slave1.infinity.com
```

File based

Open the file with the following command:

```
vi /etc/hostname
```

Alternatively, you can directly use the following command to give a hostname we want to set, for example, infinity1.techinfinity.com:

```
echo [hostname] > /etc/hostname
```

Likewise, we can set the hostname in this file for all the nodes we need to have in our cluster.

After changing it in the host file, we need to open the hosts file in the /etc/ directory, which is used for file-based networking. When we open this file using vi /etc/hosts, we will find something like the following lines:

```
127.0.0.1      localhost
127.0.1.1      <some default name>
```

We need to change these lines to:

```
127.0.0.1      localhost
#127.0.1.1      <some default name>
192.168.0.2  slave1.infinity.com
```

Use ifconfig to get the IP address assigned to your Ethernet adapter. You can use ifconfig -a. This will display all the addresses assigned to your machine; just check for the Ethernet. It is better that you assign a static IP to your system because dynamic IP addresses tend to change on reboot. After assigning an IP address and hostname to the file, we add all other machines' IPs and hostnames to all host files in all the machines in the cluster so that they can communicate with each other. Follow this method to set a static IP to the machine:

1. Type in the following command to open a file:

   ```
   sudo vi /etc/network/interfaces
   ```

2. Once the file is opened, make the following changes:

   ```
   auto eth0
   ifaceeth0inet static
   address 192.168.0.2
   netmask 255.255.255.0
   network 192.168.0.0
   ```

```
broadcast 192.168.0.255
gateway 192.168.0.1
dns-nameservers 192.168.0.1
```

3. Make changes according to your network settings. You can also make changes using GUI in Ubuntu. Have a look at the following screenshot for reference:

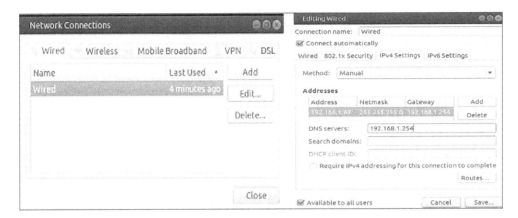

4. In the **Network Connections** window, click on **Edit...** and enter the information accordingly.

5. After making these changes, we can reboot the system or restart the networking services. These changes should be made in all the machines in the cluster. Keep in mind that you need to provide a unique name for all the machines. Restart the networking service using the following command:

```
sudo /etc/init.d/networking restart
```

>  For Red Hat/CentOS operating systems, it can be done in the same way.

6. So, once we finish configuring a hosts file, we will have a hosts file on different systems, as follows:

```
127.0.0.1      localhost
#127.0.1.1     <some default name>
192.168.0.2    slave1.infinity.com
192.168.0.3 slave2.infinity.com
```

```
192.168.0.4 slave3.infinity.com
192.168.0.5 slave4.infinity.com
192.168.0.6 slave5.infinity.com
```

Once we successfully set up the hostname and IP address correctly, a lot of problems can be avoided during cluster setup.

DNS based

For DNS-based host configurations, we need to have the IP addresses of all machines and equivalent hostnames. Then, the IP address and hostname pair must be added to the DNS server. For this, we need to have a DNS server that resolves the host to IP. Setting up a DNS server is out of the scope of this book, refer to `https://help.ubuntu.com/community/Servers#DNS` or `https://access.redhat.com/site/documentation/en-US/Red_Hat_Enterprise_Linux/6/html/Identity_Management_Guide/Working_with_DNS.html` for details.

Installing and configuring SSH

In this section, we will look at the steps to install and enable a passwordless SSH. It's always better that you have a dedicated Linux user for Hadoop and HBase processes. Let's create a user for Hadoop and HBase and name it `hbasehadoop`. We will use this user to start and stop all Hadoop/HBase daemon processes. Once the user is created, we can generate SSH for the same and set up a passwordless SSH on all machines. This user must exist on all machines in the cluster. Also, this user must be provided a root access if we need to install SSH using this user, else we can create a simple user just to start and stop the process, and we can install using the existing root user. The following figure will give you a clear picture:

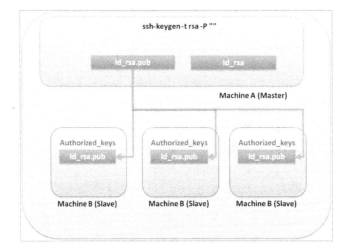

To add a user, the current user must be a root user. So, switch to the root user using the following command before setting up a password:

`useraddhbasehadoop`

To set a password for the `hbasehadoop` user, use the following command:

`passwdhbasehadoop`

From now on, we can use this user to start, stop, and configure Hadoop/HBase.

Installing SSH on Ubuntu/Red Hat/CentOS

Install SSH if it's not installed already. Use the following commands for this:

`sudo apt-get install openssh-server`

The preceding command will install an SSH server.

`sudo apt-get install openssh-client`

The preceding command will install an SSH client.

Once this installation successfully finishes, we can start configuring SSH.

Configuring SSH

Follow these steps to configure SSH:

1. The following command will generate a key-pair file in the current user's `.ssh` folder, which is in the `home` folder for the user. Just press *Ctrl + H* to show hidden files:

   `ssh-keygen -t rsa -P ""`

2. After issuing this command, just keep pressing *Enter*; don't enter the filename or anything else. It will show the following output:

   `Generating public/private rsa key pair.`

3. Next, the Linux terminal will ask you to enter the file in which to save the key; just press *Enter*.

4. After this, you will get the shell prompt back. Type in the following command:

   `cat $HOME/.ssh/id_rsa.pub>> $HOME/.ssh/authorized_keys`

This will create `authorized_keys` in the `.ssh` folder and put your public key in it so that you just need to type in `sshlocalhost` the next time, and it will log in to localhost without asking for the password.

5. Change the permission of the `.ssh` directory to `600` for security. This directory will be found in the `home` directory of the user for which key has been generated.

6. Once a public/private key pair is generated, we need to copy and paste this public key to the `authorized_keys` file on the machine, which we need to log in to or start/stop the process without a password.

Installing and configuring NTP

In this section, we will install and configure NTP on Ubuntu and CentOS/Red Hat.

First, we will look at the steps to install and configure NTP on Ubuntu. Ubuntu comes preinstalled with `ntpdate`, and this service runs automatically and updates time data at system startup. If we need a more frequent update, we can set up a cron job for the same. For this, we can create a script file such as `updateTimeDate.sh` and include the following lines:

```
#!bin/sh
ntpdate ntp.ubuntu.com
```

Set this as a `crontab` job to update the system date more frequently, keep in mind that this file must be the same, and note that the frequency of `crontab` must be the same for all the nodes in the cluster.

We can use the `sudontpq -np` command to check if the NTP service is running properly.

It can also be installed using the following commands, if it is not already installed:

```
sudo aptitude update
sudo aptitude install ntp
```

 The `aptitude` command was formerly used as `apt-get`.

On CentOS or Red Hat, we need to install the NTP client and set an NTP server to keep the time and date updated throughout the cluster. The following are the commands using which we can install and configure an NTP client service on nodes:

```
sudo yum install ntp
sudo /sbin/chkconfigntpd on
```

The first command will install an NTP service, and the second command will enable it to run on the boot-up process. If needed to be more frequent, a cron can be written for the same. Once the setup is complete, verify them as follows:

- **Java**: Use the `java -version` command. This must give a JDK version that we installed.

- **SSH**: Test SSH by connecting to all machines, for example, `ssh <hostname>`. If you can connect to the machine without using a password, the SSH setup is successful. If you get any errors, delete the `.ssh` directory in the `home` directory, regenerate the key again using the aforementioned method, and reboot your machine once.

- **NTP**: Check the time of all the systems. There must not be more than a 30-second difference between the times of the different machines.

- **DNS/host file**: Use commands such as `nslookup`, `dig`, and `ping` for correctness and reachability of the machines in the cluster. Check this using both the IP and hostname.

 Verify twice, and let's move forward.

Performing capacity planning

Hadoop and HBase were developed to run commodity hardware so that we can have hundreds of commodity machines and configure a Hadoop/HBase cluster. As data becomes costlier or important, we prefer some good machines so as to provide a robust cluster operation.

We have two scenarios—one in which we have many low-end machines, and another in which we have less number of machines for a cluster to be configured. In the first scenario, what we can do is set the replication factor more as we have many machines with storage and memory, and by setting a higher replication of data, we can make sure that data is available even if a machine fails frequently. For this scenario, we must have a good configuration machine that hosts NameNode, because it's a crucial component of the cluster and a proper back-up plan for metadata. In the second scenario, we might have less number of machines, so it is suggested that these machines must be well configured.

The following table shows the typical configuration requirements for machines for a cluster, which also depends upon the use case or the storage requirement of the user:

CPU	Number of nodes	Memory	Storage	Network
8-24 cores	• One primary node • One HMaster • One secondary node • One back-up HMaster • One JobTracker • Five to *n* nodes, TaskTracker, and RegionServers The number of nodes depends upon the attached storage and amount of data needed to be stored. It is always suggested to have more number of nodes with an average amount of storage attached.	8 GB to 128 GB of memory is required. This depends upon the kind of processing needed; if more primary memory is available, processing will be faster. It also depends upon the daemon processes we need to run on each node.	Storage depends on the number of nodes and data to be stored. We should have a higher number of nodes with low disk storage, for example, 10 nodes with 2 TB of storage attached.	A fiber-cable-based network will be great, but a cable-based network with faster switches will also work. Machines in cluster, if kept on more than one rack, are always better. Generally, we should have 1 GBPS to 10 GBPS for better network transfers and reduce network congestion.

For better configuration, we can have these HBase/Hadoop daemons hosted on separate machines. It all depends on the use case of the user and the type and amount of data to be stored and processed on the cluster. It can be calculated as: if we have a replication of 3 and 2 TB of data is to be stored, we must have around 10 TB of storage available in the cluster, around 6 TB for storage, and the rest for processing and intermediate temporary files, for which we can have either 5 DataNodes with 2 TB each or 10 DataNodes with 1 TB each, which depends on user preference.

Installing and configuring Hadoop

We will consider Hadoop installation using two methods: using a TAR file on Ubuntu and using the `.rpm` file on Red Hat distros. We will have a basic, running Hadoop cluster, and then we will set up an HBase cluster in detail. Execute the following steps:

1. Download Hadoop v2, the stable version of which is available at `http://www.webhostingjams.com/mirror/`. If you want a version other than the one we use here, you can always visit `http://www.webhostingjams.com/mirror/apache/hadoop/common/` and download the version that you want to install.

2. We can download Hadoop using the `wget` command, as follows:

```
Wget <full link of file which you get by clicking on the link
and getting copy link address in web browser>
```

Alternatively, we can also open this link in a browser and download it. Once this file is downloaded, we need to extract and copy it to the location where we need to keep it.

We can find the configuration files that need to be changed in the `Hadoop-<version>` directory. All configuration files that need to be changed can be found at `Hadoop-<version>/etc/hadoop`. We have two options for configuration: one in which we can keep the files in the same structure it exists and make changes, and another in which we copy the file to the `/etc` directory of the file system and create a symbolic link in the current directory. For a start up configuration, we will keep it as it is and start the configuration.

3. Once extracted, we have a folder structure as shown in the next screenshot:

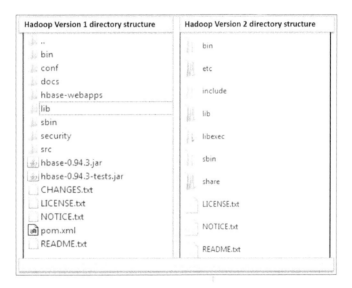

The left-hand side of the preceding screenshot shows the older directory structure of Hadoop Version 1 or previous versions, and the right-hand side shows the directory layout of Version 2 or above.

Let's discuss some important directories from the preceding screenshot briefly, which are important to be considered while configuration and working:

- `bin`: This directory contains Hadoop binary files
- `conf`: This directory contains configuration files
- `lib`: This directory contains JAR files or Hadoop precompiled library files
- `sbin`: This directory exists in the newer versions of Hadoop and contains scripts to start/stop clusters and scripts for some other administrative tasks
- `etc`: This is the directory in the newer versions of Hadoop containing configuration files

> For an older version of Hadoop, we need to change the configuration files inside the `conf` directory and start/stop cluster using files in the `bin` directory. In the newer versions of Hadoop, the configuration needs to be done in the `etc/hadoop` directory, and start/stop processes can be initiated using the scripts found in the `sbin` directory.

Now, let's start building the Apache Hadoop cluster. The following are the steps to install and configure Apache Hadoop:

1. To download Hadoop, change the directory to the desired location as follows:

   ```
   Cd ~/Downloads
   ```

2. Get Hadoop using the following command:

   ```
   wget http://www.carfab.com/apachesoftware/hadoop/common/
   stable/hadoop-2.2.0.tar.gz
   ```

   Refer to the following screenshot:

```
shashwat@infinity: ~/Downloads
shashwat@infinity:~/Downloads$ pwd
/home/shashwat/Downloads
shashwat@infinity:~/Downloads$ wget http://www.carfab.com/apachesoftware/hadoop/common/stable/hadoop-2.2.0.tar.gz
--2014-04-22 22:23:43--  http://www.carfab.com/apachesoftware/hadoop/common/stable/hadoop-2.2.0.tar.gz
Resolving www.carfab.com (www.carfab.com)... 205.186.175.60
Connecting to www.carfab.com (www.carfab.com)|205.186.175.60|:80... connected.
HTTP request sent, awaiting response... 200 OK
Length: 109229073 (104M) [application/x-gzip]
Saving to: `hadoop-2.2.0.tar.gz.1'

 2% [=>                                                                   ] 2,906,844
```

3. Once this file is downloaded, let's copy it to some location and extract it:

```
mv hadoop-2.2.0.tar.gz ~/hbinaries
tar -xvzfhadoop-2.2.0.tar.gz
mv hadoop-2.2.0 hadoop
cd ~/hbinaries
```

Have a look at the next screenshot:

```
shashwat@infinity: ~/hbinaries
shashwat@infinity:~/Downloads$ tar -xvzf hadoop-2.2.0.tar.gz
shashwat@infinity:~/Downloads$ mv hadoop-2.2.0 hadoop
shashwat@infinity:~/Downloads$ ll
total 107072
drwxr-xr-x  3 shashwat shashwat       4096 Apr 22 23:12 ./
drwxr-xr-x 28 shashwat shashwat       4096 Apr 22 21:38 ../
drwxr-xr-x  9 shashwat shashwat       4096 Oct  6  2013 hadoop/
-rw-rw-r--  1 shashwat shashwat 109229073 Oct  6  2013 hadoop-2.2.0.tar.gz
-rw-rw-r--  1 shashwat shashwat    393454 Jan 21 21:30 Rplots.pdf
shashwat@infinity:~/Downloads$ mkdir ~/hbinaries
shashwat@infinity:~/Downloads$ mv hadoop ~/hbinaries/
shashwat@infinity:~/Downloads$ cd ~/hbinaries/
shashwat@infinity:~/hbinaries$ ll
total 12
drwxrwxr-x  3 shashwat shashwat 4096 Apr 22 23:12 ./
drwxr-xr-x 29 shashwat shashwat 4096 Apr 22 23:12 ../
drwxr-xr-x  9 shashwat shashwat 4096 Oct  6  2013 hadoop/
shashwat@infinity:~/hbinaries$
```

4. Once a file is downloaded, extracted, and moved to the desired location, we can start configuring Hadoop. So, when we list them out, we find the following directory structure. We need to go to the `etc` folder where the configuration files lie:

```
shashwat@infinity: ~/hbinaries/hadoop
shashwat@infinity:~/hbinaries/hadoop$ ll
total 60
drwxr-xr-x 9 shashwat shashwat  4096 Oct  6  2013 ./
drwxrwxr-x 3 shashwat shashwat  4096 Apr 22 23:12 ../
drwxr-xr-x 2 shashwat shashwat  4096 Oct  6  2013 bin/
drwxr-xr-x 3 shashwat shashwat  4096 Oct  6  2013 etc/
drwxr-xr-x 2 shashwat shashwat  4096 Oct  6  2013 include/
drwxr-xr-x 3 shashwat shashwat  4096 Oct  6  2013 lib/
drwxr-xr-x 2 shashwat shashwat  4096 Oct  6  2013 libexec/
-rw-r--r-- 1 shashwat shashwat 15164 Oct  6  2013 LICENSE.txt
-rw-r--r-- 1 shashwat shashwat   101 Oct  6  2013 NOTICE.txt
-rw-r--r-- 1 shashwat shashwat  1366 Oct  6  2013 README.txt
drwxr-xr-x 2 shashwat shashwat  4096 Oct  6  2013 sbin/
drwxr-xr-x 4 shashwat shashwat  4096 Oct  6  2013 share/
shashwat@infinity:~/hbinaries/hadoop$
```

5. The following two categories of files are found in `etc/hadoop`:

    ° **Default**: These are the default files with default values; we need not touch or edit these files:

    `core-default.xml`: This contains common default properties for the whole cluster

    `hdfs-default.xml`: This contains HDFS-related default settings

    `yarn-default.xml`: This contains the YARN framework-related default settings

    `mapred-default.xml`: This contains MapReduce-related default settings

    ° **Site-specific files**: These are the files where we make changes, and the values in these files will override the values in default files:

    `core-site.xml`: The values given in this file override the `core-default.xml` settings

    `hdfs-site.xml`: The values given in this file override the `hdfs-default.xml` settings

    `yarn-site.xml`: The values given in this file override the `yarn-default.xml` settings

    `mapred-site.xml`: The values given in this file override the `mapred-default.xml` settings

We have some runtime files where we need to make changes, such as the `hadoop-env.sh` file that runs as an initial script for the Hadoop start up process. In this file, we set runtime variables such as a Java path and heap memory settings, and we execute the Java processes.

So, we can think of the `*-default` files as the files that are by default shipped with Hadoop with preset parameters and values. If we need to change some parameter value, we can add it to site-specific files such as `*.site.xml`.

These files are in the XML format, they start and end with a `<configuration>` tag, and all parameters lie in between the two tags. Inside `<configuration>`, we have `<property><name>{name of parameter}|</name><value>{value of the parameter}</value><description>{explanation about the tag}</description>`.

The following is a sample configuration file:

```
shashwat@infinity:~/hbinaries/hadoop$ head -200 /home/shashwat/hadoop/hadoop1/src/core/core-default.xml
<?xml version="1.0"?>
<?xml-stylesheet type="text/xsl" href="configuration.xsl"?>

<!-- Do not modify this file directly.  Instead, copy entries that you -->
<!-- wish to modify from this file into core-site.xml and change them -->
<!-- there.  If core-site.xml does not already exist, create it.     -->

<configuration>

<!--- global properties -->

<property>
  <name>hadoop.tmp.dir</name>
  <value>/tmp/hadoop-${user.name}</value>
  <description>A base for other temporary directories.</description>
</property>

<property>
  <name>hadoop.native.lib</name>
  <value>true</value>
  <description>Should native hadoop libraries, if present, be used.</description>
</property>
```

Hadoop runs in three modes. We will not discuss these in detail, only briefly so that we can understand the mode of operations:

- **Standalone mode**: This is the default mode that can run without any configuration changes as it is downloaded, extracted, and initiated. This has minimal configuration requirements. It does not use a distributed file system, but a local file system, and it does not initiate any Hadoop daemon processes. This mode is not suitable; it is just to check Hadoop testing.

- **Pseudo-distributed mode**: This can be seen as a cluster on a single machine. In this mode, Hadoop virtually runs as a cluster, but not on many machines. In this mode, Hadoop uses a distributed file system and runs all Hadoop daemons, and all these daemons run under a single JVM. This can be used to visualize a Hadoop cluster, testing purpose, code testing, or testing environment.

- **Fully distributed mode**: In this mode, the cluster is spread on many nodes as master and slave nodes. The daemons of Hadoop run on separate machines and they are best for a production environment. Each machine will have its own JVM and daemons (such as NameNode and DataNode) on separate machines.

Configuring pseudo- and fully distributed configuration is almost the same. Once configured as pseudo, we can distribute configuration files to other nodes, with some changes in configuration files, and can make it a fully distributed cluster.

Now, let's make changes in the required files. For this, what we can do is open these files in any text editor such as gedit or nano, or we can use command-line editing tools such as vi or vim.

 Make changes or put values according to your machine name; here, it is listed as per the current machine configuration.

Here, we will configure the newer version (V2) of Hadoop, which uses YARN for the MapReduce framework for configuration of older versions (1 or lower) of Hadoop and HBase. Follow these links to learn how to configure it step by step:

`https://www.youtube.com/watch?v=Mmqv-CvSTaQ`

`http://helpmetocode.blogspot.com`

Some configurations parameters are mentioned in the following sections.

core-site.xml

The `core-site.xml` configuration file overrides the default values for the core Hadoop properties.

The following is the configuration for Hadoop newer versions:

```
<configuration>
  <property>
    <name>fs.defaultFS</name>
    <value>hdfs://infinity:9000</value>
    <description>Namenode address</description>
  </property>
</configuration>
```

The following is the configuration for Hadoop older versions:

```
<configuration>
  <property>
    <name>fs.default.name</name>
    <value>hdfs://infinity:9000</value>
    <description>Namenode address</description>
  </property>
</configuration>
```

The hostname might vary according to your machine name, and you can give any unused port number.

hdfs-site.xml

The `hdfs-site.xml` file contains the site-wide property to enable/disable the features such as various paths and tuning parameters. You will see the following code in this file:

```
<configuration>

  <property>
    <name>dfs.namenode.name.dir</name>
    <value>/disk1/namenodemetacopy1,/disk2/amenodemetacopy2
      </value>
    <description>This is the directory where hadoopmetadata will
      be stored, always better to have more than one copy of
      metadata directory for robustness</description>
  </property>

  <property>
    <name>dfs.blocksize</name>
    <value>134217728</value>
    <description>This is block size of Hadoop that depends on data
     you are hosting. We can keep it from 6</description>
  </property>

  <property>
    <name>dfs.datanode.data.dir</name>
    <value>/disk1/datadirectory1,/disk1/datadirectory2</value>
    <description>This parameter defines where actual data will be
      stored on DataNodes. We can give one or more directory paths
      separated by commas. There should be proper permission on the
      directory which we specify here.</description>
  </property>

  <property>
    <name>dfs.replication</name>
    <value>5</value>
    <description>This defines the replication factor for not-so-
      valuable data and huge amount of data. We can keep it lower and
      for costly data, we can keep it higher. This defines how many
      copies of each block of a file will be kept on the cluster and
      this is how reliably the data will be stored if machines
      fail.</description>
  </property>
```

```
<property>
  <name>dfs.namenode.handler.count</name>
  <value>200</value>
  <description>Defines number of NameNode threads higher value
    means more datanodes.</description>
</property>

</configuration>
```

yarn-site.xml

The YARN framework-related configuration is stored in the `yarn-site.xml` file. Have a look at the following code:

```
<configuration>

  <property>
    <name>yarn.resourcemanager.address</name>
    <value>infinity:9002</value>
    <description>This is host where yarn manger will be hosted
    </description>
  </property>

  <property>
    <name>yarn.resourcemanager.scheduler.address</name>
    <value>infinity:9003</value>
    <description>Yarn scheduler address</description>
  </property>

  <property>
    <name>yarn.resourcemanager.admin.address</name>
    <value>infinity:9004</value>
    <description>Management interface of resource manager
    </description>
  </property>

  <property>
    <name>yarn.resourcemanager.resource-tracker.address</name>
    <value>infinity:9005</value>
    <description>resource manager resource tracker interface
    </description>
  </property>
```

```
<property>
  <name>yarn.nodemanager.aux-services.mapreduce.shuffle.class
  </name>
  <value>org.apache.hadoop.mapred.ShuffleHandler</value>
  <description>Specifies mapreduce framework to be used
  </description>
</property>

<property>
  <name>yarn.scheduler.maximum-allocation-mb</name>
  <value>1000</value>
  <description>Max memory forschedular</description>
</property>

</configuration>
```

mapred-site.xml

The `mapred-site.xml` file contains the MapReduce framework-related configurations. Have a look at the following code:

```
<configuration>
  <property>
    <name>mapreduce.framework.name</name>
    <value>yarn</value>
    <description>Framework to be used for map reduce</description>
  </property>
</configuration>
```

There are many other configuration parameters that can be found in the `*-default.xml` files and added to the `*-site.xml` files to override the default parameters. We will discuss more parameters and their optimal values in *Chapter 6, HBase Cluster Maintenance and Troubleshooting*, and *Chapter 7, Scripting in HBase*.

hadoop-env.sh

The `hadoop-env.sh` file contains the environment and runtime variables, which is as follows:

```
export JAVA_HOME=<path of Java here>
export HADOOP_CONF_DIR=<hadoopconf directory path here>
export HADOOP_HEAPSIZE=<amount of memory available to jvm>
```

yarn-env.sh

The `yarn-env.sh` file contains the YARN framework-related runtime and environment configuration:

```
export JAVA_HOME=<path of Java here>
export YARN_CONF_DIR=<configuration conf directory of yarn/hadoop>
JAVA_HEAP_MAX=-Xmx1000m
```

Slaves file

The `slaves` file contains the list of hosts where DataNode daemons will run. The following are the host names of DataNode machines:

```
datanode1
datanode2
datanode3
```

Add the nodes where you want to host DataNode services.

After all these changes are made, verify the paths and parameters in these files. Once verified, we can move forward to start Hadoop services. Once all Hadoop services start successfully, we can move forward to configure HBase.

Hadoop start up steps

Let's get started with Hadoop using the following steps:

1. Format NameNode.

   Before starting up the Hadoop daemons, we need to format NameNode. This is like formatting a new disk. We know that just as we bring a new disk drive and format it to a file system (FAT, NTFS, ExtFS), we format NameNode. This process creates a logical layer of HDFS on top of the file system.

    `<hadoop directory path>` can be added to the system path to call the `hadoop` command directly. Follow `http://www.cyberciti.biz/faq/unix-linux-adding-path/` for various options.

   The following line will format NameNode and make it available to read and write files from HDFS. This command prepares the HDFS file system:

   ```
   <hadoop directory path>/bin/hdfsnamenode -format
   <cluster name>
   ```

2. Once NameNode is formatted successfully without any errors, let's start the Hadoop daemons:

```
sbin/hadoop-daemon.sh start namenode
sbin/hadoop-daemons.sh start datanode
sbin/yarn-daemon.sh start resourcemanager
sbin/yarn-daemons.sh start nodemanager
sbin/yarn-daemon.sh start historyserver
```

3. Once all the processes start, we can check it using the following command:

```
ps -ef|grep Java
```

Use the following command found in `<Java home>/bin/jps`:

```
Jps
```

4. For easy access of `jps`, we can create an alias and just type `jps`. It will display the Java process running; `jps` stands for Java process. As all Hadoop daemons are Java processes, `jps` displays the daemons running:

```
alias jps=<Java path>/bin/jps
```

Now, we can directly access the `jps` command.

5. To stop the Hadoop cluster, we can use:

```
sbin/hadoop-daemon.sh stop namenode
sbin/hadoop-daemons.sh stop datanode
sbin/yarn-daemon.sh stop resourcemanager
sbin/yarn-daemons.sh stop nodemanager
sbin/yarn-daemon.sh stop historyserver
```

Now, let's move forward and configure HBase.

Configuring Apache HBase

As we have already set up Java, SSH, NTP, DNS, and Hadoop, let's configure HBase. HBase runs in these modes:

- **Standalone**: This mode uses file systems to store tables and data, not HDFS. All the daemon processes run under a single JVM. This mode is suitable for testing purposes, but if you want to have real power of HBase, you need to configure it with Hadoop.

- **Distributed**: This can be divided into the following two modes:

  ○ **Pseudo-distributed**: This uses HDFS file systems. All daemon processes run under a single JVM on a single machine. This is best for testing purposes; it also provides the power of Hadoop and can be configured with fewer resources on a single machine.

  ○ **Fully distributed**: This uses HDFS as an underlying file system. All of its daemon processes run under different JVMs on different machines. This mode is best for the production environment.

Configuring HBase in the standalone mode

Configuring HBase in a standalone mode is simple since we don't have to make many configuration changes. We can just download the TAR file, extract it, and start the daemons. HBase configured in this mode will not use HDFS, but file://, to store data files on top of the local file system.

Download the HBase binary from `http://apache.mirrors.pair.com/hbase/`. Here, we will use the latest compatible version of HBase. Refer to the compatibility table to understand which HBase we need to download for which Hadoop.

> Use the following command to download the desired HBase binary:
>
> `wget http://apache.mirrors.pair.com/hbase/<version to download .tar>`

Once the download is complete, extract the TAR file and move it to a location where you want to configure it, such as the ~/hbinaries/hbase path:

```
tar -xvzfhbase-0.94.18.tar.gz //extract tar
mv hbase-0.94.18 hbase          //rename to hbase
mv hbase ~/hbinaries/hbase      //move to configuration location
cd ~/hbinaries/hbase            // go to ~/hbinaries/hbase directory
```

The following is how the terminal window looks like:

```
shashwat@infinity: ~/hbinaries/hbase/bin
shashwat@infinity:~/hbinaries/hbase/bin$ tar -xvzf hbase-0.94.18.tar.gz
shashwat@infinity:~/hbinaries/hbase/bin$ mv hbase-0.94.18 hbase
shashwat@infinity:~/hbinaries/hbase/bin$ mv hbase ~/hbinaries/
shashwat@infinity:~/hbinaries/hbase/bin$ cd ~/hbinaries/hbase/bin
shashwat@infinity:~/hbinaries/hbase/bin$ ./start-hbase.sh
shashwat@infinity:~/hbinaries/hbase/bin$ hbase shell
HBase Shell; enter 'help<RETURN>' for list of supported commands.
Type "exit<RETURN>" to leave the HBase Shell
Version 0.94.12, r1524863, Fri Sep 20 04:44:41 UTC 2013

hbase(main):001:0> list
TABLE
0 row(s) in 6.2570 seconds

hbase(main):002:0>
```

Once extracted, move the file to the desired location to start the process as it is. It will store the tmp files, log files, and other files to the default locations, which are defined in the `*-default.xml` file, mostly in the `/tmp` or current directory. This is why the standalone mode is not advisable as everything gets lost once the system is started. On every reboot or start up process, the content of the `/tmp` directory is removed.

This mode can be used version of to get familiar with the directory structure, start up HBase, and run some basic HBase commands. Now, let's configure HBase in the distributed mode.

Configuring HBase in the distributed mode

We can configure a pseudo-distributed mode and distribute the configuration files to nodes that we like to have in the cluster where we need to run RegionServers. So, let's configure HBase in the distributed mode.

The following are the files that need to be changed or configured:

- `hbase-site.xml`: This is an HBase site-specific file. We can add configurations related to the HBase root and log directories in this file. All default settings from the `hbase-default.xml` file can be overridden in this file.
- `hbase-env.sh`: We can define runtime variables such as Java path, RegionServer-related options, and JVM settings in this file.
- `regionservers`: This file contains all the node names where we want to host or run our RegionServer daemon.

Now, let's set the values and start configuring.

hbase-site.xml

Let's see the configuration we need to add in the `hbase-site.xml` file:

```xml
<configuration>

  <property>
    <name>hbase.rootdir</name>
    <value>hdfs://infinity:9000/hbase</value>
    <description>Here, we need to enter Hadoop NameNode address
    followed by the hbase directory name where hbase files are to be
    stored.</description>
  </property>

  <property>
    <name>hbase.cluster.distributed</name>
    <value>true</value>
    <description>This parameter decides whether HBase will run in
    local mode or distributed mode.</description>
  </property>

  <property>
    <name>hbase.tmp.dir</name>
    <value>/mnt/disk1/tmp</value>
    <description>Using this parameter, we specify tmp directory for
     HBase.</description>
  </property>

  <property>
    <name>hbase.zookeeper.quorum</name>
    <value>infinity</value>
    <description>Using this parameter, we can specify ZooKeeper host
     machines addressee.</description>
  </property>

  <property>
    <name>hbase.zookeeper.property.clientPort</name>
    <value>2081</value>
    <description>port at which client can connect to zookeeper
    </description>
  </property>


</configuration>
```

HBase-env.sh

We can define runtime parameters in this file. This file will include the following lines:

```
export JAVA_HOME=<path of Java here>
```

In the preceding line, we mention the Java path.

```
export HBASE_HEAPSIZE=8000
```

In the preceding line, we mention the heap memory size.

```
export HBASE_MANAGES_ZK=true
```

The preceding command will be false if it is in the fully distributed mode and ZooKeepers are installed as separate instances on different machines. For the pseudo-distributed mode, or if we need to manage HBase's built-in ZooKeeper, we need to keep it to `true`; if we have a separate ZooKeeper, we can make it `false`.

regionservers

In this file, we list all the servers we need to run RegionServers:

```
infinity
```

All set, now let's start HBase. This is in the pseudo-distributed mode, so Hadoop must run first. Start the Hadoop processes, and then we will start HBase:

bin/start-hbase.sh

In the preceding command, we run the script that will start all the required processes.

Alternatively, we can start HBase in the following ways:

1. Start the ZooKeeper:

   bin/hbase-daemon.sh start zookeeper

2. Start the HMaster:

   bin/hbase-daemon.sh start master

3. Start the RegionServer:

   bin/hbase-daemon.sh start regionserver

This will start HBase in the pseudo-distributed mode with all the processes running on the same server. If we need to make HBase fully distributed, we will have to add all the DataNode addresses to a `regionserver` file, wherein we will run HBase RegionServers.

There is a small difference between the pseudo-distributed and fully distributed modes. First, we will add the following settings to `hbase-site.xml` and add the hostnames of DataNode where we need to host our RegionServer. In this setup, we will have separate instances of ZooKeeper (odd number). Start a master server on the NameNode server, RegionServers on different DataNodes, and ZooKeeper processes.

There are two ways to start it; if a passwordless SSH is configured and the master server is able to connect to all DataNodes, we can use `start-hbase.sh`, which will start HMaster on NameNode and RegionServers on the listed DataNodes.

We must first start all ZooKeepers, and then we can run the `start-hbase.sh` script. Another method is to start processes using `hbase-daemon.sh` to start HMaster on the NameNode server and RegionServer on DataNodes, for which we need to run this script in the same way we called in starting hbase in pseudo mode.

A few settings that we need to add or change in `hbase-site.xml` are as follows:

```
<property>
  <name>hbase.zookeeper.quorum</name>
  <value>zkhost1:2181,zkhost2:2181,zkhost3:2181</value>
  <description>List of zookeeper instances</description>
</property>

<property>
  <name>hbase.zookeeper.property.dataDir</name>
  <value>/mnt/disk1/zookeeperData</value>
  <description>zk data directory path</description>
</property>
```

We also need to add DataNode addresses in the `regionserver` file, as follows:

```
datanode1
datanode2
datanode3
```

Change the line `export HBASE_MANAGES_ZK=true` to `export HBASE_MANAGES_ZK=false` in hbase-env.sh file. This will instruct HBase not to use the inbuilt ZooKeeper as there exist separate ZooKeeper instances. The preceding configuration in `hbase-site.xml` will tell where ZooKeeper instances are running, and data directories for the ZooKeeper location are defined by the second parameter.

After making these changes, we can restart the cluster, and these settings will be loaded.

Once all these settings are complete, we need to copy the configuration files to other nodes too.

Now, let's see how to install and configure ZooKeeper instances. It is advisable that we configure odd number of ZooKeeper instances. Let's consider that we want three servers. Download a ZooKeeper copy on these three servers and make changes in the zoo.cfg file that lies in ZooKeeper's conf directory.

Installing and configuring ZooKeeper

The following is the step-by-step process to download, install, and configure ZooKeeper:

1. The download link for ZooKeeper is http://apache.mirrors. lucidnetworks.net/zookeeper/.

   So, let's download the latest release of ZooKeeper using the following command:

   ```
   wget http://apache.mirrors.lucidnetworks.net/zookeeper/stable
   /zookeeper-3.4.6.tar.gz
   ```

2. Extract it as follows:

   ```
   tar -xvzfzookeeper-3.4.6.tar.gz
   ```

3. Rename this file for an easy naming convention:

   ```
   mv zookeeper-3.4.6.tar.gz zookeeper
   ```

4. Move it to a desired location:

   ```
   mv zookeeper ~/hbinaries/
   cd ~/hbinaries/zookeeper/conf
   vim zoo.cfg
   ```

5. Now, add the following lines:

   ```
   dataDir=/mnt/disk1/zookeeperData#Assuming the layout of the
   reader's filesystem>
   tickTime=2000
   clientPort=2181
   ```

   Here, dataDir is the location where the memory snapshot database of ZooKeeper will be stored, tickTime is the heartbeat interval for session timeout in milliseconds, and clientPort is the port where the client connection will be accepted and ZooKeeper listens.

6. After configuring ZooKeeper, we can start ZooKeeper as follows:

```
./zkServer.sh start
```

Alternatively, we can use the following command:

```
bin/zkServer.sh start
```

So, this is the method to configure a standalone ZooKeeper. However, in a production environment, we have more than one distributed ZooKeeper instances for high availability, which can be configured by configuring ZooKeeper individually at different servers. What we can do is configure, as described earlier, and copy the same directory at different servers. We need to make the following changes in the zoo.cfg file to make it distributed and a highly available ZooKeeper cluster.

We need to copy the ZooKeeper directory to all the servers that we have for an instance, and the configuration file will be same for all; we can make changes and copy the same configuration file to all servers.

The following command will create the zoo.cfg file:

```
vim zoo.cfg
```

Add the following lines to this file:

```
initLimit=5
syncLimit=2
server.1=zookeeperinstance1:2888:3888
server.2=zookeeperinstance2:2888:3888
server.3=zookeeperinstance3:2888:3888
```

Here, initLimit is the timeout to connect to the leader ZooKeeper, syncLimit is the maximum time difference between the leader and follower ZooKeepers, and server.1, server.2, and server.3 are servers where ZooKeeper instances are running. The port number is to enable communication between instances.

Once these configurations are complete, we can start all the instances of ZooKeeper one by one. Out of these three ZooKeepers, a leader will be elected randomly, which will become active; the other two will work in coordination to master. If any one of these ZooKeepers fails, other ZooKeepers will be elected as a master.

We have an option to work with ZooKeeper CLI, a command-line shell, using which we can connect to different ZooKeepers and perform operations such as getting information about ZooKeeper components, which we will discuss in *Chapter 6, HBase Cluster Maintenance and Troubleshooting.*

We can start with ZooKeeper **command line interface (CLI)**, as follows:

```
bin/zkCli.sh -server <IP of the zookeeper>
```

Alternatively, we can use the following command:

```
./zkCli.sh -server <IP>
```

Executing this command will connect to the ZooKeeper IP and provide a command-line shell where we can execute commands.

Installing Cloudera Hadoop and HBase

Now, let's see how to install and configure the Cloudera distribution of Hadoop. There are two options for Cloudera Hadoop installation:

- Using the tarball (TAR file)

  Cloudera Hadoop tars of CDH4/CDH5 can be downloaded from
  `http://www.cloudera.com/content/support/en/documentation.html`.

- Using the package file (RPM on Red Hat distros)

If you use tarball, follow the same method as was previously mentioned for both Ubuntu and Red Hat distros. There are other methods too, which use the `.rpm` package, which we will discuss now.

Downloading the required RPM packages

In this section, we will see links to download the required RPM packages for installation.

The following is the link to download RPM packages for the CDH4 version of Hadoop:

`http://archive.cloudera.com/cdh4/redhat/6/x86_64/cdh/4/RPMS/x86_64/`

The following is the link to download RPM packages for the CDH4 version of HBase:

`http://archive.cloudera.com/cdh4/redhat/6/x86_64/cdh/4/RPMS/x86_64/`

The following are the links to download RPM packages for the CDH4 version of ZooKeeper:

- `http://archive.cloudera.com/cdh4/redhat/6/x86_64/cdh/4/RPMS/x86_64/zookeeper-3.4.5+25-1.cdh4.6.0.p0.12.el6.x86_64.rpm`
- `http://archive.cloudera.com/cdh4/redhat/6/x86_64/cdh/4/RPMS/x86_64/zookeeper-server-3.4.5+25-1.cdh4.6.0.p0.12.el6.x86_64.rpm`

After downloading these packages, we can install different components on machines assigned for specific components.

For a single node setup, we can install all these RPM packages on a single server, as follows:

```
Rpm -ivh<rpm package name.rpm>
```

For a fully distributed cluster, we will install the Hadoop and HBase RPM packages on all nodes; the NameNode, JobTracker, and master RPM packages on the NameNode server; the DataNode, TaskTracker, and RegionServer RPM packages on DataNodes; and the ZooKeeper RPM package on servers assigned for ZooKeepers.

 Keep in mind that to install RPM packages, we need root user access. After installing these RPM packages, change the permission and ownership of the Hadoop/HBase directory to the user. Usernames will be used to start, stop, and handle the cluster.

After changing the permission and ownership, the configuration process is the same as configuring TAR files. We need to add the parameters as we added them in the *Configuring Apache HBase* section; the startup and stop processes are also the same.

Installing Cloudera in an easier way

There is another easy method to install Cloudera, which is as follows:

1. Download Cloudera:

   ```
   Wget http://archive.cloudera.com/cdh4/one-click-install/redhat/6/x86_64/cloudera-cdh-4-0.x86_64.rpm
   ```

2. Install and configure local Cloudera using the downloaded RPM package:

```
sudo yum --nogpgchecklocalinstall<Cloudera rpm downloaded
cloudera-cdh-4-0.x86_64.rpm>
```

3. Install CDH4.

The following command will add a repository key:

```
sudo rpm --import
http://archive.cloudera.com/cdh4/redhat/6/x86_64/cdh/RPM-GPG-
KEY-cloudera
```

Installing the Hadoop and MapReduce packages

Let's install Hadoop and other components such as NameNode, DataNode, MapReduce, secondary NameNode, and so on using the yum command available in RHEL distributions:

1. Install the components using the following commands:

```
sudo yum clean all;
sudo yum install hadoop-hdfs-namenode
sudo yum install hadoop-hdfs-secondarynamenode
sudo yum install hadoop-0.20-mapreduce-tasktrackerhadoop-hdfs-
datanode
sudo yum install hbase
```

2. Verify whether these components installed successfully using the rpm -qa<hadoop/hbase> command:

You can start and stop the processes using the following commands:

```
/usr/lib/hadoop/bin/hadoop-daemon.sh<start/stop><daemon name>
/usr/lib/hbase/bin/hbase-daemon.sh<start/stop><daemon name>
```

3. Be careful of the sequence of starting and stopping HBase and Hadoop daemon processes.

   If we use `start-all.sh`, `start-dfs.sh`, `start-mapred.sh`, or `start-yarn.sh` to start the HBase/Hadoop cluster, it takes care of the sequence of starting and stopping the process. However, if we use `Hadoop-daemon.sh` or `HBase-daemon.sh` to start Hadoop/HBase processes, we should follow the following sequence:

   1. Hadoop startup process:

   | NameNode → DataNodes → SecondaryNameNode → JobTracker → TaskTrackers |

   2. Hadoop shutdown process:

   | JobTracker → TaskTracker → NameNode → DataNodes → SecondaryNameNode |

   3. HBase startup process:

   | ZooKeepers → HMaster → RegionServers |

   4. HBase shutdown process:

   | RegionServers → HMaster → ZooKeepers |

Installing Hadoop on Windows

We can install Hadoop on Windows in order to evaluate its power, before migrating and configuring full-sized production cluster on a Linux machine. Bear in mind that this configuration is suitable for evaluation or testing purposes only. For a full-fledged production cluster, we need to have a Linux distribution for cluster setup.

1. Download and install Cygwin from `http://www.cygwin.com`.

   This is a tool that provides native Linux programs to run on Windows.

2. Download Hadoop, HBase, and Zookeeper. It's better not to download the most recent version as Cygwin does not have full-fledged support. Cluster using Cygwin will just give us the feeling of a cluster when we don't want to directly switch to the Linux OS and first evaluate it on Windows.

3. Copy the downloaded Hadoop file to `c:\cygwin\usr\local`, which is the default location of Cygwin when installed.

4. Open Cygwin and extract Hadoop, HBase, and ZooKeeper TAR, which we copied inside the Cygwin folder. We will find it at the `/usr/local` location. After extracting, make the following changes to these particular files:

   In the `core-site.xml` file, make the following changes:

   ```
   <property>
     <name>fs.default.name</name>
     <value>hdfs://localhost:9100</value>
     <description>the value can be either localhost or
     127.0.0.1 </description>
   </property>
   ```

   In the `mapred-site.xml`, make the following changes:

   ```
   <property>
     <name>mapred.job.tracker</name>
     <value>localhost:9101</value>
     <description>the value can be either localhost or
     127.0.0.1 </description>
   </property>
   ```

   In the `hdfs-site.xml` file, make the following changes:

   ```
   <property>
     <name>dfs.replication</name>
     <value>1</value>
   </property>
   <property>
     <name>dfs.permissions</name>
     <value>false</value>
   </property>
   ```

5. After this, we just format NameNode and start the process; we also install HBase.

   Extract the HBase TAR file. Create a symbolic link to JRE, which must be present in Windows, using the following command:

   ```
   ln -s /cygdrive/c/Program\ Files/Java/<jre present in system>
   /usr/local/Java/<jre present in system >
   ```

   The preceding command will create a soft link to JRE and make JRE available to Cygwin for Hadoop and HBase.

6. Change `hbase-env.sh`; add the following lines:

```
export JAVA_HOME=/usr/local/Java/<jre name given>
export HBASE_IDENT_STRING=$HOSTNAME
export HBASE_MANAGES_ZK=true
```

7. Then, change the `hbase-site.xml` file and add the following lines:

```
<property>
  <name>hbase.rootdir</name>
  <value>file:///C:/cygwin/tmp/hbaseroot</value>
</property>

<property>
  <name>hbase.tmp.dir</name>
  <value>C:/cygwin/tmp/hbaseroot/temp</value>
</property>
```

Now, we can start HBase using the following command:

bin/start-hbase.sh

Alternatively, you can use the following command:

./start-hbase.sh

> Bear in mind that this will not be suitable for production or serious code testing. If we need a real Hadoop cluster, we must have a Linux/Mac/Oracle OS or similar.
>
> Follow the steps given on `http://wiki.apache.org/hadoop/Running_Hadoop_On_OS_X_10.5_64-bit_(Single-Node_Cluster)` to install and run Hadoop on OS X.

Another way to get Ubuntu on Windows is to install the OS in a virtual machine and configure Hadoop/HBase. Use the following links to do so.

- Configure the Hadoop, HBase, Hive, or Pig cluster using the following links:
  - `https://www.youtube.com/watch?v=Mmqv-CvSTaQ`
  - `https://www.youtube.com/watch?v=c8ReD7gLfGo`

- Configure the fully distributed Hadoop cluster using a virtual machine, by browsing the following links:
  - `https://www.youtube.com/watch?v=gIRubPl20oo`
  - `https://www.youtube.com/watch?v=pgOKKl5P0to`
  - `https://www.youtube.com/watch?v=8CrgPUaNfjk`

After installation and configuration, we can perform a file-system-related operation using Hadoop HDFS binary and HBase shell, which we will see in detail in the next chapter.

> For configuration files, it is always better to have a separated directory on a common mount point to all nodes, and a soft link in either an HBase or a Hadoop directory pointing to it. Processes can be started using the `--config` keyword on command lines while starting and stopping the processes.

Summary

In this chapter, we learned the steps to install and configure all prerequisites of Hadoop and HBase, Hadoop distributions, and HBase. We also learned how to install, configure, and test a cluster on Windows using Cygwin. We learned about various Apache/Cloudera Hadoop and HBase distributions available and started the daemon processes of Hadoop/HBase.

In the next chapter, we will see the basic operations that we can perform with the Hadoop HBase cluster using a command line, and we will then look into the optimizing and other important parameters in different files.

4
Optimizing the HBase/Hadoop Cluster

Different workloads have different characteristics, so experiment with different tuning options before finalizing. We cannot achieve the optimum performance for HBase without optimizing Hadoop as HBase runs on top of Hadoop. So, we will first see the optimization parameters of Hadoop and then continue optimizing HBase.

In this chapter, we will discuss the following topics:

- Hadoop and HBase cluster types
- Hardware requirements
- Capacity planning
- Hardware, network, and operating system considerations
- The optimization of different components in a cluster configuration
- Different configuration files in Hadoop/HBase

Setup types for Hadoop and HBase clusters

Now, let's see the files and their parameters in Hadoop, using which optimization can be performed. Mentioned next are examples of Hadoop/HBase cluster types. When we configure a Hadoop/HBase cluster, we can have the following types of clusters, according to their usability:

- **Standalone**: This cluster type is suitable for development work where one machine can host all the daemon processes or we have a single machine with many virtual machines on a single system. This type of cluster is good for evaluation and testing purposes.

- **Small**: We can have less than or equal to 20 nodes with different processes running of different machines. It is good for small productions with less data and processing requirements.

- **Medium**: This cluster type can have 20 to 1000 nodes with HA, three to five ZooKeepers, and DataNodes, which is better for full-fledged production clusters.

- **Large**: This cluster type can have 1000 or more nodes with huge storage capacity and several machines for high dataset-processing power, which is best for large-scale setups and processing clusters.

The hardware requirement for these clusters depends on the user scenario. It is best to have more machines with an average amount of storage (GBs to TBs) attached and a more-than-average amount of primary memory (8 GB to 128 GB) for DataNodes. Assigning a huge amount of primary memory for the heap is also not very advisable as lengthy garbage collection might affect the performance.

Let's see an example cluster for the following components:

- **NameNode/HMaster**: This is one of the most critical components of a Hadoop cluster, so we need to have this machine as the best and most robust machine. It must not fail as frequently as DataNodes fail, but if NameNodes fail, the whole cluster goes down.

  The recommended hardware configuration for NameNode is as follows:

  - 16 GB to 64 GB memory
  - 2 x (8 to 24) core processor or 2 x 16 core processor
  - SATA ~1 TB disk and one network mounted disk for secondary backup of metadata; this must be of 7200 RPM (Solid State Drives are preferred)
  - 2 x 1 GB Ethernet controller

  As all the metadata is cached in the main memory for faster performance, so the main memory should be of good speed and quality. More memory space means a larger number of files can be hosted by the cluster as it enables bigger namespaces on NameNode.

  Not much storage is required on NameNode, so less disk space is needed. We must have at least two disk locations for the metadata for two copies: one attached to the machine and another network-mounted fixed disk. The metadata is loaded in the main memory and the persistent copy of it with edit logs is kept on a disk.

- **JobTracker**: This can run on a NameNode machine or be separately hosted. The hardware configuration requirement will be the same as NameNode. It does not require much storage space as it distributes the job, so not much storage and processing power is required.

- **DataNode/TaskTracker/RegionServers**: The actual data resides on these nodes, so we need more storage and processing power for these machines if the number of machines is high. We can have the average storage, memory, and processing power for fewer machines. In the cluster, we need to have more powerful machines, as recommended previously:

    ° 24 to 128 GB of memory

    ° 2 x (8 to 16/24) core processor

    ° 2 x 4 (2 TB disk) with 7200 RPM

    ° 2 x 1 GB Ethernet controller

Recommendations for CDH cluster configuration

The hardware specification might vary according to the amount of data to be stored and the type of processing power required. It is recommended to use the following configurations:

- 1 to 4 TB hard disks

- Two (8 to 24 core) processors, running at least 2 to 2.5 GHz

- 64 to 512 GB of memory

- Bonded Gigabit Ethernet or 10 Gigabit Ethernets

Now, let's explain these hardware components in more detail:

- **CPU**: The workload depends on this hardware component. It is recommended that we have a medium-clock-speed CPU with two slots for DataNodes. Why medium? This is because the high-end processor cost of a setup rises quickly, so we can have a comparatively cheaper CPU with more machines than use fewer machines with high-end processors. So, it is recommended to have 8 to 24 core processors with medium CPU cycle for less power consumption.

- **Power**: This is also a component to consider when configuring a Hadoop cluster because power consumption tends to go up with high-end or a higher number of machines, and hence increases the cost to maintain air cooling and the environment setup. There must be a constant power supply with failover for constant operations. Also, there must be proper air conditioning for the cluster environment.

- **RAM**: We need only the amount of memory that will be sufficient to keep processors busy in processing instead of keeping it waiting for data to be brought to the main memory for processing. So, 8 GB to 48 GB of RAM looks adequate for a system inside a cluster. HBase tends to use a lot of memory and keeps files in the main memory (if in-memory tables are enabled). So, for clusters subhosting HBase, we can consider more memory than what we have for Hadoop-only clusters. If caching is enabled in HBase, the entire table is tried to be kept in the main memory, so depending upon the components (DataNode, RegionServer, and TaskTracker) being hosted, we might have to add or reduce RAM. Whatever requirements we specify are a global resource not only for the Hadoop/HBase heap but also for the system. If we have more memory in the system, we can change the heap memory on requirement.

- **Disk**: The disk must have high-speed (7200 RPM) SATA drives. This disk storage varies with the amount of data we need to have on the cluster and number of machines. It is not advisable to have a machine loaded with huge disk space because if it fails, there will be a huge overhead in re-replicating the blocks. We can have machines with locally attached disks, but they must also have network-attached disks. So, for local disks, if a machine fails, the data can't be used, but if it is network attached, the same disk can be attached with other machines (newly configured) and be used to report the data to NameNode. As an example, we can say that we can have one to four disks attached to machines of capacities calculated on the basis of data storage requirement if we have **Solid State Drives** (**SSDs**) that also boost the throughput a lot.

- **Network**: Hadoop/HBase tends to transfer data between nodes while running tasks, accessing data, or writing data to the cluster, so it is advisable to have a high-speed network between the nodes, and also a high-speed network switch. For a small or medium cluster, 1 GB/s network is enough to do the work; for bigger clusters, 10 GB/s network is preferable. The network load also depends on the type of analytical computing in the cluster. Some operations, such as sorting and shuffling, tend to transfer a lot of data between the nodes, and hence, the bandwidth matters a lot; if adequate bandwidth is not available, there will be more timeout errors and issues such as RegionServer failing, ZooKeeper timeouts, bad connection error, and no route to host errors. For smaller clusters, it's better to have a single switch for better performance; for bigger clusters, we can have multiple fast switches.

Capacity planning

Suppose we have around 2 TB data with a replication factor of 3, which means $3 * 2 = 6$ *TB*, which in turn means that 2 TB of extra space is still needed. So, for 2 TB of data, we can have a cluster with 4 to 8 DataNodes, totaling 8 TB of storage disk.

This extra space is needed for an intermediate temporary file that is generated during read/write operations and MapReduce jobs. If the data on which we run MapReduce is huge and the MapReduce code processes the whole data that requires a huge HDFS storage to store the temporary and intermediate result files, we will need to provide enough disk storage, the absence of which will result in a lot of failing tasks and blacklisted nodes. It is advisable to have 25 to 50 percent more storage than the original data size (without a replication factor) on the cluster; the minimum should be 25 percent more of the whole data size if we want to run a MapReduce task without much failing.

So, we can apply an approximate formula, as follows (not a universal formula, but might be used to calculate the storage required):

```
T = (S*R) *1.25 (approximately for intermediate files)
```

Here, s is the size of data to store on HDFS, R is the replication factor, and T is the total space.

This is the case of a cluster where we need to run MapReduce jobs frequently. For the clusters where we don't need to run jobs, but just store files and read/write, we can have a formula such as $S * R +$ *some extra amount of disk space*.

So, for example, if we have 2 TB of data, we can calculate the total space $A = (2*3) +6*(1/4)$ which will total to 7.5 (approximately).

Thus, if we assign 8 TB (four nodes with 2 TB each or five nodes with 1.5 TB each) for this cluster, we can ensure proper functioning of the cluster; also, this can be managed as the amount of data grows. We need to add more nodes or storage to the cluster as data grows. This size is the size available for HDFS and not for the whole system, so if we have 2 TB storage for each node, then we must have at least 2.5 or 3 TB for the system.

We can calculate the number of DataNodes in a cluster as *Number of DataNodes = (total size required / amount of disk space allocated per nodes) + Disk space for the system (for other resources)*.

So, if 100 TB is required to be stored, and each node is attached with 5 TB of space, the number of DataNodes will be 100 / 5 = 20 (at least).

If we have compression enabled, the storage requirement might reduce. There is no universal formula; however, we can use the aforementioned formula for an approximate estimation.

Hadoop optimization

If we have an optimized Hadoop cluster, a lot of problems are easily solved for other Hadoop ecosystem components on the cluster, for example HBase. So, now let's see some of the factors using which we can optimize Hadoop.

General optimization tips

These are some general optimization tips that will help us to optimize Hadoop:

- Create a dedicated Hadoop/HBase user to run the daemons.
- Try to use SSD for the NameNode metadata.
- The NameNode metadata must be backed up periodically; it can be either on an hourly or daily basis. If it contains very valuable data, it must be backed up every 5 to 10 minutes. We can write crons to copy with the metadata directory.
- We must have multiple metadata directories for NameNode, which can be specified using the parameters `dfs.name.dir` or `dfs.namenode.name.dir`; one can be located at local disk and another at network mount location (NFS). This provides redundancy of metadata, and robustness, in case of failure.
- Set `dfs.namenode.name.dir.restore` to `true` to enable NameNode to try and recover previously failed `dfs.namenode.name.dir` directories during checkpointing.
- Master node must be RAID enabled with RAID 1 architecture (mirrored pair).
- Keep a lot of space for NameNode's `log` directory. These logs help us to debug or troubleshoot.
- Since Hadoop is I/O bound, we must select the best possible (with respect to speed and throughput) storage.

Optimizing Java GC

Follow these steps for Java GC optimization:

- Use the latest version of Java
- Use parallel GC for Java
- Disable adaptive sizing in JVM and fix the lower and higher values of heap memory
- Enable JVM reuse so that we can set the values of the `mapred.job.reuse.jvm.num.tasks` parameter to the number of tasks we want to reuse JVM

Optimizing Linux OS

Use these techniques for Linux OS optimization:

- The **atime** and **noatime** attributes are the Linux file system attributes that enable Linux to record the created and accessed times for a file; disabling these attributes gives significant gains to performance. This property can be set in `fstab` (file systems table) fount at `/etc/fstab` as follows:

  ```
  /mnt/dev1/Vol1 / ext4 defaults,noatime,nodiratime1  1
  ```

- Enable a file system's read-ahead buffer to enable caching of blocks of files for faster access. We can set it using the following command:

  ```
  blockdev --setra32768 /dev/sda
  ```

- Disable `vm.swappiness` using the following command:

  ```
  sysctl -w vm.swappiness= 0
  ```

  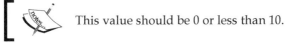 This value should be 0 or less than 10.

- Increase `ulimit` to a higher value; the default value, `1,024`, is not adequate so make it between 32K to 34K, depending upon the system resources.
- We should always have time synchronization in clusters. We will discuss how to do it using the NTP service.
- Keep your OS bug free, apply available patches, and keep it updated (before updating, check for compatibility with Hadoop/HBase).

Optimizing the Hadoop parameter

The following are the steps that will help us to optimize the Hadoop parameter:

- Enabling trash will help if a file is deleted accidently; we will see how to do this in administration chapter.

- Keep the number of threads higher for RPC calls; this can be done using the following parameters:

  ○ The `dfs.namenode.handler.count` and `mapred.jobtracker.handler.count` parameters, by default, are `10`, and we can change it to between 50 and 100, depending upon the memory available.

  ○ The `dfs.datanode.handler.count` parameter for the DataNode handler count, the default for which is `3`, makes it higher between 5 and 10 if more HDFS clients have to read/write from a cluster. The higher the number of threads, the higher the consumption of memory, so set this parameter accordingly, don't make it too high.

  ○ Set `dfs.replication` to lower or higher according to the cost and size of data. If the size of data is huge and it's not very costly, we can keep it between 2 and 3; if data size is very valuable and less costly, keep it between 3 and 5 or so.

  ○ The `dfs.block.size` parameter defines the block size. It's better to keep it between 64 MB and 256 MB, depending upon the file's size on HDFS. For files less than 100 MB, a block of 64 MB will be better, and for files greater than 100 MB, or files whose size is in GBs, a 256 MB block will be better.

> These and other parameters must be adjusted according to the setup and amount of resources available.

Optimizing MapReduce

To optimize MapReduce, use the following techniques:

- `mapreduce.tasktracker.http.thread` (renamed to `mapreduce.tasktracker.http.threads` in Hadoop 2.0) defines the number of worker threads for the HTTP server. By default, it is 40; make it between 80 and 100 for large clusters.

- `mapreduce.task.io.sort.factor` defines the sort factor and must be kept higher to reduce disk access. This also defines the number of open files at a time.

- If `mapreduce.map.speculative` is set to `true`, jobs will be executed in parallel; it speeds up the execution process in case some tasks fail (jobs that take a lot of time, that is, more than an hour or two, should be set to `false`).

- Compression of Map and Reduce outputs must be set to `true` for larger clusters and `false` for smaller clusters (`-jobconfmapred.output.compress=true`).

- Use the maximum number of mappers and reducers. This should be set according to the number of the CPU core in node. We will see how to set it later.

- There are a few other parameters that must be fiddled with according to the cluster size and type of jobs running.

Rack awareness in Hadoop

In a production environment, we should enable rack awareness for a more robust cluster as it might happen that the whole rack will go down due to a problem with the central switch for this specific rack, or there might be a fire that will affect all the machines on the rack. If we enable and set up a cluster with rack awareness, we can avoid the whole cluster going down and always access the data that lies on nodes on other racks; meanwhile, the affected rack can be brought up. Now, let's see how to enable and configure this feature.

To make the cluster rack aware, we can write a script that enables the master node to assign data blocks according to the topology for high availability in case of a rack failure. For this, we need to include a parameter in the `hadoop-site.xml` file, which is `topology.script.file.name` (`net.topology.script.file.name` in Hadoop 2); for this, we give the path of the executable script that returns a list of IPs or hostnames and the rack where they reside:

```
<property>
  <name>topology.script.file.name</name>
  <value>/home/shashwat/hadoop/conf/hadoopRackAwareness.sh
  </value>
</property>
```

The following is the `hadoopRackAwareness.sh` script:

```
#!/bin/sh
#SourceFrom : http://wiki.apache.org/hadoop/topology_rack_awareness_
scripts
#Credit : Apache Wiki
```

```
HADOOP_CONF=/home/shashwat/hadoop
while [ $# -gt 0 ] ; do
nodeArg=$1
exec< ${HADOOP_CONF}/IPRackFile.list
  result=""
while read line ; do
ar=( $line )
if [ "${ar[0]}" = "$nodeArg" ] ; then
result="${ar[1]}"
fi
done
shift
if [ -z "$result" ] ; then
echo -n "/default/rack "
else
echo -n "$result "
fi
done
```

The following is the content of `IPRackFile.list`:

```
192.168.1.10      /rack1
192.168.1.11      /rack1
192.168.1.12      /rack1
10.3.0.3          /rack2
10.3.0.4          /rack2
10.3.0.5          /rack2
192.3.0.4         /rack3
192.3.0.5         /rack3
192.3.0.6         /rack3
```

After making these changes, restart the cluster and issue this command that will show a new line with the rack information:

```
bin/hadoop dfsadmin -report
```

Number of Map and Reduce limits in configuration files

For the number of Map and Reduce limits, we need to consider the following parameters:

- The maximum number of Map task slots to run simultaneously on a single TaskTracker:

  ```
  mapred.tasktracker.map.tasks.maximum
  ```

- The maximum number of Reduce task slots to run simultaneously on a single TaskTracker:

```
mapred.tasktracker.reduce.tasks.maximum
```

To set these two values, we need to consider available CPU cores, disk, and memory. Suppose we have an eight core processor, and if the job is CPU intensive, we can set four Maps that will finish. Then, the reducer will start; for less CPU-intensive jobs, we can keep map task at 40 and reduce task at 20. After fixing these, we need to see if there is a long wait, and then we can reduce the number so as to make the process faster. We must understand that if we set too big a number, there will be a lot of context switching and swapping of data between memory and disk, which might reduce the overall slow processing, so we need to make it balanced according to the system resources we have.

 For further reading, go to `http://wiki.apache.org/hadoop/HowManyMapsAndReduces`.

Considering and deciding the maximum number of Map and Reduce tasks

Let's see how we can set the maximum number of Map and Reduce tasks. It is not always correct to run a lot of tasks (MapReduce) at a time because if they can't fit in the memory, tasks tend to fail or take a lot of time. So, we need to consider the maximum number of MapReduce tasks that can run at a time on TaskTracker, and according to the number of CPU cores available in the system, we fit only a certain number of task data in memory and don't swap in or swap out data as it increases I/O and hence degrades performance.

The following table lists the number of Map and Reduce tasks according to the existing number of CPU cores and memory:

CPU core	Memory	Number of Map task(s)	Number of Reduce task(s)
1	1 GB	1	1
1	5 GB	1	1
4	5 GB	4	2
16	32 GB	16	8
16	64 GB	16	8
24	64 GB	24	12
24	128 GB	24	12

Programmatically, we can set the number of Map and Reduce tasks too, which can override the value we set in configuration files. Generally, we can calculate it as follows:

```
mapred.tasktracker.map.tasks.maximum = 2 + cpu_numer * 2/3
mapred.tasktracker.reduce.tasks.maximum = 2 + cpu_numer * 1/3
```

Optimizing HBase

For some systems, memory-related settings that we discussed for Hadoop are common to HBase. So, let's discuss HBase-specific optimization in brief. We will also look at component-wise HBase optimization.

Let's start with Hadoop.

Hadoop

Add the following parameter to the `hdfs-site.xml` and `hbase-site.xml` files:

```
<property>
  <name>dfs.support.append</name>
  <value>true</value>
</property>
```

The preceding code will enable sync on HDFS, which is essential for durable HBase data synchronization and durability. After making this change, we need to restart the cluster.

The following code decides the number of open files on DataNode and should be kept high as HBase keeps a lot of files open. This must be kept to 4096 or above, according to the size of the HBase cluster and amount of data and operation being run on it:

```
<property>
  <name>dfs.datanode.max.xcievers</name>
  <description>dfs.datanode.max.transfer.threads in newer version
  </description>
  <value>4096</value>
</property>
```

The following code enables a network socket to wait for a longer time to write, and it is a good tweak up for environments where heavy transactions take place:

```
<property>
<name>dfs.datanode.socket.write.timeout</name>
<value>0</value>
<description>In hdfs-site.xml</description>
</property>

<property>
<name>dfs.socket.timeout</name>
<value>0</value>
<description>default is 60000 increase it to 360000 if not adequate
then make it 0 for unlimited in hdfs-site.xml</description>
</property>
```

The following code enables the compression of intermediate files when we run `mapreduce` jobs; this reduces writing time drastically:

```
<property>
<name>mapreduce.map.output.compress</name>
<value>true</value>
</property>
<property>
<name>mapreduce.map.output.compress.codec</name>
<value>org.apache.hadoop.io.compress.GzipCodec</value>
</property>
```

Also, adjust the following parameters and check the performance:

- `mapred.map.tasks`
- `mapred.tasktracker.map.tasks.maximum`
- `mapred.reduce.tasks`
- `mapred.tasktracker.reduce.tasks.maximum`
- `mapred.map.child.java.opts`
- `mapred.reduce.child.java.opts`

Change Linux `epoll limit fs.epoll.max_user_instances = 1024` to `/etc/systel.conf`. This will set the Linux open-file-limit polling (this setting limits the number of files that a single user/process can have open).

Memory

HBase needs a lot of memory space. There are options to enable tables to be in memory while creating a table. If there are in-memory tables, we will require a good amount of RAM, which provides not only memory but also better allocation to different daemons. Out of 100 percent of memory, use around 70 percent for the Hadoop/HBase heap of main memory; this also depends upon the amount of memory available. It is not advisable to assign very huge heap sizes because during GC, there might be huge pauses that may result in RegionServers being reported as down. So, for HBase and Hadoop, 16 to 48 GB of memory is good enough for an average cluster. Always keep in mind to leave a good amount of memory for the system too so that if the system starves, the daemons of Hadoop and HBase will starve too.

Java

Use the following steps:

1. Install the latest version of Java (read more about Java 7 and garbage collection at `http://www.infoq.com/articles/G1-One-Garbage-Collector-To-Rule-Them-All`).

2. Disable OS swapping.

3. Enable parallel GC using the following parameter:

    `-XX:+UseParallelGC`

4. Increase the `ParallelGCThread` number:

    `-XX:ParallelGCThreads=<4 or More >`

5. Disable adaptive memory sizing by fixing the `Max` and `Min` heaps to the same value.

6. Disable explicit GC to prevent developers perform GC using code:

    `-XX:+DisableExplicitGC`

 These settings can be implemented in the Hadoop and HBase `env` configuration file.

OS

The techniques for optimization are as follows:

- `/proc/sys/fs/file-max`: This is the number of maximum concurrently open files. Change its limit to at least between 32K and 64K in the `cat /proc/sys/fs/file-max` file by setting `fs.file-max`.

- `/proc/sys/net/ipv4/tcp_max_syn_backlog`: This is the maximum number of remembered connection requests, which still did not receive an acknowledgment from the connecting client. The default value is `1024` for systems with more than 128 MB of memory and `128` for low-memory machines. If a server suffers and gets overloaded, try to increase this number to a somewhat bigger value and analyze. This setting can be changed in `/etc/sysctl.confusing configuration net.ipv4.tcp_max_syn_backlog`.

- `/proc/sys/net/core/somaxconn`: This decides the limit of socket listen backlog, known in user space as SOMAXCONN. The default value is `128`. The value should be increased substantially to support bursts of request. For example, to support a burst of 512 requests, set SOMAXCONN to `512`. Changes can be made using the `/etc/rc.d/rc.local` or `/etc/sysctl.conf` script to keep these changes persistent.

- Use a 64-bit OS for a bigger RAM and address space.

HBase

Now, let's discuss a parameter that we can play with to have an optimized HBase cluster. Before finalizing the parameters, we must have a benchmarking on our target cluster; there are a lot of benchmarking options available, which we will discuss later, and once we see a good response time, we can finalize and put the cluster in production.

We have many disks attached to DataNodes. These settings tell us when DataNodes should be shut down if a disk fails; it's better to set it to 1 because if a volume fails, it can be treated as dead and the whole correct data can be replicated to a healthy DataNode so as to prevent corruption. This setting can be added to a Hadoop site file.

```
<property>
  <name>dfs.datanode.failed.volumes.tolerated</name>
  <value>1</value>
</property>
```

The following configuration decides the number of threads kept alive to handle the request of data from the user table; this value can be lowered in the case of a higher number of writes and can be increased if there are few writes.

```
<property>
  <name>hbase.regionserver.handler.count</name>
  <value>10</value>
</property>
```

The default value for the following property is `true`. If HBase cluster is running on Hadoop, it can be turned off using the `false` value. If required can be turned on for special cases such as nodes getting blacklisted frequently due to many failed tasks the specific TaskTracker performed:

```
<property>
  <name>mapred.map.tasks.speculative.execution</name>
  <value>true</value>
</property>
```

The default value of the following property is `true`. If the HBase cluster is running on Hadoop, it can be turned off using the `false` value. If the Reduce task is running, it can be turned on for special cases such as TaskTrackers getting blacklisted due to many task failures:

```
<property>
  <name>mapred.reduce.tasks.speculative.execution</name>
  <value>true</value>
</property>
```

The default value for the following property is `30`, which is the number of RPC listeners. If there are a huge number of write and read requests, try increasing and decreasing according to the number of requests:

```
<property>
  <name>hbase.regionserver.handler.count</name>
  <value>30</value>
</property>
```

The following property defines the HStore file size, the default for which is 10 GB. If we need to run a HBase MapReduce job on the cluster, we can reduce this splitting size to a lower value because the number of Maps depends on the region size. There is one mapper for one region, and if a region size is very big, Map tasks will take more time:

```
<property>
  <name>hbase.hregion.max.filesize</name>
  <value> 10737418240 </value>
</property>
```

The following property defines the buffer for an HTable client. We can increase to reduce RPC calls, but increasing it requires more memory, so a balance value should be given, and there should be more buffer and memory and faster and less RPC calls:

```
<property>
   <name>hbase.client.write.buffer</name>
   <value>2097152</value>
</property>
```

The following property defines the number of rows fetched when `scan.next` (method to read records from an HBase table) is called. The default value is `100`, but we can increase (1000 to 10,000) it for better and faster fetching of rows; a bigger value will, however, eat up more memory:

```
<property>
   <name>hbase.client.scanner.caching</name>
   <value>10</value>
</property>
```

So, the preceding are the settings which, when given correct values, increase HBase performance. These settings are fiddled with according to the cluster setup and size and the amount and type of data on the cluster.

Optimizing ZooKeeper

As mentioned in *Chapter 1*, *Understanding the HBase Ecosystem*, ZooKeeper provides distributed synchronization and group service to HBase. It is one of the necessities of HBase, and hence, we have to optimize it. Use the following setting for optimization:

```
<property>
   <name>zookeeper.session.timeout</name>
   <value>3000</value>
</property>
```

The default value for this setting is 3 minutes. This decides how often master should check for server crashes. We can decrease it so that the server crashes can be noticed quickly, but if this value decreases, we need to take care of GC. In the case of full GC, the server might not respond while running fine, and it might be reported as crashed. This configuration can be overridden in the `hbase-site.xml` file.

This value should be increased if there is a timeout while writing to the HBase cluster. If it is too small, and while writing huge amounts of data to HBase, GC happens, resulting in the pause of server responses, and hence timeout, this is due to improper JVM tuning. If JVM is tuned correctly, we can keep this value lower for more responsiveness.

The number of ZooKeeper instances must always be an odd number (we already discussed the reason behind this). Try to configure a higher number of ZooKeepers. So, for nodes around 20, we should have five to seven ZooKeepers. You can increase the number later, according to the sizing of the cluster.

Enable the ZooKeeper data directory at a safe location, and not the default HBase temp, so that the logs and data can be checked in the case of some failure.

Important files in Hadoop

We will look at some important files that we need to consider. We will also see why these files are important in Hadoop. The following is the list of files:

- **Hadoop-default files**: The following is the list of files that are shipped with Hadoop, which contains the default settings. Users must not change settings inside this file; rather, the changes must be done in site-specific files, which are listed in Hadoop overridden files.
    - ° mapred-default.xml
    - ° core-default.xml
    - ° hdfs-default.xml
    - ° yarn-default.xml
    - ° httpfs-default.xml

- **Hadoop configuration files to override default values**: These are the files that are site specific or the values inside these files override the default parameters. So, changes must be made or new parameters must be added to these files:
    - ° mapred-site.xml
    - ° core-site.xml
    - ° hdfs-site.xml
    - ° yarn-site.xml
    - ° httpfs-site.xml

- **Hadoop configuration files to specify runtime parameters**: These are the runtime files that provide Java-related settings and memory and daemon-related settings:
    - ° hadoop-env.sh
    - ° httpfs-env.sh
    - ° mapred-env.sh
    - ° yarn-env.sh

We can make changes in site-specific and `env` files. In `env` files, we need to add Java settings, JVM-related settings, Java path, Hadoopconfdir, log directory, and some other settings.

Important files in HBase

Similar to Hadoop, we have a few files in HBase that need to be considered. Let's have a look at them:

- **HBase-default files**: The following file needs to be considered from this category:
    - `hbase-default.xml`

- **HBase overridden files**: The following file needs to be considered from this category:
    - `hbase-site.xml`

- **HBase runtime files**: The following file needs to be considered from this category:
    - `hbase-env.sh`

Summary

In this chapter, we learned that we should run more than one instance of HMaster for high availability and whether we can run two to three HMasters per rack if the cluster is big enough. We should run separate instances of five to seven ZooKeepers on separate hardware machines in a production cluster. Some ZooKeepers can be cohosted (on a production cluster, ZooKeeper machines must be hosted separately). We should keep the time synchronized between all the nodes in an HBase cluster. Run HBasehbck, which checks HBase and tells us if there are any errors in HBase; also, we should make it as a cron job to see the status of the cluster. Run the HBase balancer with data throughout the region server; how to do this will be discussed in *Chapter 6, HBase Cluster Maintenance and Troubleshooting*.

We will discuss more about HBase's data types, how data is stored in HBase (Logical View/Actual Physical view), and services such as table, row, column family, column, and cells that HBase offers in the next chapter. It will also focus on data operations, versioning, schema designing, and some other interesting and important topics as per data design, data layout, and internal and external views.

5
The Storage, Structure Layout, and Data Model of HBase

As the chapter name implies, this chapter is an in-depth discussion on the storage and structure layout of HBase. It will also cover data models and their operations in HBase. We will look at some important topics such as tables, columns, column families, cells, and metadata in HBase. The chapter will end with a section that is based on schema designing, and it will cover types of table design and its benefits.

In this chapter, we will discuss the following topics:

- A data model of HBase
- Namespaces
- Data model commands
- Versioning of records
- Row key design tips
- Schema designing basics

Let's get started with a conceptual and physical view of data stored in HBase tables. Then, we will discuss the various components of HBase storage.

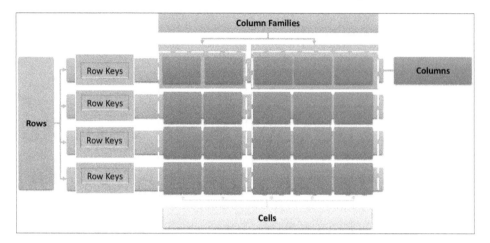

HBase is not very relational design centric, but it is open to a more flexible design, based on a user's requirements, which enables the user to have a more flexible and scalable table layout. It provides a single index facility on row keys, which is called the primary key in the relational world. We can avoid very large read-and-write operations in HBase by dividing rows into column families and columns, and this supports both horizontal and vertical scaling of tables.

An HBase table consists of the following components:

- Row
  - Column family
    - Column
      - Cell

So, we can think of rows consisting of a column family, a column family is made up of columns, and the columns are made up of cells. The data in a table is accessed using row keys.

We can give any name to the row key (but we have some suggested parameters for row key design, which we will discuss later). When we name a column family, it should be logical to group columns. Column qualifiers are specified as follows:

```
<columnFamily>:<columnName>
```

We are now aware of the data model in HBase. Let's move forward to explore the data types in HBase.

Data types in HBase

There are no fancy data types such as `String`, `INT`, or `Long` in HBase; it's all byte array. It's a kind of byte-in and byte-out database, wherein, when a value is inserted, it is converted into a byte array using the `Put` and `Result` interfaces. HBase implicitly converts the data to byte arrays through a serialization framework, stores it into the cell, and also gives out byte arrays. It implicitly converts data to equivalent representation while putting and getting the value.

So, in short, we can say that HBase cells only hold byte arrays. `Put` and `Result` methods handle encoding and decoding of objects.

Anything that can be converted into bytes, from a simple string to an image file, can be stored in HBase, but it too is converted into bytes and can then be stored (or as long as it's a serializable object). We can have values up to 10 to 15 MB stored in an HBase cell. If any value is bigger, we need not store it into HBase, what we can do is store the file on HDFS and then store the filepath in HBase. It is not advisable to convert a huge file or value into byte arrays and store it in HBase; however, HDFS can be used to host files with an underlying distribution and file metadata into an HBase table.

HBase provides APIs that serialize and deserialize different data to be put into an HBase table and fetched from an HBase table. We will see this in Java coding for HBase in *Chapter 8*, *Coding HBase in Java*, and *Chapter 9*, *Advance Coding in Java for HBase*.

Storing data in HBase – logical view versus actual physical view

At a conceptual level, an HBase table can be seen as a sparse set of rows, but in actual storage, it is stored as per a column family. While defining a table, columns can be added or specified on the run in a column family. We must decide the number and name of the column family at the time of table creation, but columns can be added as required at any point in time while storing the data, and this is the beauty of schema-free when we use HBase.

The following is the logical view of how data is stored in HBase, but in actual these are stored separately with column families:

Row keys	Time_Stamp	Column family 1 (CF1)		Column family 2 (CF2)		
		CF1:Col 1	CF1:Col 2	CF2:Col 3	CF2:Col4	CF2:Col 5
Row1	Time stamp 1			Value 3	Value 4	Value 5
Row2	Time stamp 2	Value 6	Value 7	Value 8	Value 9	Value 10
Row2	Time stamp 3	Value 11	Value 12	Value 13		

So, in physical storage, this table will be stored in two parts, column family 1 and column family 2, and data can be accessed from different column families.

A column is always represented and accessed using the column family name as prefix (`columnfamilyname: columnname`) so that we know which column family is accessed. The columns that do not contain values are not stored. We can see this column-family-wise representation in the following two tables that represent the logical view of data storage, as shown in the preceding table.

The following tables represent the tables that will be stored as column-family-based tables:

Row keys	Time_Stamp	Column family 1 (CF1)	
		CF1:Col 1	CF1:Col 2
Row2	Time stamp 2	Value 6	Value 7
Row2	Time stamp 3	Value 11	Value 12

Row keys	Time_Stamp	Column family 2 (CF2)		
		CF2:Col 3	CF2:Col4	CF2:Col 5
Row1	Time stamp 1	Value 3	Value 4	Value 5
Row2	Time stamp 2	Value 8	Value 9	Value 10

In the earlier releases of HBase, we did not have a database concept; however, there was the table concept. The newer version of HBase introduces a concept called namespace (supported in HBase 0.96 and later versions) that groups tables logically, giving a more structured, organized representation, and storage of tables. Let's discuss it now.

Namespace

A namespace is a logical grouping of tables, similar to relation databases in group-related tables. The following is the typical representation of namespaces:

Now, let's now discuss the components of a namespace:

- **Table**: All tables are member of some namespace. If a namespace is not defined, the table belongs to a default namespace. One table can only be the member of a single namespace.

- **RegionServer group**: A namespace might have a default RegionServer group. Therefore, the table created will be a member of the RegionServer group of the defined namespace.

- **Permission**: A namespace enables us to define **Access Control Lists** (**ACLs**). For example, the write permission will give permission for table creation and other operations such as read, delete, and update.

- **Quota**: This enforces the limit of the number of tables and regions a namespace can contain.

- **Predefined namespaces**: The following are the predefined namespaces:

    ◦ **default**: This namespace is for all the tables for which a namespace is not defined.

    ◦ **system**: The .ROOT. and .META. tables and tables in ACLs are loaded before any other table.

Commands available for namespaces

The following are the commands available for namespaces:

- `alter_namespace`
- `create_namespace`
- `describe_namespace`
- `drop_namespace`

- `list_namespace`
- `list_namespace_tables`

We will see the uses of these commands when we discuss shell commands in HBase. Keep in mind that these commands are available with HBase Version 0.96.0 and above. So, namespaces can be created, removed, and altered. A table belongs to the namespace that's decided at time of table creation, which adds the table to the specified namespace. We can create namespaces as follows:

```
Create_<namespace name>
```

Have a look at the following example:

```
create_namespace student_namespace
```

Then, we can create tables in specific namespaces, as follows:

```
create'<namespace_name : table_name>', 'column_family_name'
```

Have a look at the following example:

```
create 'student_namespace:student_table','student_detail'
```

Once a namespace is created and a table is added to it, the path on HDFS will look like the following:

```
<ROOT PATH>/data/<NAMESPACE NAME>/<TABLE NAME>
```

Services of HBase

The HBase data model terminology is listed as follows:

- Table
- Row
- Column family
- Column
- Cell

Let's have a look at each of them in detail.

Row key

This is a unique key for each record in an HBase table. It is represented as a byte array internally. No matter what data (string, long, date, or serialized) we choose as the row key, internally, on the disk, or in memory, it will be converted to byte arrays, and then stored. For example, `Emp_ID` can be the row key for an `employee` table.

Column family

This entity of an HBase table groups different columns of the table. Suppose we have columns such as `name`, `dob`, `salary`, `city`, `phone`, `pin`, and `landmark` in an `employee` table. We can group these columns as `Basic_Detail(name, dob, salary)` and `Address(city, phone, pin, landmark)` as two column families. The benefit is that you can retrieve the columns faster as column families are stored separately in HBase on the disk.

Column

Each field in a row is called a column family. We can have columns such as `name`, `dob`, `salary`, `city`, `phone`, and `pin` in an `employee` table.

Cell

These are the smallest or basic units of storage inside a column where the actual value of a field is stored. Cells can be accessed using the `<row, column family:column, version>` tuple. The default version is `1`.

Version

HBase is able to maintain more than one value for a cell of tuple (row, column family, and column), which is called the version of a record. The version is specified in long integers and based on a timestamp. By default, HBase keeps three versions of records. However, we can change it to the number of versions we need. For example, if we have frequent data change and need to retain previous values too, we can have versioning. Fetching the value form HBase gives the latest value, and we can get the specific version by specifying it.

Timestamp

With every insertion of data, the current timestamp becomes associated with the value. This denotes when the specific value was inserted into a table.

We can visualize the version and timestamp in the following diagram:

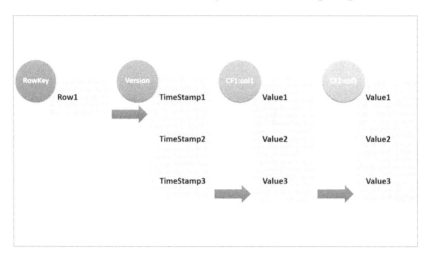

So, for each version of record, we have a timestamp attached to it, and we can have more than one version or copy of a record in an HBase table. If you want to save space, you can set the version to 1; if you want the number of previous records, you can set the value to 3. Once the maximum version is reached, the earliest record is overwritten.

Data model operations

The operations that are the basic blocks of data model are Get, Put, Scan, and Delete, using which we can read, write, and delete records from an HBase table. We will discuss these operations in detail now.

Get

The Get operation can fetch certain records from an HBase table. It is similar to the select [fields] where RowKey=<Row Key value here> statement in relational databases, where we fetch a row from the table.

The following is the representation of `Get`:

```
public Result get(Get get)throws IOException
```

In the preceding code, the `Get` operation can be provided as a single `get` object out of a list of `get` objects as `get(List<Get> gets)`. It is specified by `Get` in the `HTableInterface` interface given by HBase. The `Get` operation receives the `get` parameter, which objects the data that is to be fetched from the table. It returns data of the particular row, which is specified in the `get` object as an HBase `Result` object, and this throws `IOException` when not able to read.

We will see how to use these methods in Java in *Chapter 8, Coding HBase in Java*, and *Chapter 9, Advance Coding in Java for HBase*.

On HBase shell, it can be used as follows:

```
get 'table name', 'row key',<filters>
```

Put

The `Put` operation adds a new row of data to a table or updates/overrides a specific row of data. It is executed through `HTable.put()` or `HTable.batch()`, which is a batch write operation.

This takes `put` as parameter. We can see its use as follows:

```
public void put(Put put) throws InterruptedIOException,RetriesExhauste
dWithDetailsException
```

This also takes a single `put` object or a list of `put` objects to write a set of values in a table.

Scan

The `Scan` operation can be used to read multiple rows of data in contrast to `Get` where we need to specify a set of rows to read data. However, in the case of a scan, we can iterate through a range of rows or all the rows in a table.

It can be used as follows (Java code):

```
HBaseConfiguration conf = HBaseConfiguration.create();
HTable table1 = new HTable(conf, "hbaseTable");
Scan scanObj = new Scan();
ResultScannerrs = htable.getScanner(scanObj);
```

Also, we can iterate through a result-set object and get each row in the result object.

Delete

The `Delete` operation removes a row or a set of rows from a table. It is executed through `HTable.delete()`. Once a row is set to be deleted, it is marked as *tombstone*, and once compaction takes place, the row is finally deleted or removed from a table.

```
public void delete (Delete delete) throws IOException
```

`delete` is specified as an interface of `HTableInterface`, takes the `delete` object or `delete` list as a parameter, and throws IOException if any intermediate exception occurs.

The `Delete` happens for the following:

- **Delete**: This is for a specific version of a column
- **Delete column**: This is for all versions of a column
- **Delete family**: This is for all columns of a particular column family

Versioning and why

As we already discussed version for a record, there is a tuple consisting of {row, column, version} that defines a cell and its value. We can have as many versions as we want, but the number of versions should be decided optimally as it is storage dependent. It means the more versions, the more disk space it requires (it is possible to have an unbounded number of cell versions).

The version is denoted using a long value. The versioned values are stored in descending order so as to keep the most recent value on top. So, when we fetch records, the most recent version is returned.

Let's consider a scenario to version HBase.

Suppose we have an employee database with the `employee_history` table where we need to keep all the details of a person's previous company. We can enable versioning (increase to whatever number we like to have after a default of 3) and keep all previous and current details of the employee, such as their employment history and scenarios similar to this.

We can visualize the version and its value in the following diagram, where we have `Employee_Employment_History_Table` (which can be associated with the `employee` table) containing a column family as `Employment_History` and columns as `Companies`, `Salaries`, and `Posts Held`, with version of records as 3; this means we can have three values for each column. As we store the value, the current value will always be fetched. So suppose there is a person named A, then `Companies` column can contain values such as `Acompany1`, `Acompany2`, and `Acompany3` specifying the companies the person worked with.

The following table shows how we can get the salary or other column value of an employee (current and previous):

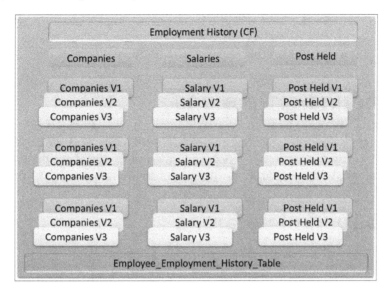

Now, let's see how to fetch the versions of the record.

As we discussed, Get is used to fetch records from a table, so we can use Get. setMaxVersion(number of version we need to return). Using this function, we can read a specified number of records. We can see the code example as follows:

```
Get get = new Get(Bytes.toBytes("rowkey"));
get.setMaxVersions(5);
Result resultSet = HTableObj.get(get);
```

So, this will return five versions of a record. Likewise, we can specify 1, 2, 3, or the other versions we want to fetch. This will not return not only Version 5, but all five versions of the record.

A detailed explanation of versions in various operations such as Get, Put, and Delete will be discussed in the upcoming chapters.

Deciding the number of the version

Now, let's discuss the maximum and minimum numbers of a version we can consider for a table. This information is maintained using `HColumnDescriptor`, which contains information about a column family, such as the number of versions and compression settings. This acts as input for table creation and addition of columns.

Lower bound of versions

The default lower bound of version is `0`, which means it is disabled. The minimum number of rows a version uses is in conjunction with **Time To Live** (TTL), and we can have 0 or more for a version, according to the requirements of the use case. Using 0 for version will prevent the writing of more than one value to the cell.

Upper bound of versions

The default upper bound for a version is 3, which keeps three copies (inserted on the basis of a timestamp) of a row. It is advised that the maximum number should not be very large as it is storage-centric too. So, more or less 100 can be thought of as the upper bound, which is not a hard limit, as we can go with bigger numbers too. The maximum number of version is solely based on the use case data to be stored in an HBase table.

Once the maximum limit of the version is reached, and if we try to insert any new data, the latest value will be overwritten and we will get the latest inserted value plus the previously maintained version.

Keeping the value very high will drastically increase the size of a store file (if all the cells contain value), leading to the requirement of more storage and overhead on reading the store file too.

On HBase shell, we can define it as follows:

```
hbase>create 'Tablewithversion', {NAME => 'colFamily1', VERSIONS =>
50}
```

The preceding command will create a table that will maintain 50th version of previous data for a row in a table. Suppose we need to change the version already defined, we can use the following command:

```
hbase>alter <Tablewithversion> {NAME =>'colFamily1', VERSIONS => 100}
```

The preceding command will change the number of version from `50` to `100`.

This version feature of HBase can be used as a data-retention technique of HBase where we can use more versions to keep the history data. The option-defining TTL is also a method to keep the data up to a certain point in time; the TTL will keep the specific data until the timestamp is defined. Using these two features, we can have historical data for a table. It is just table based, so we can have different versions for different tables according to the requirements of data stored in the table.

When TTL expires, the whole data will be deleted and no version will be available, so we need to choose TTL so that the table data is not marked to be deleted after a specific timestamp. In the newer version of HBase, we have an option to define versions to be kept even after the time is expired or TTL is overpassed.

 For instance, have a look at the following:

```
keep <specific number of version of data>
```

The maximum number of data copies can be the number of versions we define.

Keep the data till <TTL>. This will keep the data till <TTL> (time to live) expires. In newer version of HBase, data remains there even after TTL is expired.

If we need to keep the deleted value and not remove it from the table, we can define it as follows:

hbase>KEEP_DELETED_CELLS=>true

This is done using HBase shell, and if we need to do it through Java code API, we can do so as follows:

HColumnDescriptor.setKeepDeletedCells(true)

Schema designing

HBase does not support any kind of joins, but it provides the single-indexing strategy on the row key. HBase schema design supports denormalization with nested entities. These nested entities are nothing but a column whose name is the unique identifier for the nested entity and whose value is the entire record mashed together. Since HBase allows dynamic column definition, there's no problem. Here's a great way to scale your joins. Additionally, with column families, large rows can be partitioned to small data chunks that can be read individually from a disk.

Schema or table design must be done at the initial phase, and we can add or remove columns on the fly, but we need to design our RowKey of table and column families at the initial schema design phase.

Some points that we might consider while designing a schema are as follows:

- The row key is a very important aspect of schema design to consider. Row keys are indexed and provides the O(1) operation, which provides constant scheduling of fetching the data with a constant lookup speed.
- Create a composite key by combining multiple values together, which can be used to set the relation between more tables.
- In HBase, schema design revolves around application design.
- HBase minimizes IO by keeping the column family and row together.
- While designing the row key, column names are to be chosen intelligently as these are stored with the value in memory. So, design should minimize the column names; instead of a big column name such as `employee_salary`, we can have a name such as `esal` or similar.
- We should use row atomicity as a design tool. HBase supports atomicity at the row level, which means if we need to update two tables atomically, we will find it difficult to update in one go. If we need atomicity on two tables, migrate one of the tables into another as nested entities.

Now, let's discuss it further.

As we have already discussed, the HBase data model is quite different from relational database systems. So, let's ask some questions that will help us design it in a better way:

- What should the row key structure be? What all should it contain? What fields of different tables should it be made up of?
- How many versions should there be for each row?
- What information should be stored in the cell?
- How many column families should there be and how should they be named?
- Although we can add columns to column families on the fly even at the operation time, is it better to define or decide what and how many columns there are, and what their names should be?
- How many columns are there for each column family?

Row key design is one of the most important design considerations. This is very important to read and write data into an HBase table. So, to define and design, we should consider different factors, which are as follows:

- Number of tables in the design.
- Indexing will be done on a row key.
- A table is sorted on the basis of a row key. Each region tells about the start and stop row in the region, and the region stores the sorted list of rows from the start to end row key.
- Everything is sorted as a byte array. There are no other data types such as string, integer, long, and so on when it comes to data stored in HBase table internally.
- HBase guarantees atomicity only on a row key and multirow transaction is not supported; these might be introduced in future versions of HBase (above 0.98).
- Column families to be defined at the time of table creation.
- Column creation/addition is dynamic and can be added or defined at write time too.
- HFile is sorted on the row key, qualifier, and timestamp.

Let's consider a scenario-based schema design now.

Suppose we have a scenario in which we need to design a table on a student-course relationship; we will have the following relation types as shown in the following figure:

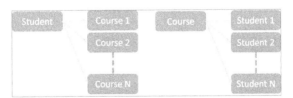

Now, let's consider some use cases of table requirement design, such as how it is represented in RDBMS and HBase.

We generally have this scenario while designing a Student-Course relationship; so in RDBMS, we know that this can be represented as follows:

Student	Studcourse_Relation	Courses
Stud_ID (Primary Key)	Stud_ID	Course_ID (Primary Key)
Stud_Name	Course_ID	Course_Title
Stud_Age	Type	Note
Stud_Sex		Instructor_ID
Stud_Address		

In HBase, the same thing can be represented as follows as there is no relation constrains, so we can implement this in many ways. Here is one we can implement:

So, the `Student` table and detail might look like the following:

Row_Keys	Column_Family (Student_Details_CF)	
Stud_ID	Column (Student_Deatils)	Column (courseID)
	Student_Deatils:Stud_Name	CourseID:course_ID
	Student_Deatils:Stud_Age	
	Student_Deatils:Stud_Sex	
	Student_Deatils:Stud_Address	

The `Course` table looks like the following:

Row_Keys	Column_Family (Course_Details_CF)	
Course_ID	Column (Course_Deatils)	Column (StudentID)
	Course_Deatils:Course_Title	StudentID:Stud_ID
	Course_Deatils:Course_Note	
	Course_Deatils:Course_Instructor_ID	

So, here we can set the relation on the basis of `Student_ID` and `Course_ID`; for example, getting the student ID and details from the first `Student` table and their equivalent courses from the `Course` table based on `Student_ID` from the `Course` table.

The second use case we will consider in this situation is how a user performs some task. So, we will see how to design a table and keep track of user activities.

Since we are recording a user activity, we will design the row key accordingly, which will contain a combination of userID, timestamp, and eventID.

User_Events	Event
RowKey (userID + timestamp + eventID) (Primary Key) User_Name Note	EventID EventName

So, the first table, `User_Events`, will contain user details with the row key as a combination of a unique keys, current timestamps, event IDs, and user name, and will keep a note about the user or activity. The second table, which will be for event details, will have a set of events such as write, read, delete, update, edit, and so on. This information will be stored in the second `Event` table, and we can fetch all the operation performed by the user using these two tables.

Types of table designs

We can have two types of designs while considering a table. They are as follows:

- **Short and Wide**: This design pattern can be considered in the following cases:
  - There is a small number of columns
  - There is a large number of rows

- **Tall-Thin**: This design pattern can be considered in the following cases:
  - There is a large number of columns
  - There is a small number of rows

Now, let's consider a use case of blogging data, which needs to be created to store the blog entries to HBase. In this scenario, a user writes blog entries and saves data to HBase cell.

So, let's consider the scenario of a blogging website such as `http://blogspot.com`, `http://wordpress.com`, or any other blogging website where a user logs in, enters the content, and posts it. Internally, the content is stored in a table either as a column value or as a text file on a file system, and then it's linked to the database.

There can be two conditions that we can consider in the case of a design HBase table, which are as follows:

- Each row might represent a single user (one row for a user and columns with the blog entries)
- Each blog as a single row for which we will need to read multiple rows to read the blogs of a single user

Now, let's consider the following cases.

In a short-and-wide table design, we have all blogs stored in a single row and column family in an HBase table. Each newly created blog is stored in a dedicated column.

We will refer to the row ID here as User ID and to the column family as BlogEntriesCF; we will represent it as BECF.

Columns are added on the fly whenever a user creates a blog entry, and as columns, we will have a fixed string plus a timestamp attached to it, such as BEntry plus TimeStamp, which we will represent as BT.

RowKey (User_ID)	BECF						
	BECF:BT	BECF:BT	BECF:BT	BECF:BT	BECF:BT	BECF:BT	...
WriterA	HbaseEntry	HadoopEntry	...	...	...	...	...
WriterB	HadoopEntry	MongoEntry	...	...	...	HiveEntry	...
Writerc	...	...	...	SqoopEntry	...	HBaseEntry	...
...	...	...	...	...	...	...	...
sWriter(N)	...	...	...	...	...	Nth	...

This table grows horizontally with new columns that are added on the fly as the contents are added. In this case, the table grows towards the right-hand side, and not downwards, with new columns being added more quickly.

So, here we can read a whole row to get entries by a specific writer.

In a Tall-Thin table design, the table grows downwards more quickly than towards the right-hand side. Once new rows (user IDs attached with timestamps) are added with new blog entries, the blog entries are attached to a fixed column family and column. We can visualize this scenario as follows:

| RowKey (UserID+TimeStamp) | BlogEntriesCF |
	BlogEntriesCF:Entries
WriterATimeStamp1	HBaseEntry
WriterBTimeStamp2	HadoopEntry
WriterATimeStamp3	HadoopEntry
...	...
...	...
...	...
WriterCTimeStampN	EntryN

Benefits of Short Wide and Tall-Thin design patterns

Now, let's see the benefits of both the design patterns:

Tall-Thin	Short Wide
If we query using a row ID, it will skip rows faster	This has to be queried using a column name that will not skip rows or store files
Not good for atomicity	Better for atomicity
Better for scalability	Not as good for scalability as Tall-Thin is

It's best to consider the Tall-Thin design as we know it will help in faster data retrieval by enabling us to read the single column family for user blog entries at once instead of traversing through many rows. Also, since HBase splits take place on rows, data related to a specific user can be found at one region server.

We will talk more about use case base schema design and coding in *Chapter 10, HBase Use Cases*. Now, here are some more tips about row key considerations:

- Avoid generating continuous row key-like sequences or timestamps as this might result in the hanging up of the reading process during heavy writes.

- Always keep the names of column families and row keys smaller in size as we know when a cell is stored it is preceded by a column name and column family name, so if we have bigger name, it will add up to the data storage size. So, for example, instead of StudentNameColumn, we can keep the column name as SNC, or something of this sort.

- Row keys can be stored in their binary representations as opposed to string representations as it will require less space of storage.

- If we need to reverse the scan of our table, we can add a reverse timestamp with the row key for faster scanning, for example, *row key + (maxTimestamp-current)*.

Designing an efficient row key results in faster and optimized scanning/reading and writing process. This is why we need to consider a good row key, column family, and column name design.

Composite key designing

Composite keys can be created comprising various fields clubbed together to form a row key. This can be done as *UserID + Seperator + DateString + SeperatorCharter + UserSessionID*.

We can use the start and stop row keys in the HBase scan key to read a specific range of data we want to read. Let's see a scenario where we need to read the data and how to set the start and stop keys in the scan:

- To read all the sessions for a given user, we can specify the start row as `userId`:

```
HBase > table 'tableToScan',{STARTROW=>'userId'}
```

In Java, we can specify it as:

```
Scan s=new Scan(userID)
Table.getScanner(s)
```

It's the same in the following cases.

- To find a specific session of a user, we can specify the full row key as the start row key
- To find all sessions of a user or the session in a specific date range, we can specify *UserID + SeperatorCharacter + DateString* as the start and end row keys

Likewise, we can do different combinations to get specific ranges and the required data.

Real-time use case of schema in an HBase table

Here, we will list some use cases in the industry that use HBase as a backend to manage their applications and infrastructure.

There are many companies that use HBase in their production environment successfully, such as Trend Micro, eBay, Yahoo!, Facebook, and many other analytical-based companies. Some of the examples where this is being used include communications in Facebook messages, which are maintained in HBase, Trend Micro for security purposes, Nielsen for measurement purposes, Jive Software for enterprise collaboration, OCLC for digital media, Ancestry.com Inc. for DNA matching, and Box Inc. for machine data analysis.

Schema change operations

Schema and table management of an HBase table can be done through the `Alter` command. Using this command, we can perform the following operations:

- Modify column family schema
- Add column families
- Remove column families
- Change table-related settings such as maximum file size, MemStore flush size, read-only, and so on

In 0.94 and later versions of HBase, we rename a table using the snapshot feature, as follows:

```
hbase> disable 'TableToRename'
hbase> snapshot 'TableToRename', 'NewTable'
hbase>clone_snapshot 'NewTable', 'newTableToRename'
hbase>delete_snapshot 'NewTable'
hbase> drop 'TableToRename'
```

Now, let's discuss some schema-change-related operations.

We can change the versioning of a column family. Suppose we have a default version for a column family as 3, and lately, we realize that we need to have version 4, we can change the versioning as follows:

```
hbase> alter 'tableToAlter', {NAME => 'ColFam',VERSIONS => 4}
```

To remove or delete an existing column family, we can do it as follows:

```
hbase> alter 'tableToAlter', {NAME => 'colFam',METHOD => 'delete'}
```

If we need to enforce the maximum size of a column family to 256 MB, we can use the following command:

```
hbase> alter 'tableToAlter',{NAME=> 'colFam', METHOD => 'table_att',
MAX_FILESIZE => 268435456}
```

If we need to add a new column family to an HBase table, we need to disable it first and then define a new name with already existing names, as shown in the following snippet. Suppose we have a table with colFam1, and we need to add colFam2, we can do it as follows:

```
hbase>disable 'tableToAlter'
hbase> alter 'tableToAlter' {NAME=>'colFam1',NAME=>'colFam2'}
hbase>enable 'tableToAlter'
```

We have the option of performing multiple operations in a single command. Suppose we need to change the versions of two column families, we can do it as follows:

```
hbase> alter
'tableToAlter',{NAME=>'colFam1',VERSIONS=>2}'{NAME=>'colFam2',VERSION
S=>5},{NAME=> 'toDeleteColFam',METHOD => 'delete}
```

Likewise, we can perform many operations in a single line of alter command. We can also see the status of the alter command, as follows:

```
hbase>alter_status 'tableToAlter'
```

We will talk more about the shell command in *Chapter 6, HBase Cluster Maintenance and Troubleshooting*, with more options.

 We should always keep in mind that changes do not take immediate effect; they take place at the next major compaction. Until then, the old definition remains active.

There exists a project on GitHub using which we can easily create XML-based schema. For more information on the project, visit:

- `https://github.com/larsgeorge/hbase-schema-manager`
- `https://github.com/ivarley/scoot`

Calculating the data size stored in HBase

In the case of any database, whether it is RDBMS or NoSQL, we always need to find out the record size in order to plan the storage size needed, or to in order do a capacity planning. Even a few bytes per record might bring drastic changes to the data storage size that we estimate. For example, suppose we have one extra byte attached to each record, and we have around one billion records, and this extra byte requires around 1 GB of storage space on the disk.

Now, let's consider this data size calculation in case of HBase. Let's consider a table named `employee`, where we have fields such as the row key, the column family, the column, and the value. In HBase, each value is stored as fully qualified, so for each column of a record, it is accompanied with the row key we assign. So, let's now consider the space requirement.

As HBase stores data in the key-value format, let's now do the approximation. We will consider the row key as `student1`.

Key size	Value size	Row size	Row data	Col fam size	Col fam data	Column size	Timestamp	Key type	Actual value
Int (4)	Int(4)	Short(2)	Byte array	Byte (1)	Byte array	Byte array	Long (8)	Byte (1)	Byte array

Let's calculate the requirement of fixed size, which is 4 + 4 + 2 + 1 + 8 + 1 and equals 20 bytes. For other parts, we need to calculate the byte array sizes of the different values, so the total size is *Total = fixed size + variable size.*

Suppose we have one billion records, then the total size will be around *40 bytes * one billion = 40 billion bytes*, which will be around 40 GB, and therefore, we can calculate according to the number of columns and rows in HBase. There is the option of compression in an HBase table, using which we can minimize the requirements of storage drastically.

We can implement compression while creating the table, as follows:

```
hbase>create 'tableWithCompression',
{ NAME =>'colFam',COMPRESSION =>'SNAPPY'}
```

This will implement the Snappy compression algorithm on the records inserted in an HBase table. There are also other compression algorithms we can use as Snappy, such as LZF, LZO, and ZLIB.

Some benchmarking on the use of algorithm follows, so use of algorithms should be decided accordingly. Have a look at the following table:

Algorithm	IO performance	Compression ration achieved
ZLIB	Performance degraded	Best compression provided around (45 percent to 50 percent)
LZO	Around 4 percent to 6 percent	Around 41 percent to 45 percent
LZF	Around 20 percent to 22 percent)	Around 38 percent to 40 percent
Snappy	Around 24 percent to 28 percent)	Around 38 percent to 41 percent

Also, the compression depends on the type of data present in the table, so compression ration should be accordingly selected. Suppose we need more compression but less performance, we can always go with ZLIB, and if we need performance with an average compression, we can choose Snappy or whichever suits our data in the table.

Summary

In this chapter, we discussed schema designing basics, the data model of HBase, and data model operations that we can perform on an HBase table.

We also focused on designing different types of row keys, naming preferences, and suggestions for better optimization. The chapter also covers different use cases and how a schema can be designed based on it. There was a section that discussed namespaces and versioning of the records. In the next chapter, we will discuss the administration tasks and processes in HBase in detail.

6
HBase Cluster Maintenance and Troubleshooting

We have already learned about setting up the Hadoop and HBase clusters. Now, we will learn the aspects we need to consider to maintain the cluster and keep it up and running. This chapter will help readers make their HBase cluster more reliable by making it high available.

In this chapter, we will concentrate on the operational part of HBase. We will discuss the following topics:

- Introduction to the HBase administration
- HBase shell
- Different administration tools for HBase
- Using Java in HBase shell for various tweaks
- HBase and shell scripting for HBase
- Connecting hive with HBase to run **Hive Query Language** (**HQL**) queries from hive
- Implementing securities in HBase
- Frequently occurring errors and their solutions
- Other miscellaneous topics

As HBase runs on top of Hadoop, before starting with the HBase administration, let's look at Hadoop administration tasks and aspects in brief.

Here is the list of available Hadoop shell commands and steps on how to use them.

Hadoop shell commands

A binary is present inside the `bin` directory. We can call the following Hadoop command if we need to know all the commands available:

```
<Hadoop directory path>bin/hadoop
```

In the version previous to Hadoop v1, we can use the preceding command. However, in the later versions, we have to use the following command:

```
<Hadoop directory path>bin/hdfs
```

A binary without any parameter will display the list of available commands. We can check the actual implementation of Hadoop shell and its Java source at `https://github.com/shot/hadoop-source-reading/blob/master/src/core/org/apache/hadoop/fs/FsShell.java`.

> We can use `bin/hadoop` or `bin/hdfs` based on the version of Hadoop we have. In the newer versions of Hadoop, it is advisable to use HDFS instead of Hadoop. Here, we will use `bin/hadoop`, but you can use any one of the commands, depending on the version you are using.

Types of Hadoop shell commands

Let's take a look at the Hadoop shell commands. However, first we will look at the generic options available with the aforementioned `bin/hadoop` and `bin/hdfs`. The following is the syntax:

```
hdfs [--config <configuration dir>] [command] [generic_options]
[command_options]
```

The following table will explain to you the parameters of the preceding command:

Parameters	Explanation

`--config`	Using this parameter, we can define the current and active configuration directory as we might have more than one configuration parameter or directory for the cluster. We can define it as follows:
	
	`hadoop --config`
	`/home/shashwat/hadoop2/config1`

`-D parameter-name=parameter value`	Here, we can give runtime parameters that are found in the configuration files. We can pass command-line runtime parameters.

Parameters	Explanation
`-jt <local>` or `<jobtrackerHostname:port>`	Using this, we can pass the JobTracker address host address while dealing with MapReduce.
`-files <files list separated by comma>`	In this parameter, we provide a list of files to be copied and required for a job running on the Hadoop cluster while submitting. This copies the required resource files for the job.
`-libjars <list of jar files required for job to run command separated file list>`	Here, we can list out the library JAR files that are needed for the job to run, which will be included in the Java classpath.
`-archives <list of archieve files comma separated>`	Here, we can list the files that are to be extracted for the job resource.

 All the earlier options are valid in the cases of the `fs`, `dfs`, `dfsadmin`, `fsck`, `job`, and `fetchdt` commands.

We categorized Hadoop shell commands into the following three types:

- Administration commands
- User commands
- File-system-related commands

Let's explore the commands under the above mentioned types.

Administration commands

The following is the list of administration commands:

- `balancer`: Using this command, we can balance data distribution throughout the cluster. Sometimes, it so happens that a few of the DataNodes become overloaded when write operations happen at pace. This might also happen when a new DataNode is added but underutilized. We can stop this command anytime using *Ctrl + C*.

  The syntax for this command is as follows:

  ```
  hdfs balancer [-threshold <threshold value>]
  ```

  The following is the example:

  ```
  hdfs balancer - threshold 20
  ```

The balancer process is iterative. The threshold value gives us a long value in the range of 1 to 100. The balancer generally tries to equalize the data uses throughout all the DataNodes, and tries to keep it within the range `[average - threshold, average +threshold]`.

The smaller the value of the given threshold, the more balanced the cluster is.

While balancing the cluster, it uses a lot of network bandwidth. We can control it using another administration command, `dfsadmin -setBalanacerBandwidth <bandwidth>`, so the balancer will use a specified percentage of the available bandwidth. This should be set to prevent read/write exceptions during the cluster operation. This setting can also be changed using the `dfs.balance.bandwidthPerSec` (value in bytes per second) parameter found in the default file in Hadoop, wherein we can specify it, or we can set it at runtime using the `dfsadmin` command.

The balancer will pick DataNodes with disk usage above the higher threshold (seen as over utilized DataNode) and try to find blocks from these DataNodes to be copied into a DataNode that's underutilized. In the second round, a balancer selects DataNodes that are overutilized, and moves the blocks to nodes where utilization is below average. The third round will choose nodes with utilization above average to move data to underutilized nodes.

> For more details on balancer (flow, architecture, and administration), visit `https://issues.apache.org/jira/browse/HADOOP-1652`. Here, PDF files are available on the balancer architecture; you can also visit `http://hadoop.apache.org/docs/current/hadoop-project-dist/hadoop-common/CommandsManual.html#balancer`.

- `daemonlog`: This command is used to set the logging level for each Hadoop daemon process. This comes handy when we debug a problem with Hadoop, and therefore this command can be used to increase or decrease the log level for debugging purposes. This log-level modification can be done through configuration or Hadoop daemon web pages. However, it is better that an administrator does it through a command line.

This command accepts two parameters, namely get and set. Get is used to get the information about the log level, and set is used to set the log level.

The following is the syntax to get the log level information:

```
-getlevel <host:port> <name>
```

The preceding command gets the log level information of the daemon processes running at the specified host and port by internally connecting to http://<host>:<port>/logLevel?log=<name>.

The host, <host>, gets the log level information from the port, <port>, on which the service is running.

The <name> parameter specifies the hostname from which to get the log level. This is a fully qualified classname of the daemon performing the logging process.

Example of it is org.apache.hadoop.mapred.JobTracker for the JobTracker daemon.

The following is the syntax to set the log level:

```
-setlevel <host:port> <name> <level>
```

The preceding command sets the log level of the daemon running at the specified host by internally connecting to http://<host>:<port>/logLevel?log=<name>.

The host, <host>, sets the log level on the port, <port>, on which the service is running. The <name> parameter specifies the daemon on which to set the log level. The <level> parameter specifies the log level to set the daemon.

The following command is an example of how to get the log level:

```
hdfs daemonlog -getlevel host:<port>
org.apache.hadoop.mapred.JobTracker
```

The following command is an example of how to set the log level:

```
hdfs daemonlog -setlevel host:
<port>org.apache.hadoop.mapred.JobTracker <ERROR or DEBUG>
```

 You can also find the description of the daemonlog command at http://hadoop.apache.org/docs/current/hadoop-project-dist/hadoop-common/CommandsManual.html#daemonlog.

- `datanode`: This command is used to start or stop the DataNode daemon processes. The following is the syntax:

```
hdfs datanode [-rollback]
```

The rollback option helps to roll back DataNode to the previous version. If the upgrade process is in progress and something goes wrong, we need to restore the DataNode metadata to the previous existing version. If the command is specified without any parameter, it will start the DataNode daemon, if it's not already running.

> You can also find the description of the `datanode` command at `http://hadoop.apache.org/docs/current/hadoop-project-dist/hadoop-common/CommandsManual.html#datanode`.

- `dfsadmin`: This command runs the `dfsadmin` client for the Hadoop cluster to perform administration commands. We can check the actual implementation in Java at `https://github.com/facebook/hadoop-20/blob/master/src/hdfs/org/apache/hadoop/hdfs/tools/DFSAdmin.java`. The following is the syntax:

```
hdfs dfsadmin [GENERIC_OPTIONS] [-report] [-safemode enter |
leave | get | wait] [-refreshNodes] [-finalizeUpgrade]
[-upgradeProgress status | details | force]
[-metasave filename] [-setQuota <quota><dirname>]
[-clrQuota <dirname>......<dirname>] [-help [cmd]]
[-restoreFailedStorage true|false|check]
```

The following list will give us an explanation of different parameters in this command. We already discussed the generic options earlier, and it remains the same here.

- `report`: This parameter with the `hdfs` command displays the basic status of the cluster and HDFS file system.

  For example, have a look at the following command:

```
hdfs dfsadmin -status
```

The following is what you will get as output:

```
bash-4.1$ hdfs dfsadmin -report
Configured Capacity: 11888480666 (11.07 GB)
Present Capacity: 8688660480 (8.09 GB)
DFS Remaining: 8626753536 (8.03 GB)
DFS Used: 61906944 (59.04 MB)
DFS Used%: 0.71%
Under replicated blocks: 101
Blocks with corrupt replicas: 0
Missing blocks: 0


- - - - - - - - - - - - - - - - - - - - - - - - - - - - - - - - - - - -
Datanodes available: 1 (1 total, 0 dead)

Live datanodes:
Name: 127.0.0.1:50010 (localhost.localdomain)
Hostname: localhost.localdomain
Rack: /default
Decommission Status : Normal
Configured Capacity: 11888480666 (11.07 GB)
DFS Used: 61906944 (59.04 MB)
Non DFS Used: 3199820186 (2.98 GB)
DFS Remaining: 8626753536 (8.03 GB)
DFS Used%: 0.52%
DFS Remaining%: 72.56%
Last contact: Fri Jul 25 10:36:46 PDT 2014
```

- ○ safemode: Safe mode is the condition when Hadoop prevents reading of data from the cluster, and meanwhile, loads and updates the metadata during a start up process. We have a command to get and set information. Safe mode is the state of NameNode in which it is in a read-only mode, where NameNode does not accept changes to the namespace and deleted blocks are not replicated.

  This command has parameters such as -safemode <enter /leave / get | wait>, where leave forces Hadoop to come out of the safe mode explicitly, get gets the status of NameNode, whether it is in the safe mode, and wait makes NameNode wait till it comes out of the safe mode.

  If you force Hadoop to come out of the safe mode, it means you are asking Hadoop to come out without updating the metadata, and this will lead to corruption of data most of the time. However, if at all it's necessary to force Hadoop to leave the safe mode, first verify, check, and try to see what is there in the logs of NameNode.

  Hadoop enters the safe mode automatically at startup, and it leaves the safe mode by itself once it has reached the minimum percentage of blocks needed for a replication condition to fulfill (based on the replication factor).

NameNode can also enter the safe mode manually, but then, it can also only be taken out of this safe mode manually.

This parameter of `dfsadmin` can be used as follows:

```
hdfs dfsadmin -safemode [<get/enter/leave/wait>]
```

Let's see one example:

```
hdfs dfsadmin -safemode get
```

The following screenshot shows the output of the preceding command:

```
File  Edit  View  Search  Terminal  Help
bash-4.1$ hdfs dfsadmin -safemode
Usage: java DFSAdmin [-safemode enter | leave | get | wait]
bash-4.1$ ^C
bash-4.1$ hdfs dfsadmin -safemode get
Safe mode is OFF
bash-4.1$ hdfs dfsadmin -safemode wait
Safe mode is OFF
bash-4.1$ hdfs dfsadmin -safemode enter
Safe mode is ON
bash-4.1$ hdfs dfsadmin -safemode get
Safe mode is ON
bash-4.1$ hdfs dfsadmin -safemode wait
^Cbash-4.1$ hdfs dfsadmin -safemode leave
Safe mode is OFF
```

- `refreshNodes`: This parameter of the command makes Hadoop read configurations such as hosts again, and excludes files to update the set of DataNodes that are allowed to connect to NameNodes that should be or are already decommissioned. For example, have a look at the following command:

  ```
  hdfs dfsadmin -refreshNodes
  ```

- `finalizeUpgrade`: When we issue the `dfsadmin` command with this parameter, it will make an upgrade permanent. It does so by deleting the previous version of directories on DataNodes and NameNode. This completes the upgrade process and is not downgradable.

- `upgradeProgress`: This parameter of the command has three options: `status`, `detail`, and `force`. It also fetches the information on the Hadoop upgrade process.

- `metasave`: This parameter saves the NameNode primary data structures to a file. The file contains one line for each of the following:

  - DataNodes' hearts beating with NameNode
  - Blocks waiting to be replicated
  - Blocks currently being replicated
  - Blocks waiting to be deleted

- ◦ `setQuota`: This parameter is used to set the quota for each directory as a long integer value that puts a hard limit on the number of names in the directory tree. It reports errors if one of the following is true:
  - *N* is not a positive integer
  - The user is not an administrator
  - The directory does not exist or is a file
  - The directory exceeds the new quota

- ◦ `clrQuota`: This parameter clears the quota for each directory. An error is reported if one of the following is true:
  - The directory does not exist or is a file
  - The user is not an administrator; `clearQuota` does not fault if the directory has no quota

- ◦ `help`: This displays the help for all the commands.

- ◦ `restoreFailedstorage`: This parameter turns automatic attempts on or off to restore failed storage data. If a failed storage comes online again, the system will attempt to restore edits and/or fsimage during checkpoint. The `check` option will return the current setting. This parameter has options such as `true`, `false`, and `chec`.

 You can also find the description of the `dfsadmin` command at `http://hadoop.apache.org/docs/current/hadoop-project-dist/hadoop-common/CommandsManual.html#dfsadmin`.

- `mradmin`: This command runs a MapReduce client. The following is the syntax:

```
hadoop mradmin [ generic_options ] [-refreshqueueacls]
```

The `-refreshqueueacls` parameter refreshes the queue ACLs used by Hadoop to check access during submissions of the job by the user. The properties present in `mapred-queue-acls.xml` are reloaded by the queue manager.

Some other options of this command are as follows:

- ◦ The `-refreshQueues` option to refresh a job queue
- ◦ The `-refreshUserToGroupsMappings` option to refresh user groups
- ◦ `-refreshSuperUserGroupsConfiguration`
- ◦ `-refreshNodes`
- ◦ `-help [cmd]`

You can also find the description of the mradmin command at http://hadoop.apache.org/docs/ current/hadoop-project-dist/hadoop-common/ CommandsManual.html#mradmin.

- jobtracker: This command runs an instance of a MapReduce node if the daemon is not already started. The following is the syntax:

```
Hadoop jobtracker [-dumpConfiguration]
```

The -dumpConfiguration option dumps the configuration used by JobTracker, along with the queue configuration in JSON format, into a standard output used by JobTracker, and then exits.

 You can also find the description of the jobtracker command at http://hadoop.apache.org/docs/ current/hadoop-project-dist/hadoop-common/ CommandsManual.html#jobtracker.

- namenode: This command runs a NameNode instance. The following is the syntax:

```
hadoop namenode [-format] / [-upgrade] / [-rollback] /
[-finalize] / [-importCheckpoint]
```

The following table describes the parameters of this command:

Command options	Description
-format	This parameter of the command should be used only once, at the first time, when a new cluster is configured. The command with this parameter formats the file system to HDFS and prepares the file system. This parameter must not be used for a working and in-production cluster as whole data will be destroyed.
-upgrade	This initiates the upgrade process to a newer version.
-rollback	This roll backs the upgrade process if something goes wrong. This must be used after stopping the cluster and distributing the old Hadoop version files on it.
-finalize	Once all NameNodes and DataNodes are upgraded successfully, this command commits the changes; this removes the previous state of the HDFS file system. After using this command, rollback will not work.

Command options	Description
-importCheckpoint	This loads the image file data from a checkpoint directory and saves it into the current directory. The checkpoint directory is read from the fs.checkpoint.dir property.

For more details on this, go to http://hadoop.apache.org/ docs/current/hadoop-project-dist/hadoop-hdfs/ HdfsUserGuide.html and http://hadoop.apache.org/ docs/current/hadoop-project-dist/hadoop-common/ CommandsManual.html#namenode.

- secondarynamenode: This command starts the secondary NameNode instance. The following is the syntax:

```
hadoop secondarynamenode [-checkpoint [force]] /
[-geteditsize]
```

The following list explains the parameters of this command:

- checkpoint [-force]: This performs checkpointing at the secondary NameNode if the EditLog size is greater than or equal to the fs.checkpoint.size.

   If -force is used, perform checkpoint irrespective of the EditLog size.

- geteditsize: This prints out the EditLog size.

You can also find the description of this command at http://hadoop.apache.org/docs/current/hadoop-project-dist/hadoop-common/CommandsManual. html#secondarynamenode.

- tasktracker: This starts the TaskTracker node; the syntax for this is as follows:

```
hadoop tasktracker
```

You can also find the description of this command at http://hadoop.apache.org/docs/current/hadoop-project-dist/hadoop-common/CommandsManual. html#tasktracker.

User commands

The following is the list of user commands:

- `archive`: This command is used to create Hadoop achieve files. Its syntax is as follows:

```
hadoop archive -archiveName NAME <src> <dest>
```

- `distcp`: This command is used to copy a file from one cluster to another or to the same cluster at a different location. This uses the MapReduce task to copy files parallel. Its syntax is:

```
hadoop distcp <source url> <destination url>
```

Have a look at the following example:

```
hadoop distcp hdfs://hadoop1:9000/files
hdfs://hadoop2:9000/filesdir
```

- `fs`: Instead of this command, we use `hdfs dfs`, which we will discuss in the next section with all of its various options.
- `fsck`: This command is used to find the inconsistencies in HDFS. It reports problems with various files, for example, missing blocks for a file or under-replicated blocks. This is not a Hadoop shell command. It can be run as:

```
hdfs fsck [GENERIC_OPTIONS] <path> [-move | -delete |
-openforwrite] [-files [-blocks [-locations | -racks]]]
```

The following is the description of the parameters of this command:

Command options	Description
`path`	This defines the path to be checked
`-move`	This moves corrupted files to `/lost+found`
`-delete`	This deletes corrupted files
`-files`	This prints out files being checked
`-openforwrite`	This prints out files opened for write
`-list-corruptfileblocks`	This prints the list of missing blocks and files they belong to
`-blocks`	This prints out the block report
`-locations`	This prints out locations for every block
`-racks`	This prints the network topology for DataNode locations

By default, the `fsck` command ignores files opened for write; we can use `-openforwrite` to report such files. They are generally tagged `CORRUPT` or `HEALTHY` depending on their block allocation status.

The following screenshot shows the output of `fsck`:

```
File Edit View Search Terminal Help
/user/oozie/share/lib/sqoop/netty-3.4.0.Final.jar:  Under replicated BP-763425243-127.0.0.1-1373884718246:blk_683760715
64232_1178. Target Replicas is 3 but found 1 replica(s).
.

/user/oozie/share/lib/sqoop/oozie-sharelib-sqoop-3.3.2-cdh4.3.0.jar:  Under replicated BP-763425243-127.0.0.1-137388471
blk_3590926773842375075_1180. Target Replicas is 3 but found 1 replica(s).

/user/oozie/share/lib/sqoop/sqoop-1.4.3-cdh4.3.0.jar:  Under replicated BP-763425243-127.0.0.1-1373884718246:blk_659296
01445689_1182. Target Replicas is 3 but found 1 replica(s).
Status: HEALTHY
 Total size:    60582743 B
 Total dirs:    49
 Total files:   101
 Total blocks (validated):      101 (avg. block size 599829 B)
 Minimally replicated blocks:   101 (100.0 %)
 Over-replicated blocks:        0 (0.0 %)
 Under-replicated blocks:       101 (100.0 %)
 Mis-replicated blocks:         0 (0.0 %)
 Default replication factor:    3
 Average block replication:     1.0
 Corrupt blocks:                0
 Missing replicas:              202 (66.666664 %)
 Number of data-nodes:          1
 Number of racks:               1
FSCK ended at Fri Jul 25 13:36:05 PDT 2014 in 102 milliseconds

The filesystem under path '/' is HEALTHY
```

- `fetchdt`: This retrieves delegation tokens from NameNode. Authentication is a two-party authentication protocol based on Java SASL Digest-MD5. The token is obtained during job submissions and submitted to JobTracker as part of the job submission. Find more details at `http://hortonworks.com/wp-content/uploads/2011/10/security-design_withCover-1.pdf`.

The following is the syntax:

```
fetchdt <opts> <token file>
```

The following table will describe to you the different command options:

Command options	Description
`--webservice <url>`	This is the URL to contact a NameNode on
`--renewer <name>`	This is a name of the delegation token renewer
`--cancel`	This cancels the delegation token
`--renew`	This renews the delegation token, which must be fetched using the `--renewer <name>` option
`--print`	This prints the delegation token

- `jar`: This runs a JAR file. Users can bundle their MapReduce code in a JAR file and execute it using the command, the syntax of which is as follows:

```
hadoop jar <jar> [mainClass] arguments
```

The following is an example of this command:

```
hadoop jar hadoop-mapreduce-examples-*.jar pi 20 20
```

- `Job`: This is used to submit a job. It can be known as a Hadoop or mapred job. The following is the syntax :

```
JobClient <command> <args>
  [-submit <job-file>]
  [-status <job-id>]
  [-counter <job-id> <group-name> <counter-name>]
  [-kill <job-id>]
  [-set-priority <job-id> <priority>]
  [-events <job-id> <from-event-#> <#-of-events>]
  [-history <jobOutputDir>]
  [-list [all]]
  [-list-active-trackers]
  [-list-blacklisted-trackers]
  [-list-attempt-ids <job-id> <task-type> <task-state>]
  [-kill-task <task-id>]
  [-fail-task <task-id>]
```

The following table will guide you through the command options:

Command options	Description
`-submit job-file`	This is used to submit the job.
`-status job-id`	This prints the map and reduces the completion percentage and all job counters.
`-counter job-id group-name counter-name`	This prints the counter value of a job.
`-kill job-id`	This is used to kill the job.
`-events job-id from-event-# #-of-events`	This prints the events' details received by JobTracker for the given range of values.

Command options	Description
-history [all] jobOutputDir	This prints job details of failed and killed jobs. More details about the job, such as successful tasks and task attempts, made for each task can be viewed by specifying the [all] option.
-list [all]	This is used to display jobs that are yet to be completed. The -list all option displays all jobs.
-kill-task task-id	This is used to kill the task using a task ID.
-fail-task task-id	This lists out the failed tasks of a failed job and the number of attempts.
-set-priority job-id priority	Using this switch, we can change the priority of a job to any one of these priority values: VERY_HIGH, HIGH, NORMAL, LOW, and VERY_LOW.

- pipes: This command enables Hadoop to MapReduce code written in C++. This library is supported on 32-bit Linux installations. The following is the syntax:

```
hadoop pipes [-conf <path>] [-jobconf <key=value>, <key=value>,
...] [-input <path>] [-output <path>]
[-jar <jar file>] [-inputformat <class>] [-map <class>]
[-partitioner <class>] [-reduce <class>] [-writer <class>]
[-program <executable>] [-reduces <num>]
```

The following are the descriptions of the command options:

Command options	Description
-conf path	This is the path to where configuration for a job exists
-jobconf key=value, key=value, ...	This adds/overrides configurations for jobs
-input path	This is the path to the input directory
-output path	This is the path to the output directory
-jar jar file	This is the JAR filename
-inputformat class	This is a InputFormat class
-map class	This is Java Map class
-partitioner class	This is a Java partitioner
-reduce class	This is a Java Reduce class
-writer class	This is a Java RecordWriter class
-program executable	This is an executable URI
-reduces num	This is the number of Reduces

- `version`: This displays the Hadoop version. Its syntax is as follows:

```
hadoop version
```

File system-related commands

The `hdfs dfs` command provides shell-based Hadoop commands that directly interact with **Hadoop Distributed File System (HDFS)** as well as other file systems that Hadoop supports, such as Local FS, HFTP FS, S3 FS, or others.

This command can be executed using the following syntax:

```
[hadoop fs <args>]
```

Alternatively, we can also use:

```
[hdfs dfs args]
```

Let's discuss these `dfs` commands briefly:

Options	Description
`-appendToFile`	This appends files to HDFS. These files can be local or inputs to be written on HDFS.
	Have a look at the following example:
	- `hdfs dfs -appendToFile file /user/data/appendedfile`
	- `hdfs dfs -appendToFile file file0 /user/data/appendedfile`
	- `hdfs dfs -appendToFile localfile hdfs://<namenode>/user/data/appendedfile`
	- `hdfs dfs -appendToFile - hdfs://<namenode>/user/data/appendedfile`
	This parameter reads the input from `stdin`.
`-cat`	This displays the content of a file on `stdout`. The following is the syntax:
	`hdfs dfs -cat <file URI>`
	Here is an example:
	`hdfs dfs -cat hdfs://<namenode>/file`

Options	Description

** -chgrp	This changes the group of a file or directory. -R is used for recursive. The syntax is:
	
	`hdfs dfs -chgrp [-R] [owner][:[group]]<URI>`
	
	Here are some examples:
	
	`hdfs dfs -chgrp -R hadoop:hadoop hdfs://namenode/dir`
	
	`hdfs dfs -chgrp hadoop:hadoop hdfs://namenode/file`
	
	For permission-related information, visit http://hadoop. apache.org/docs/r1.2.1/hdfs_permissions_guide. html.

** -chmod	This changes the access mode of a file or directory. -R is used for recursive.
	
	The syntax is as follows:
	
	`hdfs dfs -chmod <mode> <URI>`
	
	Here are some examples:
	
	`hdfs dfs -chmod 777 hdfs://namenode/filename`
	
	`hdfs dfs -chmod -R 777 hdfs://namenode/directory`
	
	For more on permission and mode, visit http://hadoop. apache.org/docs/r1.2.1/hdfs_permissions_guide. html.

** -chown	This changes the owner of a directory or file, we use -R for recursive.
	
	The syntax is as follows:
	
	`hdfs dfs -chown [-R] <user or owner:group><URI>`
	
	Here is an example:
	
	`hdfs dfs -chown -R shashwat:hadoop hdfs://namenode/directory`

-copyFromLocal	This copies files from a local drive to an HDFS file system.
	
	The syntax is as follows:
	
	`hdfs dfs -copyFromLocal <Local file/ Local Directory><URI>`
	
	Here are some examples:
	
	`hdfs dfs -copyFromLocal /user/home/Shashwat/file1 hdfs://namenode/newdir`
	
	`hdfs dfs -copyFromLocal /user/home/Shashwat/dir hdfs://namenode/newdir`

Options	Description
-copyToLocal	This copies files from HDFS to local drives. Adding `ignorecrc` will force it not to check crc after copying, and the `crc` option will print the crc details.
	This is the syntax:
	`hdfs dfs -copyToLocal [-ignorecrc] [-crc] <URI><Local file/ Local Directory>`
	Here are some examples:
	`hdfs dfs -copyToLocal hdfs://namenode/newdir /user/home/Shashwat`
	`hdfs dfs -copyToLocal hdfs://namenode/newdir /user/home/Shashwat`
## -count	This counts the number of directories, files, and bytes under the given path. `-q` is also added to get quota.
	The following is the syntax::
	`hdfs dfs -count [-q] <path>`
	Here's an example:
	`hdfs dfs -count /dir`
## -cp	This is used to copy files from one HDFS location to another on the same Hadoop cluster or other Hadoop clusters.
	This is the syntax:
	`hdfs dfs -cp <Source URI> <Destination URI>`
	Here are some examples:
	`hdfs dfs -cp /user/file1 /user/dir1/`
## -du	This displays the size of the directories and files under the given path.
	This is the syntax:
	`hdfs dfs -du [-S] [-h] <URI>`
	Adding options `-S` will give the summarized (aggregated) size, and `-h` will give it in a human-readable format (in MB, GB, and so on).
	Here are some examples:
	`hdfs dfs -du -s /user/dire`
	`hdfs dfs -du /user/dir`
	`hdfs dfs -du -s -h /user/dir`
## -dus	This is equivalent to `-du -s` and displays the size of directories or files as an aggregated summary.

Options	Description
## -expunge	When we delete files, and trash is enabled on HDFS, deleted files go to trash, but not directly deleted from HDFS. This command enables us to empty the trash.
	This is the syntax:
	`hdfs dfs -expunge`
-get	This is equivalent to `-copyToLocal`.
	This is the syntax:
	`hdfs dfs -get <HDFS location> <local destination>`
	Here is an example:
	`hdfs dfs -get hdfs://namenode/dir /tmp`
-getmerge	This concatenates the source and destination, and copies them to a local directory.
	This is the syntax:
	`hdfs dfs -getmerge <src> <localdst> [addnl]`
-ls	This lists out files and folders in a given path.
	Here is the syntax:
	`hdfs dfs -ls <directory path>`
	This is the example:
	`hdfs dfs -ls /`
-lsr	This lists out files and folders recursively; the syntax and uses are same as `-ls`.
-mkdir	This creates a directory on HDFS.
	This is the syntax:
	`hdfs dfs -mkdir <directory path to be created>`
	Here are some examples:
	`hdfs dfs -mkdir /user/hadoop/dirtocreate`
	`hdfs dfs -mkdir /user/hadoop/dirtocreate /user/hadoop/dirtocreate1`
-moveFromLocal	This copies a file from the local directory and deletes the source file on the source path.
	This is the syntax:
	`dfs -moveFromLocal <localsrc> <dst>`
-moveToLocal	This moves the file from HDFS to a local destination.
	This is the syntax:
	`hdfs dfs -moveToLocal [-crc] <src> <dst>`

Options	Description

** -mv	This moves a file or directory from one HDFS location to another, either on the same cluster or to different clusters.
	
	This is the syntax:
	
	`hdfs dfs -mv <source> <dest>`
	
	Here are some examples:
	
	`hdfs dfs -mv /user/shashwat/file /user/shashwat/file1`
	
	`hdfs dfs -mv hdfs://namenode/file hdfs://namenode/file`

-put	This copies a single source or multiple sources from the local file system to the destination file system. It also reads the input from `stdin` and writes to the destination file system.
	
	This is the syntax:
	
	`hdfs dfs -put <source local> <destination HDFS>`
	
	Here are some examples:
	
	`hdfs dfs -put /tmp/userfilelocal hdfs://namenode/dirtarget`
	
	`hdfs dfs -put - hdfs://nn.example.com/hadoop/hadoopfile`
	
	Giving – (hyphen) instead of source path will take input from `stdin`.

** -rm	This deletes a specified file. If the `-skipTrash` option is specified, the trash, if enabled, will be bypassed, and the specified file or files will be deleted immediately. This can be useful when it is necessary to delete files from an over-quota directory.
	
	This is the syntax:
	
	`hdfs dfs -rm [-skipTrash] URI [URI …]`
	
	Here are the examples:
	
	`hdfs dfs -rm hdfs://namenode/file`
	
	`hdfs dfs -rm hdfs://namenode/file hdfs://namenode/file1`
	
	`hdfs dfs -rm /user/files/file`

** -rmr	This deletes files/directories recursively.
	
	This is the syntax:
	
	`hdfs dfs -rmr [-skipTrash] URI [URI …]`
	
	Here is an example:
	
	`hdfs dfs -rmr /user/shashwat/dirTodelete`

Options	Description
## -setrep	This is a helpful command for specifying the replication of existing files on HDFS explicitly. -R is added to set the replication factor recursively.
	This is the syntax:
	`hdfs dfs -setrep [-R] <path>`
	Here is an example:
	`hdfs dfs -setrep -w 5 -R /user/shashwat/dir`
	Here, -w will wait until it is replicated and -R will perform the operation recursively.
## -stat	This displays the statistics of the given argument file/directory.
	This is the syntax:
	`hdfs dfs -stat URI [URI ...]`
	Here is an example:
	`hdfs dfs -stat /user/Shashwat/file`
-tail	This displays the trailing content of a file on HDFS, which is the same as the `tail` command in Linux. -f is added to continuously tail the file content.
	This is the syntax:
	`hdfs dfs -tail [-f] URI`
	Here are some examples:
	`hdfs dfs -tail /user/Shashwat/file.log`
	`hdfs dfs -tail -f /user/Shashwat/file.log`
-test	This tests the condition with the following options:
	• -e checks to see whether the file exists; it returns 0 if true
	• -z checks to see whether the file is of zero length; it returns 0 if true
	• -d checks to see whether the path is a directory; it returns 0 if true
	This is the syntax:
	`hdfs dfs -test -[ezd] URI`
	Here are some examples:
	`hdfs dfs -test -e /user/Shashwat/file`
	`hdfs dfs -test -z /user/Shashwat/file`
	`hdfs dfs -test -d /user/Shashwat/file`

Options	Description
## -text	hdfs dfs -cat will display the file content correctly when the file is text based. If we need to read a sequential binary file or compressed file, cat will not do, so we have to use this command. The allowed formats are ZIP and TextRecordInputStream.
	This is the syntax:
	hdfs dfs -text <src>
	Here is an example:
	hdfs dfs -text /user/Shashwat/mr/_part01
-touchz	This command creates a zero-length file on HDFS.
	This is the syntax:
	hdfs dfs -touchz URI [URI …]
	Here are some examples:
	hdfs dfs -touchz hdfs://namenode/user/Shashwat/file
	hdfs dfs -touchz /user/Shashwat/file

Commands preceding ## are important admin commands.

Commands preceding ** are the commands to be used with caution as they might result in data loss.

Difference between copyToLocal/copyFromLocal and get/put

If HDFS contains the path /user/files/file, and if the local disk also contains the same path, the HDFS API won't know which one we mean, unless we specify a scheme such as file:// or hdfs://. It might pick the path we did not want to copy.

Therefore, we have -copyFromLocal, which prevents us from mistakenly copying the wrong file by limiting the parameter we give to the local file system.

The put command is for users who know which scheme to put in front. It is confusing, sometimes, for new Hadoop users to decide or specify which file system they are currently in and where their files actually are.

copyFromLocal is similar to the put command, except that the source is restricted to a local file reference.

copyToLocal is similar to the get command, except that the destination is restricted to a local file reference.

For the latest Hadoop documentation, visit `http://hadoop.apache.org/docs/` and select the Hadoop version.

Now, let's start with HBase administration and operation tasks.

HBase shell commands

HBase shell is a JRuby-based shell that provides an interface to HBase to perform operations such as creating tables and other operations. We can go to HBase shell using the following command:

```
hbase shell
```

Alternatively, we can use the following command, depending on the directory you are in or whether the environment variable is set:

```
bin/hbase shell
```

Once we type in one of the previous commands, we will get a prompt:

```
hbase(main):026:0>
```

At this prompt, we can type in the commands. We can always type `help` to get the list of available commands, and `help command_name` to get help on the particular command, as follows:

```
hbase(main):026:0> help
```

Similarly, with a particular command, it is as follows:

```
hbase(main):026:0> help 'scan'
```

Let's look at the commands and their descriptions.

Commands	Description
General Commands	
status	This shows the server status, for example: `5 servers, 0 dead, 25.0000 average load` This has three switches, as follows: `hbase> status 'simple'` `hbase> status 'summary'` `hbase> status 'detailed'`

Commands	Description
whoami	This shows the current HBase user. The following is the example: `hbase> whoami`
version	This shows the version of HBase.

list	This shell command will list out the existing tables in HBase.
	
	The syntax is as follows:
	
	`list`
	`list 'stud.*'`

count	This counts the number of records in a specified table. The syntax is as follows:
	
	`count 'tableName'`
	
	The count shows every 1,000 rows by default. The count interval might be optionally specified. Scan caching is enabled on count scans by default. The default cache size is 10 rows. If our rows are small in size, we increase this parameter.
	
	Have a look at the following example:
	
	`hbase> count 't1'`
	`hbase> count 't1', INTERVAL => 100000`
	`hbase> count 't1', CACHE => 1000`
	`hbase> count 't1', INTERVAL => 10, CACHE => 1000`
	
	This default HBase counter takes a lot of time to count if there is a lot of records. So, we have the HBase MapReduce JAR file to fasten this operation, which can be called as follows:
	
	`hadoop jar hbase.jar rowcount tablenametocount`
	
	This counter runs the MapReduce task much faster than the count in HBase.

describe	This describes the table given as parameter; information about the table structure will be displayed. The syntax is as follows: `describe 'NameOfThetableToDescribe'`
exist	If we have thousands of tables, and we need to check whether a table exists in HBase, we can use this command. If there are fewer tables, we can easily verify using a list, and if there are lots of tables, we might find it difficult to scroll through the list of tables, so we can use this command to check. The syntax is as follows: `exists 'tableToCheck'`

Commands	Description
`is_enabled`	This checks whether a table is enabled. The syntax is as follows: `is_enabled 'tableToCheck'`
`is_disabled`	This checks whether a table is disabled. The syntax is as follows: `is_disabled 'tableToCheck'`
`show_filters`	This displays a list of filters available in HBase. Have a look at the following example: `hbase> show_filters`
Data-manipulation commands	

`alter`	Using this command, we can alter the table and column family schema. Here, we pass the table name and a dictionary specifying a new column family schema.
	
	The following command adds a new column family `colFam` to table:
	
	`alter 'table', {NAME => 'colFam', VERSIONS => 1}`
	
	Alternatively, to keep a maximum of two cell versions, use the following command:
	
	`hbase> alter 'table', NAME => 'fam1', VERSIONS => 2`
	
	To delete the `f1` column family in table `t1`, use the following command:
	
	`hbase> alter ''table'', NAME => 'fam1', METHOD => 'delete'`
	
	A shorter version of the previous command is:
	
	`hbase> alter 'table', 'delete' => 'fam1'`
	
	We can also change table-scope attributes such as `MAX_FILESIZE`, `MEMSTORE_FLUSHSIZE`, `READONLY`, and `DEFERRED_LOG_FLUSH`.
	
	For example, to change the maximum size of a family to 128 MB, we use:
	
	`hbase> alter ''table'', METHOD => 'table_att', MAX_FILESIZE => '134217728'`
	
	There can be more than one alteration in a single line of command:
	
	`hbase> alter ''table'', {NAME => 'fam1'}, {NAME => 'fam2', METHOD => 'delete'}`

`alter_status`	This gives the status of the `alter` command. Have a look at the following example: `hbase> alter_status 'talblebingaltered'`

Commands	Description
alter_async	This command does not wait for all regions to receive the schema changes, whereas alter does.
	Have a look at the following example:
	`hbase> alter_async 't1', NAME => 'f1', METHOD => 'delete'`
disable	This disables a table for dropping or modification. The syntax is as follows:
	`disable 'tableToDisable'`
disable_all	This disables all the tables matching the given regex.
	Have a look at the following example:
	`hbase> disable_all 'tab*'`
drop	This deletes a table from HBase. So, before dropping the table, it must be disabled, otherwise it will throw an exception that the table is not disabled.
	Have a look at the following examples:
	`disable 'tableToDrop'`
	`drop 'tableToDrop'`
drop_all	This drops all of the tables matching the given regex.
	Have a look at the following example:
	`hbase> drop_all 'tab*'`
enable	This enables the table after modification.
	The syntax is as follows:
	`enable 'NameOfDisabledTableToEnable'`
enable_all	This enables all of the tables matching the given regex.
	Have a look at the following example:
	`hbase> enable_all 'tab*'`
delete	This deletes a cell value in a row.
	The syntax is as follows:
	`Delete 'table','row1','colFam1:name'`
	So, this will delete a name value in row1.

Commands	Description

`deleteall`	This deletes an entire row of a table or a column specified.
	
	The syntax is as follows:
	
	`deleteall 'table','row1'`
	
	This will delete the entire `row1`:
	
	`deleteall 'table','row1','colFam:name'`
	
	This will also delete column names from `row1`.

`truncate`	This disables the table, drops the table, and recreates schema. So, when we use `drop`, we need to disable the table manually, and then drop. If we just want to drop data and not the schema, we can use `truncate`; it automatically drops and recreates the schema of the dropped table: `hbase> truncate`
Data-creation commands	

`create`	This command is used to create a new table with a specified schema.
	
	The syntax is as follows:
	
	`create 'tablename','cf1'`
	
	This will create a table with a column family `cf1`, and we can then put data in the table and dynamically add columns.
	
	Have a look at the following examples.
	
	The following command will create a `tableToCreate` table with the column family `colFam1`, with five versions of records:
	
	`hbase> create 'tableToCreate', {NAME => 'colFam1', VERSIONS => 5}`
	
	This will create a `tableToCreate` table with column families `colFam1`, `colFam2`, and `colFam3`:
	
	`hbase> create 'tableToCreate', {NAME => 'colFam1'}, {NAME => 'colFam2'}, {NAME => 'colFam3'}`
	
	The shorthand of the previous commands are:
	
	`hbase> create 'tableToCreate', 'colFam1', 'colFam2', 'colFam3'`
	
	`hbase> create 'tableToCreate', {NAME => 'colFam1', VERSIONS => 1, TTL => 2592000, BLOCKCACHE => true}`

`put`	This puts/writes a value at a specified cell in a table or timestamp coordinate. To put a cell value into table `t1` at row `r1` under column `c1` marked with the time `ts1`, use: `hbase> put 't1', 'r1', 'c1', 'value', ts1`

Commands	Description
Data-reading commands	
scan	This command iterates through the rows in the table and displays on `stdout`. This lists all the records in the table. A scanner might contain TIMERANGE, FILTER, LIMIT, STARTROW, STOPROW, TIMESTAMP, MAXLENGTH, or COLUMNS. If no columns are specified, all columns will be scanned. To scan all members of a column family, leave the qualifier empty, as in `'col_family:'`.
	Have a look at the following example:
| | ```
hbase> scan '.META.'
hbase> scan '.META.', {COLUMNS =>
'info:regioninfo'}
hbase> scan 't1', {COLUMNS => ['c1', 'c2'], LIMIT
=> 10, STARTROW => 'xyz'}
hbase> scan 't1', {FILTER =>
org.apache.hadoop.hbase.filter.ColumnPaginationFilt
er.new(1, 0)}
hbase> scan 't1', {COLUMNS => 'c1', TIMERANGE =>
[1303668804, 1303668904]}
``` |
| | For experts, there is an additional option, `-- CACHE_BLOCKS --`, which switches block caching for the scanner on (`true`) or off (`false`). By default, it is enabled. |
| | Have a look at the following example: |
| | ```
hbase> scan 't1', {COLUMNS => ['c1', 'c2'],
CACHE_BLOCKS => false}
``` |
| get | This gets row or cell contents and passes table names, rows, and optionally, a dictionary of column(s), timestamps, time ranges, and versions. |
| | The following is the example: |
| | ```
hbase> get 'tableName', 'row1'
hbase> get 'tableName', 'row1', {TIMERANGE =>
[ts1, ts2]}
hbase> get 'tableName', 'row1', {COLUMN => 'c1'}
hbase> get 'tableName', 'row1', {COLUMN =>
['c1', 'c2', 'c3']}
hbase> get 'tableName', 'row1', {COLUMN =>
'c1', TIMESTAMP => ts1}
hbase> get 'tableName', 'row1', {COLUMN =>
'c1', TIMERANGE => [ts1, ts2], VERSIONS => 4}
hbase> get 'tableName', 'row1', {COLUMN =>
'c1', TIMESTAMP => ts1, VERSIONS => 4}
hbase> get 'tableName', 'row1', 'c1'
hbase> get 'tableName', 'row1', 'c1', 'c2'
hbase> get 'tableName', 'row1', ['c1', 'c2']
``` |
```

Commands	Description
get_counter	This returns a counter cell value at a specified table/row/column location. A cell should be managed with an atomic increment function on HBase, and the data should be binary encoded.
	The following is the example:
	`hbase> get_counter 't1', 'r1', 'c1'`
incr	This increments a cell value at a specified table/row/column location.
	To increment a cell value in table t1 at row r1 under column c1 by 1 (which can be omitted) or 10, do:
	`hbase> incr 't1', 'r1', 'c1'`
	`hbase> incr 't1', 'r1', 'c1', 1`
	`hbase> incr 't1', 'r1', 'c1', 10`
get_table	Using this, we can assign a table to a variable and perform operations such as put, get, and scan.
	Have a look at the following example:
	`t = get_table 'stud'`
	`t.scan()`
Miscellaneous admin commands	
close_region	This closes a single region. The close operation is done without the master's involvement (it will not know of the closing operation). Once the region is closed, it will stay closed. Use assign to reopen/reassign. Use unassigned or move to assign the region elsewhere on cluster.
	Have a look at the following example:
	`hbase> close_region 'REGIONNAMEToMove'`
	`hbase> close_region 'REGIONNAME', 'REGIONSERVER_IP:PORT'`
assign	This assigns a region and adds true to force the assignment of a region. If a region is already assigned, this will just go ahead and reassign the region.
balance_ switch	This enables/disables the balancer and returns the previous balancer state.
	Have a look at the following example:
	`hbase> balance_switch true`
	`hbase> balance_switch false`
balancer	HBase has a built-in feature that is called balancer, which by default runs every 5 minutes, and once started, it will try to equal out the assigned region per RegionServer. This will show if the balancer for HBase is enabled.

Commands	Description
compact	This compacts all regions in a specified table.

flush	This flushes all regions in a specified table.
	
	Have a look at the following example:
	
	`hbase> flush 'TABLENAMEToFlush'`
	`hbase> flush 'REGIONNAMEToFlush'`

major_ compact	This command runs a major compaction on a specified table.

move	This moves a region.
	
	Have a look at the following example:
	
	`hbase> move 'ENCODED_REGIONNAME'`
	`hbase> move 'ENCODED_REGIONNAME', 'SERVER_NAME'`

split	This splits the table or an individual region.
unassign	This command unassigns the RegionServer.

zk_dump	This gives the dump status of an HBase cluster, as seen by ZooKeeper.
	
	HBase is rooted at /hbase. The following is how it shows the dump status:
	
	`Master address: shashwat.com:60000`
	`Region server holding ROOT: shashwat.com:60020`
	`Region servers:`
	`shashwat.com:60020`
	`Quorum Server Statistics:`
	`shashwat.com:2181`
	`Zookeeper version: <version number>, built on <date time>`
	`Clients:`
	`/127.0.0.1:50641[1] (queued=0,recved=3,sent=65)`
	`/127.0.0.1:50637[1] (queued=0,recved=13,sent=226)`
	`/127.0.0.1:50644[1] (queued=0,recved=14,sent=198)`
	`/127.0.0.1:50643[1] (queued=0,recved=63,sent=65)`
	`/127.0.0.1:51874[0] (queued=0,recved=1,sent=0)`
	`/127.0.0.1:50713[1] (queued=0,recved=63,sent=63)`
	`Latency min/avg/max: 0/8/210`
	`Received: 53`
	`Sent: 626`
	`Outstanding: 0`
	`Zxid: 0x32f0`
	`Mode: standalone`
	`Node count: 1`

Commands	Description
`hlog_roll`	This starts writing log messages to a new file. The name of RegionServer should be given as the parameter. Have a look at the following example: `hbase> hlog_roll`

`add_peer`	This adds a peer cluster to replicate to. The ID must be short and the cluster key must be composed as: `hbase.zookeeper.quorum:hbase.zookeeper.property.clientPort:zookeeper.znode.parent`.
	
	This gives a full path for HBase to connect to another cluster.
	
	Have a look at the following example:
	
	`hbase> add_peer '1', "server1.cie.com:2181:/hbase"`
	`hbase> add_peer '2', "zk1,zk2,zk3:2182:/hbase-1"`

`list_peers`	This lists all replication peer clusters. Have a look at the following example: `hbase> list_peers`
`disable_peer`	This stops the replication stream to the specified cluster, but still keeps track of new edits to replicate. Have a look at the following example: `hbase> disable_peer '1'`
`enable_peer`	This restarts the replication to the specified peer cluster, continuing from where it was disabled. Have a look at the following example: `hbase> enable_peer '1'`
`remove_peer`	This stops the specified replication stream and deletes all the meta information kept about it. The following is the example: `hbase> remove_peer '1'`
`start_replication`	This restarts all the replication features. Have a look at the following example: `HBase> start_replication`
`stop_replication`	This stops all the replication features. The state in which each stream stops is undetermined. Have a look at the following example: `hbase> stop_replication`

Commands	Description
Security commands	
grant	This command is used to grant user-specific rights. Grant permissions are either zero or more letters from the set RWXCA: R for read, W for write, X for execute, C for create, and A for admin.
	Have a look at the following example:
	hbase> grant 'shashwat', 'RWXCA'
	hbase> grant 'shashwat', 'RWC', 'table1', 'colFam', 'sal'
revoke	This takes back/revokes access rights.
	Have a look at the following example:
	hbase> revoke 'shashwat', 'table', 'ColFam', 'sal'
user_ permission	This shows all permissions for a particular user.
	Have a look at the following example:
	hbase> user_permission
	hbase> user_permission 'tabStud'
Namespace-related commands	
create_ namespace	This command is used to create a namespace.
	Have a look at the following example:
	hbase>create_namespace 'tableStudgroup'
	hbase>create 'snamespace:table', 'colfam'
	This will create a table in the snamespace namespace with the column family colfam.
drop_ namespace	This is used to drop a namespace. Have a look at the following example:
	hbase>drop_namespace 'snamespace'
alter_ namespace	This alters an existing namespace.
	The syntax is as follows:
	hbase>alter_namespace 'snamespace', {METHOD => 'set', 'PROPERTY_NAME' => 'PROPERTY_VALUE'}
list_ namespace	This lists out namespaces.
	Have a look at the following example:
	hbase>list_namespace

Commands	Description
list_ namespace_ tables	This lists tables in the namespace.
	Have a look at the following example:
	`hbase> list_namespace_tables 'namespace'`
describe_ namespace	This displays the namespace description.
	Have a look at the following example:
	`hbase > describe_namespace 'name'`

 For internal implementation and source code, visit `https://github.com/apache/hbase/blob/master/hbase-shell/src/main/ruby/shell.rb`.

 Keep in mind that not all commands will run on all the versions of HBase. However, most of the commands will run on the latest version of HBase shell.

HBase administration tools

Here, we will discuss HBase administrating tools that are already available. We will also study the HBase check (hbck) and the HBase health check script a bit more.

hbck – HBase check

The hbck command is used to check/repair HBase. This command finds out inconsistencies in the HBase cluster, if they exist, and gives a formatted output for them. This command/tool checks for region consistency and table integrity problems. It works in two modes:

- **Read-only mode**: This only displays inconsistencies if they exist
- **Read-write-repair mode**: This reports inconsistencies and tries to repair them

It is good to repair inconsistencies that have lower risk while executing a repair hbck command. These region consistency repairs are localized-single-region repairs, which only modify in-memory data, wrong ZooKeeper data, or patch holes in the metadata table (an inconsistency exists if every possible row key doesn't resolve to exactly one region, and if every region isn't assigned and deployed on exactly one RegionServer and metadata-related issue).

The options to repair region consistencies include:

- `-fixAssignments`: This repairs unassigned, incorrectly assigned, or multiple time assigned regions. To fix these problems, we can run the following command:

  ```
  hbase hbck -fixAssignments
  ```

- `-fixMeta`: This removes meta rows when corresponding regions are not present in HDFS and adds a new metarow if the regions are present in HDFS and not in META. Use the following command to fix assignment and Meta:

  ```
  hbase hbck -fixAssignments -fixMeta
  ```

There are a few table integrity problems that are of low risk. The first two are: degenerate where `startkey == endkey` regions and backwards regions where `startkey > endkey`. These problems are automatically handled by sidelining the data to a temporary directory (`/hbck/xxxx`). The third low-risk class is HDFS region holes. This can be repaired using the `-fixHdfsHoles` option to fabricate new empty regions on the file system. If holes are detected, we can use `-fixHdfsHoles` and should include `-fixMeta` and `-fixAssignments` to make the new region consistent.

Have a look at the following example:

```
hbase hbck -repairHoles
```

Now, let's see the region-related fixes.

We need to run the `hbase hbck -details` command so that you isolate repair attempts only upon problems that the checks identify, so that we can really understand where the exact problem lies and where the specific problem can be targeted.

Some other repair options are as follows:

- `-fixHdfsOrphans`: This is used to adopt a region directory that has missing region metadata
- `-fixHdfsOverlaps`: This has the ability to fix overlapping regions
- `-repair`: This can be used to repair all the region inconsistencies
- `-maxMerge<n>`: This can be used to merge a maximum number of overlapping regions

- **-sidelineBigOverlaps**: This sidelines the regions to non-overlapping regions if more than one big regions overlap
- **-maxOverlapsToSideline<n>**: This option works by sidelining large overlapping regions, and sidelines a maximum of <n> regions

Some other cases that are to be considered are as follows:

- Use the following command to fix if Meta is not properly assigned:

  hbase hbck -fixMetaOnly -fixAssignments

- Use the following command if the HBase version file is missing:

  hbase hbck - fixVersionFile

- Use the following command if Root and META are corrupt:

  hbase org.apache.hadoop.hbase.util.hbck.OfflineMetaRepair

- Use the following command when an offline split parent occurs:

  hbase hbck -fixSplitParents

> You can check for help with the following command:
> **hbase hbck -help**

HBase health check script

The HBase health check script is available in the example directory of HBase, the source of which we can find at `http://svn.apache.org/viewvc/hbase/trunk/hbase-examples/src/main/sh/healthcheck/healthcheck.sh`.

The following parameters can be configured in order to automate this script and set the interval of the health check:

`hbase.node.health.script.location`

`hbase.node.health.script.timeout`

`hbase.node.health.script.frequency`

`hbase.node.health.failure.threshold`

The default frequency is after every 60 seconds, but we can set it accordingly.

The failure threshold defaults to 3, which is the number of times the health check will be tried before being set as a failure of check.

Writing HBase shell scripts

We can write a set of commands in a file and run it as:

```
hbase shell <path_to_script/scriptname>
```

Alternatively, we can write it as follows:

```
hbase org.jruby.Main <path_to_script/scriptname>
```

HBase shell might contain all the available HBase shell commands. Also, we can write a Linux shell command embedded with HBase commands.

Using the Hadoop tool or JARs for HBase

In a driver class provided by Hadoop, we can run HBase JAR files utilizing the features of Hadoop and using the following command:

```
hadoop jar <HBase Jar file path>/hbase-*.jar<program name>
```

The program names we can use here are:

- `completebulkload`: This is for a bulk data load
- `copytable`: This is to export a table data from the local to peer cluster
- `export`: This is to export data from an HBase table to HDFS as a sequence file
- `import`: This is to import data written by `export`
- `importtsv`: This is to import data in TSV format to HBase
- `rowcounter`: This is to count rows in an HBase table using MapReduce
- `verifyrep`: This is to compare the data from tables of different clusters

We will discuss the preceding methods in the next chapter, where we will also discuss the backup/restore process. Likewise, we can call the HBase JAR file with Hadoop. The following are the Hadoop tools:

- **HFile tool**: This tool helps us to read an HFile content in text format. We can use it as:

  ```
  hbase org.apache.hadoop.hbase.io.hfile.hfile
  ```

  This is a very useful tool, as `hfile` is not in human-readable format, and if we need to see the content, this tool fits well.

- **FSHLog tool**: This tool can be used to read WAL files in human-readable format. We can use it as:

```
hbase org.apache.hadoop.hbase.regionserver.wal.FSHLog --dump
<hbaselocationlogfile>
```

We can also use it to split log files, as follows:

```
hbase org.apache.hadoop.hbase.regionserver.wal.FSHLog --split
<hbaselocationlogfile>
```

We have `HLogPrettyPrinter`, which prints the contents of the HBase log file and WALPlayer to replay WAL log files.

- **Counting rows or cell efficiently**: An inbuilt HBase counter is much slower as it scans through the HBase tables and huge tables take a lot of time. So, if we need to count the number of records or number of cells for a table, we have an option, using which we can do it in less time. This runs the MapReduce task for the same.

Use the following command to count rows as a MapReduce task:

```
hbase org.apache.hadoop.hbase.mapreduce.RowCounter <tablename>
```

The preceding command will show the number of rows in a specified HBase table. For more detailed statistics of records, we can use `CellCounter` or `RowCounter`, which we will see next.

A cell counter results in detailed counts; it provides the following once completed:

  ◦ The number of rows in the table
  ◦ The number of column families across all rows
  ◦ The number of qualifiers across all rows
  ◦ The number of occurrences of each column family
  ◦ The number of occurrences of each qualifier
  ◦ The number of versions of each qualifier

We can use `CellCounter` as follows:

```
hbase org.apache.hadoop.hbase.mapreduce.CellCounter
<tablename><outputDir> [regex or prefix]
```

- **Offline compaction tool**: This can be used to run compactions in the offline mode. It can be run as follows:

```
hbase org.apache.hadoop.hbase.regionserver.CompactionTool
```

Connecting HBase with Hive

We can map an HBase table to Hive (browse `https://hive.apache.org` if you don't know about Hive already) and run Hive queries that support **Hive Query Language** (**HQL**) almost in the same way as SQL on an HBase table. This is good for developers or users who possess a good knowledge of SQL.

For this, we need to create a table in HBase. Let's start the process:

Create a table in Hive as follows:

```
create 'hivehbasetable', 'name'
```

Put some data into it:

```
put 'hivehbasetable', 'row1', 'name:firstname', 'shashwat'
put 'hivehbasetable', 'row1', 'name:lastname', 'shriparv'
put 'hivehbasetable', 'row1', 'name:title', 'mr'
```

We need some JAR files for this association (Hive needs to be told where these JARs are), which are as follows:

- `Guava.<version>.jar`
- `Hive-Hbase handler.<version>.jar`
- `HBase.<version>.jar`
- `Zookeeper.<version>.jar`

Then, we will create an external table in Hive, which will map the HBase table to Hive. Start Hive with following command:

```
hive --auxpath /usr/lib/hive/lib/hbase.jar,/usr/lib/hive/lib/hive-
hbase-handler-<version>.jar, /usr/lib/hive/lib/zookeeper.jar,
/usr/lib/hive/lib/guava-<version>.jar
```

To prevent library-related errors, use the following command:

```
CREATE EXTERNAL TABLE hivehbasetablemapped (key string, userid
string, bookid string, rating int) STORED BY
'org.apache.hadoop.hive.hbase.HBaseStorageHandler' WITH
SERDEPROPERTIES ("hbase.columns.mapping" =
":key,name:firstname,name:lastname,name:title") TBLPROPERTIES
("hbase.table.name" = "hivehbasetable");
```

Alternatively, you can use the following command:

```
CREATE TABLE hivehbasetablemapped (key string, userid string, bookid
string, rating int) STORED BY
'org.apache.hadoop.hive.hbase.HBaseStorageHandler' WITH
SERDEPROPERTIES ("hbase.columns.mapping" =
":key,name:firstname,name:lastname,name:title") TBLPROPERTIES
("hbase.table.name" = "hivehbasetable");
```

Difference between external and internal tables in Hive

When we drop an internal table, it drops both the data and metadata.

When we drop an external table, it only drops the metadata. This means Hive is ignorant about the data now. It does not touch the data itself.

Here, the first column is the key column, which will be taken as HBase RowKey. If we have some numeric column, we can use `age:age#field` in the mapping.

Once we finish the preceding process successfully, we can execute a SQL query in Hive as follows:

```
hive > select * from hivehbasetablemapped;
```

We can also perform other operations on Hive.

For further details on this, visit `https://cwiki.apache.org/confluence/display/Hive/HBaseIntegration`.

HBase region management

In this section, we will discuss various operations, such as compaction, merging, and splitting, which we can perform on the HBase region.

Compaction

Compaction is done to reduce the number of StoreFiles. Once the number of StoreFiles is reduced, more efficiency and performance can be gained. It is a high-resource-hungry process. Running this will result in a single StoreFile per store. Major compactions also process delete markers and maximum versions.

We already discussed compaction, so we will see how to perform this:

```
hbase >major_compact
```

In Java, use `HBaseAdmin.majorCompact`, which we will look at in *Chapter 7, Scripting in HBase*, and *Chapter 8, Coding HBase in Java*.

 Read more on compaction in detail at `http://hbase.apache.org/book/regions.arch.html#compaction`.

Merge

We can use the merge command in adjoining regions in the same table to increase performance:

```
hbase org.apache.hadoop.hbase.util.Merge <tablename>
<region name> <region name>
```

HBase node management

In this section, we will discuss adding (commissioning) and removing (decommissioning) nodes from an HBase cluster.

Commissioning

Let's discuss the commissioning of nodes in an HBase cluster.

Prepare the machine, check the permissions twice, and check the connectivity, host entry, and host resolution. Once done and twice checked, copy the configuration file following the same path structure at the new machine, and start RegionServer using the following command:

```
hbase-daemon.sh start regionserver
```

Once this command is executed, RegionServer will automatically register with HMaster and start receiving local data. At the beginning, the newly added node will not have any data, and if balancer is not disabled, it will start moving new regions to the new RegionServer.

If the start and stop process is done using ssh and HBase script, add the newly added node host name to the `conf/regionservers` file.

So, commissioning is just like checking the new machine, copying the configuration files, and starting the process if we want to say it in one line.

Decommissioning

Decommissioning means removing a node (RegionServer) from the cluster. This process is not easy as commissioning a node. However, here we need to take care of things before removing the node from the cluster. Let's discuss this here.

First, disable the load balancer, because if it is running, it might create some inconsistencies due to the ongoing data transfer process. So, let's list the decommissioning process in steps:

1. Stop/disable the load balancer using the following command:

   `hbase>balance_switch false`

2. Stop RegionServer on the node, which must be decommissioned as follows:

   `hbase> hbase-daemon.sh stop regionserver`

3. When RegionServer is stopped, it will close all the regions and shut down.
4. The ephemeral node of RegionServer will expire in ZooKeeper.
5. The master will notice that RegionServer is down and treat it as crashed.
6. Reassignment of regions served by RegionServer will be done.

Since this stopping method might take time, we can use the graceful shutdown. It unloads regions from RegionServer, allowing the node to be terminated without impacting data availability. It is in contrast to the first option that results in a short window of data unavailability, which HBase takes to recognize the failure and does the recovery. The script that is used for this is available in the `bin` directory of HBase and named `graceful_stop.sh`.

So, let's have a look at the steps:

1. Issue the following command:

   `bin/graceful_stop.sh <RegionServer_Hostname>`

2. Always enable the balancer switch in the case of a graceful stop.
3. For the remaining steps, refer to the steps 2 to 6 in the preceding set of instructions.

Implementing security

Let's discuss various security implementations provided by HBase. Here, we will consider that Kerberos is set up and Hadoop is secured using this type of authentication. Now, let's see the security aspects in HBase.

Secure access

With a new version of HBase after Version 0.92, we get an option of enabling ACL-based protection on column families or table levels, and an optional SASL authentication of clients.

Now, let's see how to configure HBase and the client for connecting to secure HBase resources.

Requirement

First, let's see the Hadoop requirement. We must set the following parameters to `true` as we need good user authentication for Hadoop too:

`hbase.security.authentication`

`hadoop.security.authentication`

So, securing HBase is not enough, we need to secure Hadoop too.

Kerberos KDC

We need to have a **Kerberos Key Distribution Centre** (**Kerberos KDC**) configured. A Hadoop setup should be secured for an HBase, which is configured to handle requests from a secure client. HBase needs Kerberos credentials to be able to interact with the secured Kerberos-enabled Hadoop (HDFS).This authentication should be done using a `keytab` file. We need to create a `keytab` file (read more at `https://kb.iu.edu/d/aumh` for this), and it should be put where HMaster and RegionServer daemons are deployed. This file should be readable only to user accounts, using which these daemons are started.

A Kerberos principal is made up of three parts of the `<user name>/<domain name>@domain.com` form, and we need to add the following configuration to the `hbase-site.xml` file on all the machines:

```
<property>
<name>hbase.regionserver.kerberos.principal</name>
<value>hbase/_hostname@REALM.COM</value>
</property>
<property>
<name>hbase.regionserver.keytab.file</name>
<value>/home/hbase/conf/keytab.krb5</value>
</property>
<property>
```

```
<name>hbase.master.kerberos.principal</name>
<value>hbase/_hostname@REALM.COM</value>
</property>
<property>
<name>hbase.master.keytab.file</name>
<value>/home/hbase/conf/keytab.krb5</value>
</property>
```

All the HBase client users should be given a Kerberos principal that should have a password assigned with it. The client principal's `maxrenewlife` can be set so that it can be renewed only after the HBase client process is complete:

```
addprinc -maxrenewlife 4days
```

Client-side security configuration

To configure client-side security, add the following lines to `hbase-site.xml`:

The client must be logged in to Kerberos from KDC or `keytab` via the `kinit` command before it can communicate with an HBase cluster:

```
<property>
<name>hbase.security.authentication</name>
<value>kerberos</value>
</property>
<property>
<name>hbase.rpc.protection</name>
<value>privacy</value>
</property>
```

The second parameter will encrypt communication. When writing a client for HBase, we need to include the following piece of code in the client code:

```
Configuration config = HBaseConfiguration.create();
config .set("hbase.rpc.protection", "privacy");
HTable tablename= new HTable(conf, tablename);
```

If we enable encrypted communication, performance will degrade, so decide accordingly.

Client-side security configuration for thrift requests

For a thrift request configuration, we need to add the following lines in
`hbase-site.xml`:

```
<property>
<name>hbase.thrift.keytab.file</name>
<value>/user/shashwat/hbasekey.keytab</value>
</property>
<property>
<name>hbase.thrift.kerberos.principal</name>
<value>$USERNAME/_HOSTNAME@HDOMAINNAME</value>
</property>
```

`$USERNAME` and `$KEYTAB` should be changed according to the setup on the system.
For the rest of the APIs, we need to add `hbase.rest.keytab.file` and `hbase.rest.kerberos.principal` with the parameters.

Server-side security configuration

We can enable security at the server level too, for which we need to add the
following lines of code in the `hbase-site.xml` file:

```
<property>
<name>hbase.security.authentication</name>
<value>kerberos</value>
</property>
<property>
<name>hbase.security.authorization</name>
<value>true</value>
</property>
<property>
<name>hbase.coprocessor.region.classes</name>
<value>org.apache.hadoop.hbase.security.token.TokenProvider
</value>
</property>
```

After adding the configuration, we need to fully shut down and restart the cluster.

Simple security

This method is not secure to operate an HBase cluster. This setup prevents a user
from making mistakes. It can be used as an access control on a development system
without setting up Kerberos. This method does not prevent hacking attacks, but
stops wrong data operations by users on the database.

Server-side configuration

Add the following lines of xml code in `hbase-site.xml` on the server machine's file in versions before 0.94:

```
<property>
<name>hbase.security.authentication</name>
<value>simple</value>
</property>
<property>
<name>hbase.security.authorization</name>
<value>true</value>
</property>
<property>
<name>hbase.coprocessor.master.classes</name>
<value>org.apache.hadoop.hbase.security.access.AccessController
</value>
</property>
<property>
<name>hbase.coprocessor.region.classes</name>
<value>org.apache.hadoop.hbase.security.access.AccessController
</value>
</property>
```

For HBase Version 0.94 and above, add the following in the `hbase-site.xml` file:

```
<property>
<name>hbase.rpc.engine</name>
<value>org.apache.hadoop.hbase.ipc.SecureRpcEngine</value>
</property>
<property>
<name>hbase.coprocessor.master.classes</name>
<value>org.apache.hadoop.hbase.security.access.AccessController
</value>
</property>
<property>
<name>hbase.coprocessor.region.classes</name>
<value>org.apache.hadoop.hbase.security.access.AccessController
</value>
</property>
```

After making this change, a restart of a cluster is needed to load the configuration changes.

Client-side configuration

Add the following code to all the `hbase-site.xml` files at client machines with HBase version before 0.94:

```
<property>
<name>hbase.security.authentication</name>
<value>simple</value>
</property>
```

For HBase Version 0.94, add the following lines in the `hbase-site.xml` file on client machines:

```
<property>
<name>hbase.rpc.engine</name>
<value>org.apache.hadoop.hbase.ipc.SecureRpcEngine</value>
</property>
```

If `hbase.security.authentication` in client and server-side site files does not match, the client will not be able to communicate with the cluster.

We need to assign proper rights to thrift and rest so that the client can communicate through these services. Also, we need to assign administrator rights to thrift and rest APIs users, which can be done as follows:

For rest, use the following command:

```
grant 'rest_server', 'RWCA'
```

For thrift, use the following command:

```
grant 'thrift_server', 'RWCA'
```

The tag security feature

As we already know, every cell in an HBase table is attached with metadata. HBase Version 0.98 and later provides features of tag with cell format. HFile version 3 and Versions 0.98 onwards support tags, and this feature can be turned on using the following configuration:

```
<property>
<name>hfile.format.version</name>
<value>3</value>
</property>
```

Every cell can now have zero or more tags attached to it. All the tags have a type and tag byte array. The types 0 to 31 are reserved for system tags, 1 is reserved for ACL, and 2 is reserved for visibility tags.

To attach a tag to a cell during the put operation, we can do it as:

```
Put.add(byte[] colfamily, byte [] col, byte [] val, Tag[] tagname)
Put.add(byte[] colfamily, byte[] col, long timestamp, byte[] value,
Tag[] tagname)
```

> The following are the links you can visit for other security-related resources:
> - `http://hadoop.apache.org/docs/r2.3.0/hadoop-project-dist/hadoop-common/SecureMode.html`
> - `http://www.cloudera.com/content/cloudera-content/cloudera-docs/CDH4/4.3.0/CDH4-Security-Guide/CDH4-Security-Guide.html`
> - `http://dev.hortonworks.com.s3.amazonaws.com/HDPDocuments/HDP2/HDP-2.0.9.0/bk_installing_manually_book/content/rpm-chap14-2-3-hbase-zk.html`

Access control in HBase

HBase Version 0.92 and later supports an optional ACL-control-based protection on column families and tables. The access control mechanism is mature enough in relational databases. It was lacking in the earlier versions of HBase, however, in the newer versions, HBase is capable of implementing the security mechanism. ZooKeeper also needs to be configured for secure access. Secure authentication to ZooKeeper must be enabled, or else, it will be possible to ruin HBase access control by direct client access to ZooKeeper.

Enabling **Remote Procedure Calls** (**RPC**) and ACL enables users to be authenticated clients on HBase. User data is private until a special permission is granted to it explicitly. So, according to importance, we have four operation permission types: READ, WRITE, CREATE, and ADMIN.

The following table shows the permission types and mapping in HBase:

Permissions	Operations	Operation description
Read	Get	Reading a record
	Exists	Checking the existence of a table
	Scan	Scanning and reading all records of a table
Write	Put	Writing to table
	Delete	Deleting records
	Lock/UnlockRow	Locking a record
	IncrementColumnValue	Incrementing a column value
	CheckAndDelete/put	Writing and updating
Create	Create	Creating tables
	Alter	Altering tables
	Drop	Deleting tables
	Bulk load	Loading bulk data in HBase
Admin	Enable/disable	Enabling/disabling a table
	Snapshot/Restore/clone	Backing up plans and operations
	Split	Splitting a region
	Flush	Flushing a region
	Compact	Compacting a region
	Major compact	Major compacting a region
	Grant	Granting user permissions or rights
	Revoke	Revoking access rights
	Shutdown	Shutting down clusters
More references can be found at `http://hbase.apache.org/0.94/book/hbase.accesscontrol.configuration.html`.		

These permissions can be granted on any level with the CREATE and ADMIN permissions on a table level.

The following are the access controls which can be implemented on tables:

- Read: Reading from any column family in a table
- Write: Writing to any column family in a table
- Create: Altering table attributes; adding, altering, or dropping column families; and dropping the table.
- Admin: Altering table attributes; adding, altering, or dropping column families; and enabling, disabling, or dropping the table.

The following are the access controls which can be implemented on column families:

- Read: Reading from the column family
- Write: Writing to the column family

Besides these permissions, we should have a global super user permission too.

The super user is the principal user specified in the HBase conf file that has access to HBase as the root user in a UNIX system. Normally, this is the principal user that the HBase processes authenticate themselves and run on a box. A super user can create tables, switch the balancer on or off, or take other actions with global consequences; it has permissions on all resources. Tables in HBase have a metadata attribute: OWNER, who owns the table and has all the permissions (global) on the table. A user who creates the table has, by default, global permission and can be modified at the time of table creation or during an alter operation by setting or changing the OWNER table attribute. Only a single user principal can own a table at a time. A table owner has all permissions over a given table.

Now, let's look at the ACL matrix:

ACL	Description
Scope	Scope is the top-down approach. For example, global permissions will have rights from NameSpace to Cell, and permissions on cell will have permissions only on cell values.
	Global
	Namespace
	Table
	Column family
	Columns
	Cell

ACL	Description
Permissions	Permission goes in a one-to-one manner. For example, permission to read does not give permission to write, and permission to write will not give permission to read. Permission should be given explicitly, as needed.
	Super user
	Administrator (A)
	Create (C)
	Read (R)
	Write (W)
	Execute (X)
More references can be found at `http://hbase.apache.org/0.94/book/hbase.accesscontrol.configuration.html`.	

The `hbase:meta` table is accessible to all the users. The administrator has all the rights and permissions.

For `CheckAndPut` and `CheckAndDelete`, a user needs both read and write permissions. Increment and append operations do not require read rights.

Permission should be specified explicitly, for example, if a user needs permission to read, write, and execute, it should be specified as RWX. D and do not grant any other permissions.

Now, let's see the interfaces that facilitate these permissions and rights for an HBase user.

We can see the internal layout of it in the source code at the following links:

- `https://github.com/apache/hbase/blob/master/hbase-server/src/test/java/org/apache/hadoop/hbase/security/access/TestAccessController.java`
- `https://github.com/apache/hbase/blob/master/hbase-server/src/main/java/org/apache/hadoop/hbase/security/access/AccessController.java`

We can also check the source code of HBase inside the downloaded HBase directory.

The following table shows the interfaces that facilitate the permission aspect in HBase:

Interfaces	Operations	Minimum scope	Minimum permission(s)
Master	createTable	Global	A
	modifyTable	Table	A | CW
	deleteTable	Table	A | CW
	truncateTable	Table	A | CW
	addColumn	Table	A | CW
	modifyColumn	Table	A | CW
	deleteColumn	Table	A | CW
	disableTable	Table	A | CW
	disableAclTable	None	Not allowed
	enableTable	Table	A | CW
	move	Global	A
	assign	Global	A
	unassign	Global	A
	regionOffline	Global	A
	balance	Global	A
	balanceSwitch	Global	A
	shutdown	Global	A
	stopMaster	Global	A
	snapshot	Global	A
	clone	Global	A
	restore	Global	A
	deleteSnapshot	Global	A
	createNamespace	Global	A
	deleteNamespace	Namespace	A
	modifyNamespace	Namespace	A
	flushTable	Table	A | CW
	getTableDescriptors	Global | Table	A
	mergeRegions	Global	A

Interfaces	Operations	Minimum scope	Minimum permission(s)
Region	preOpen	Global	A
	openRegion	Global	A
	preClose	Global	A
	closeRegion	Global	A
	preStopRegionServer	Global	A
	stopRegionServer	Global	A
	mergeRegions	Global	A
	append	Table	W
	delete	Table|CF|CQ	W
	exists	Table|CF|CQ	R
	get	Table|CF|CQ	R
	getClosestRowBefore	Table|CF|CQ	R
	increment	Table|CF|CQ	W
	put	Table|CF|CQ	W
	flush	Global	A|CW
	split	Global	A
	compact	Global	A|CW
	bulkLoadHFile	Table	W
	prepareBulkLoad	Table	CW
	cleanupBulkLoad	Table	W
	checkAndDelete	Table|CF|CQ	RW
	checkAndPut	Table|CF|CQ	RW
	incrementColumnValue	Table|CF|CQ	RW
	ScannerClose	Table	R
	ScannerNext	Table	R
	ScannerOpen	Table|CQ|CF	R
Endpoint	invoke	Endpoint	X
AccessController	grant	Global|Table|NS	A
	revoke	Global|Table|NS	A
	userPermissions	Global|Table|NS	A
	checkPermissions	Global|Table|NS	A

More references can be found at http://hbase.apache.org/0.94/book/hbase.accesscontrol.configuration.html.

Server-side access control

For server-side access control, add the following lines in `hbase-site.xml`:

```
<property>
<name>hbase.coprocessor.master.classes</name>
<value>org.apache.hadoop.hbase.security.access.AccessController
</value>
</property>
<property>
<name>hbase.coprocessor.region.classes</name>
<value>org.apache.hadoop.hbase.security.token.TokenProvider,
    org.apache.hadoop.hbase.security.access.AccessController</value>
</property>
```

Cell-level access using tags

In versions of HBase before 0.98, permission facility was on table-and-column family levels only; in Version 0.98, a new feature of tag was introduced that provided the facility to implement security on a cell level.

For this, ACL can be specified, as follows, using APIs (in Java):

`Mutation.setACL(String username, Permission permissions)`

`Mutation.setACL(Map<String, Permission>permissions)`

For example, suppose a user needs write access, we can implement it while putting data in tables, as follows:

`put.setACL("username", new Permission(Permission.Action.READ))`

For the tag feature to be enabled, we need to enable HFile V3, as follows:

```
<property>
<name>hfile.format.version</name>
<value>3</value>
</property>
```

This code can be added to `HBase-site.xml`.

Using shell, we can add it as follows:

- The `grant` permission:
  ```
  grant <user|@group> <permissions> [ <table> [ <column family>
  [ <column qualifier> ] ] ]
  ```

- The `revoke` permission:

  ```
  revoke <user|@group> [ <table> [ <column family>
  [ <column qualifier> ] ] ]
  ```

- The `alter` permission:

  ```
  alter 'tablename', {OWNER => 'username|@group'}
  ```

- The user permission:

  ```
  user_permission <table>
  ```

Configuring ZooKeeper for security

Let's look at how we can configure security in ZooKeeper:

1. Create a service principal for the ZooKeeper server using the syntax
    `zookeeper/<domain Name>@<REALM>`, where `<domain.name>` is the host
    where the ZooKeeper server runs REALM—the name of the Kerberos realm:

    ```
    kadmin: addprinc -randkey zookeeper/infinity@KERBINFI.COM
    ```

2. Create a `keytab` file for the ZooKeeper server:

    ```
    kadmin

    kadmin: xst -k zookeeper.keytab zookeeper/domainname
    ```

3. Copy the `zookeeper.keytab` file to the ZooKeeper `conf` directory on the
    ZooKeeper server. The owner of this file should be the user under which
    ZooKeeper will run.

4. Add the following lines to the ZooKeeper conf file, `zoo.cfg` (`/etc/`
    `zookeeper/conf/`):

    ```
    authProvider.1=org.apache.zookeeper.server.auth.SASLAuthentica
    tionProvider

    jaasLoginRenew=3600000
    ```

5. Set up Java authentication and authorization service by creating a `jaas.conf`
    file in the ZooKeeper configuration directory, and content should be as
    follows:

    ```
    Server {
      com.sun.security.auth.module.Krb5LoginModule required
      useKeyTab=true
      keyTab="/etc/zookeeper/conf/zookeeper.keytab"
      storeKey=true
      useTicketCache=false
      principal="zookeeper/<your domain>@<KERBEROS REALM>";
    };
    ```

6. Add the following setting to the `java.env` file located in the ZooKeeper configuration directory, or create and add the following lines:

```
export JVMFLAGS="-Djava.security.auth.login.config=
/etc/zookeeper/conf/jaas.conf"
```

   If there are multiple ZooKeeper servers in the ensemble, steps should be repeated for each ZooKeeper server.

7. Restart ZooKeeper to take effect.

To verify whether the preceding changes took effect, we can perform the following steps:

1. Start the client as follows:

```
zookeeper-client -server hostname:port
```

2. Create a protected znode from within the ZooKeeper CLI using the following command:

```
create /znode1 znode1data sasl:zkcli@{{REALM}}:cdwra
```

3. Verify the znode is created and the ACL is set correctly, as follows:

```
getAcl /znode1
```

4. The results from `getAcl` should show the proper scheme and permissions were applied to the znode.

 Read more about Kerberos at http://web.mit.edu/kerberos/ and kadmin at http://linux.die.net/man/8/kadmin.

Troubleshooting the most frequent HBase errors and their explanations

The following are the places that index information about Hadoop/HBase and other project exceptions, and where we can search for information about Hadoop/HBase errors:

- http://search-hadoop.com
- #hbase on irc.freenode.net
- A mailing list of HBase at http://hbase.apache.org/mail-lists.html

Now, let's see the frequent errors and solutions for these:

For troubleshooting, a log is an excellent place to look into. Now, let's see the default log locations of various daemon processes:

- **NameNode:** `<hadoop home path>/logs/hadoop-<user>-namenode-<hostname>.log`
- **DataNode:** `<hadoop home path>/logs/hadoop-<user>-datanode-<hostname>.log`
- **JobTracker:** `<hadoop home path>/logs/hadoop-<user>-jobtracker-<hostname>.log`
- **TaskTracker:** `<hadoop home path>/logs/hadoop-<user>-tasktracker-<hostname>.log`
- **HMaster:** `<hadoop home path>/logs/hbase-<user>-master-<hostname>.log`
- **RegionServer:** `<hadoop home path>/logs/hbase-<user>-regionserver-<hostname>.log`

Also, look in `/var/log/<rest are same>` for logs of different HBase components.

The following are the different logging levels we can set in order to change the size. According to the details in logs, we require:

- `ALL`
- `TRACE`
- `DEBUG`
- `INFO`
- `WARN`
- `ERROR`
- `OFF`

What might fail in cluster

Different Java versions on cluster machines can cause problems. Different versions of Hadoop and HBase cause problems too.

The following are the components that might fail in operation, which we can look into while debugging:

- **Disk**: Corrupt disk
- **Operating System**: Bugs, wrong optimization parameters, and over utilization on hardware
- **Network**: Connectivity and bandwidth chocking
- **Memory**: Bad memory and overloaded memory

Monitoring HBase health

In this section, we will see the various methods for administrators to monitor and manage HBase.

HBase web UI

There are two tools under this category:

- Master web interface
- RegionServer web interface

Master

`http://<hbase-master>:<port>` is the hostname where HMaster is running and port is 60010 for older version and 16010 for newer versions (0.98 and above).

RegionServer

`http://<hbase-regionserver>:<port>` is the hostname where RegionServers are running and port is 60030 for older version and 16030 for newer versions (0.98 and above).

ZooKeeper command line

The ZooKeeper shell can be started as follows:

```
hbase zkcli -server host:port <cmd><args>
```

The arguments we can have in the preceding command are:

- `connect host:port`
- `get path [watch]`
- `ls path [watch]`

- `set path data [version]`
- `delquota [-n|-b] path`
- `quit`
- `printwatches on|off`
- `create [-s] [-e] path data acl`
- `stat path [watch]`
- `close`
- `ls2 path [watch]`
- `history`
- `listquota path`
- `setAcl path acl`
- `getAcl path`
- `sync path`
- `redo cmdno`
- `addauth scheme auth`
- `delete path [version]`
- `setquota -n|-b val path`

For help, type in just a command name without any parameter.

Linux tools

The following are the Linux tools that we can use:

- `top`: This is the Linux command to see live processes and resource uses
- `free -m`: This is used to see memory uses
- `jps`: This command is used to see the Java running process. This binary is in the Java `bin` directory
- `tail`/`head`: This is used to see the content of log files
- `ps -ef|grep Java`: This is used to see HBase running daemons
- `jstack`: This prints Java stack traces of Java threads for a given Java process, core file, or remote debug server

Set up OpenTSDB to monitor HBase more closely using the information given at `http://opentsdb.net/setup-hbase.html`.

For Cloudera distribution, the Cloudera manager can be used for monitoring and administration.

Now, let's see some exceptions and solutions:

Exceptions	Solution
`java.io.IOException: Call to /<host name> failed on local exception: java.io.EOFException org.apache.hadoop.ipc.Client.wrapException(Client.java:1139) at org.apache.hadoop.ipc.Client.call(Client.java:1107)`	This is used to add/replace the `hadoop-core.jar` file from Hadoop, being used in the HBase `lib` directory.

`FATAL org.apache.hadoop.hbase.master.HMaster: Unhandled exception. Starting shutdown.java.lang.IllegalArgumentException: 13955@<hostname>`
`at ***`
`INFO org.apache.hadoop.hbase.master.HMaster: Aborting`
`INFO org.apache.zookeeper.ClientCnxn: EventThread shut down`
	This is used to add/replace the `commons-lang-*.jar` file from Hadoop, being used in the HBase `lib` directory.

`ERROR org.apache.hadoop.hbase.master.HMasterCommandLine: Failed to start master`
`java.lang.RuntimeException: Failed construction of Master: class org.apache.hadoop.hbase.master.HMaster`
`Caused by: java.lang.ClassNotFoundException: org.apache.commons.configuration.Configuration`
	This is used to add/replace the `commons-configuration-*.jar` file from Hadoop, being used in the HBase `lib` directory.

`ERROR org.apache.hadoop.hbase.master.HMaster: Cannot start master` `Caused by: java.net.ConnectException: Call to <hostname>/<ipaddress> failed on connection exception: java.net.ConnectException: Connection refused`	This is used to remove the localhost and `127.0.1.1` entry from the `/etc/hosts` file.
`ScannerTimeoutException or UnknownScannerException`	This is used to reduce the `setCaching` value, which might be an option.

Exceptions	Solution
Master starts, but RegionServers do not	Master believes RegionServers have an IP of `127.0.0.1`, which is a local host and resolves to master's local host. RegionServers erroneously inform the master that their IP addresses are 127.0.0.1. It changes the `127.0.0.1` entry to `<hostname>`.
`java.io.IOException.(Too many open files)`	This increases `ulimit` and `nproc`.
`xceiverCount exceeds`	This increases the value in the `dfs.datanode.max.transfer.threads` property.
`java.lang.OutOfMemoryError: unable to create new native thread in exceptions`	This increases `ulimit` and `nproc`
`RegionServer lease timeouts`	This tunes up GC/check whether NTP is installed and configured or not.
`No live nodes contain current block` and/or `YouAreDeadException`	These errors can occur either when running out of OS file handles or in periods of severe network problems where the nodes are unreachable. Check for `nproc` and `ulimit`.
`ZooKeeper SessionExpired events`	Increase the `zookeeper.session.timeout` and `hbase.zookeeper.property.tickTime` parameters.
Visit `http://hbase.apache.org/book/trouble.html` for more exceptions and the latest error documentations.	

Summary

In this chapter, we discussed administrative parts of HBase such as the introduction to HBase administration, HBase shell, and different administrating tools for HBase. This chapter also covered topics such as how to use Java in HBase shell for various tweaks, HBase, shell scripting for HBase, and how to connect Hive with HBase to run HQL queries from Hive. We also looked at how we can implement security in HBase, the frequently occurring errors, and their solutions. In the next chapter, we will look into scripting and backup strategies.

7
Scripting in HBase

This chapter will talk about various scripts and other options that we can consider and write to master HBase operations and functions. We will also look at the remaining value additions, techniques, and some more exceptions and errors that you might face in HBase.

In this chapter, we will discuss the following topics:

- HBase backup and restore methodologies
- HBase on Windows
- Scripting in HBase
- Value addition
- More on exceptions and errors in HBase

HBase backup and restore techniques

Now, we will see the HBase backup and restore methods as it is very important for any technology to be able to restore and create a backup of the data to avoid data loss.

We will now discuss these methods in detail. There are two kinds of HBase methodologies in general. The following are HBase backup methods that we can choose according to our requirement and setup:

- Offline backup / full-shutdown backup
  - ° Use the `hadoop distcp` command

- Online backup
  - ° Snapshots
  - ° Replication
  - ° Export
  - ° CopyTable
  - ° HTable API
  - ° Offline backup of HDFS data
  - ° Backup using a Mozilla tool
  - ° HDFS replication

Let's get started with offline backup.

Offline backup / full-shutdown backup

This method includes full-shutdown backup of HBase on a file system, using the `distcp` command that runs the MapReduce task. It copies the parallel data from one location to another, which can be a backup location on the same cluster or another backup cluster. This method is not recommended on a live cluster or a cluster that needs zero downtime. If users can invest in a downtime, we can go with this method.

Backup

Suppose we have an HDFS location as `hdfs://namenode:9000/hbase`, where the complete HBase data is located. Here, we can copy the whole location to either the same cluster or another cluster using `distcp`.

The following is the syntax of `distcp`:

```
hadoop [ Generic Options ] distcp
    [-p [rbugp] ] [-i ] [-log ] [-m ] [-overwrite ]
    [-update  ] [-f <URI list> ] [-filelimit <n> ] [-sizelimit <n> ]
    [-delete ] <source>  <destination>
```

 More on this command can be found at `http://hadoop.apache.org/docs/r1.2.1/distcp2.html`.

If you prefer the former way, use the following command to create the backup in the same cluster.

```
hadoop distcp hdfs://Infinity1:9000/hbase
hdfs://Infinity1:9000/hbaseBackup/backup1
```

This preceding command will copy the hbase directory as it is in /hbaseBackup/backup1 on the HDFS location of the same cluster.

If you prefer the latter way, you can create a backup in different clusters using the following command:

```
hadoop distcp hdfs://Infinity1:9000/hbase
hdfs://Infinity2:9000/hbaseBackup/backup1
```

This preceding command will copy the hbase directory as it is in /hbaseBackup/backup1 on the HDFS location on another cluster.

> Note that for the distcp command to work, we need to have JobTracker and TaskTracker running as they are needed for MapReduce tasks.
>
> While copying, we have parameters such as -overwrite and -update; we can use these combinations too.

If something goes wrong, we can copy the target directory to the HBase directory. This method copies the full file system directory, so will take the same amount of space on HDFS. It is better to have a separate backup cluster or copy this data offline to the tapes.

Restore

In the restore method, restoring can be done in the same way by copying data using distcp from the target to source cluster from where data was copied.

> This method is not always preferable as it requires a full shutdown of clusters, which needs a downtime that will impact the business requirement and SLAs. So, this method is the least preferable way of backup.

Online backup

The online backup process is preferred as there is no need to shut down the cluster, and it does not hamper the operation of the cluster, and thus, we don't need a downtime. This class of backup category has the following methods to take and restore the backup. Let's discuss these.

The HBase snapshot

The HBase snapshot enables us to take a snapshot of a table without fiddling with RegionServers. Snapshot in HBase is a set of metadata information that allows the administrator to get back to the previous working state of the table. A snapshot is not a copy of the table data, but just a layout of the data present on the HBase cluster. We can think of it as a set of operations to keep track of metadata (table info and regions) and data (HFiles, MemStore, and WALs). No data is copied during the process of taking a snapshot of a table.

There are two types of snapshots, online and offline.

Online

Online snapshots can be taken when a table is enabled and active for I/O operations. In this case, the master receives the snapshot request and asks each RegionServer to take a snapshot of the regions for which it is responsible.

Offline

Offline snapshots can be taken when the table is disabled and not ready for I/O operations. The master performs this operation, and the time required to perform this operation is determined mainly on the time taken by HDFS NameNode to provide the list of files.

> Read more about snapshots at the following links:
>
> - https://blog.cloudera.com/blog/2013/03/introduction-to-apache-hbase-snapshots/
> - http://blog.cloudera.com/blog/2013/06/introduction-to-apache-hbase-snapshots-part-2-deeper-dive/

Now, we will see how to take a snapshot and back up data using the offline method:

1. Set the required configuration. We need to add the following lines in `hbase-site.xml` to enable this feature:

```
<property>
    <name>hbase.snapshot.enabled</name>
    <value>true</value>
 </property>
```

   Restart the cluster once this change is made.

2. Go to HBase shell and execute the following command to take a snapshot:

```
hbase > snapshot 'emptable', 'baksnapshot01082014'
```

3. Use the following command to list snapshots:

```
hbase > list_snapshots
```

4. Delete a snapshot using the following command:

```
hbase > delete_snapshot 'baksnapshot01082014'
```

5. Clone a table from a snapshot, as follows:

```
hbase >  clone_snapshot 'baksnapshot01082014', 'newSnapTable'
```

6. Restore a snapshot as follows:

```
hbase >  disable 'table'
hbase >  restore_snapshot ' baksnapshot01082014'
```

7. We can use MapReduce to take snapshot to another HDFS cluster.

   The `org.apache.hadoop.hbase.snapshot.ExportSnapshot` tool copies all the data related to a snapshot (HFiles, logs, and snapshot metadata) to another cluster:

```
hbase class org.apache.hadoop.hbase.snapshot.ExportSnapshot -
snapshot snapshot01082014 -copy-to hdfs://infinity:9000/hbase
-mappers 8 -bandwidth 100
```

   So, here eight map jobs will run to export all snapshots to another cluster with a limiting bandwidth of 100 MB/s.

The HBase replication method

The HBase replication method provides a mechanism to copy or replicate data from one HBase cluster setup to another. It can serve as a disaster recovery solution and contribute to provide higher availability at the HBase layer. This method works when the data is being pushed from one cluster to another, where pusher is the master and taker is the slave setup. This replication, or pushing, happens asynchronously. This provides high availability of an HBase cluster too. The basis of this replication is based on HLog from each RegionServer. There are three types of replication as follows:

- **Master-slave**: In this type of replication, the data is pushed from one cluster to the target cluster. This happens in a single direction. So, the source cluster can have its own tables, and the target cluster might have its own too. We can use the target cluster for the source data replication.

- **Master-master**: In this method, data (that might be in the same or a different table) is sent in both the directions between two clusters. So, both the clusters might act as master as well as slave at the same time, pushing and getting the data.

- **Cyclic**: In this setup, more than two HBase clusters take part in the replication setup. One cluster can have various possible combinations of master-slave and master-master setups between any two clusters.

Setting up cluster replication

The following are the prerequisites to set up cluster replication:

- All machines from both the clusters should be able to communicate with each machine in the two clusters

- Both the clusters must have the same Hadoop/HBase version

- Each table to be replicated should contain the same column families; in other words, the same schemes and tables must exist on every cluster with the exact same name

- For multiple slaves, master-master, or cyclic replications, HBase Version 0.92 or higher is needed

- The package that is responsible for cluster replication is `org.apache.hadoop.hbase.replication`

The following are the deployment steps to set up cluster replication:

1. Open the `hbase-site.xml` file and put the following lines of code in it:

```
<property>
  <name>hbase.replication</name>
  <value>true</value>
</property>
```

These changes will need a full cluster restart for configuration to be loaded.

2. Run the following command from the master-cluster-HBase shell:

```
add_peer 'ID' 'CLUSTER_KEY'
```

Here, `ID` should be a short integer and for `CLUSTER_KEY`, follow this template:

```
hbase.zookeeper.quorum:hbase.zookeeper.property.
clientPort:zookeeper.znode.parent
```

3. Once we have the peer added, we need to enable replication on column families. The first method is to alter the table and change the replication scope for the column family using the following command:

```
disable 'table'
alter 'table', {NAME => 'colFam', REPLICATION_SCOPE => '1'}
enable 'table'
```

Here, putting `0` means it will not replicate, and putting `1` means it has to replicate.

4. To list the peers, execute the following command:

```
hbase > list_peers
```

For replication-related commands, refer to the previous chapter.

5. We can verify the setup by looking into any RegionServer log where we can find:

```
Considering 1 rs, with ratio 0.1
Getting 1 rs from peer cluster # 0
Choosing peer <ipaddress_regionserver>:<regionServerPort>
```

6. If the preceding lines are present in the RegionServer logs, setup is replicating, and we can also verify this from the target cluster.

7. To stop replication at any point in time, we can use the `stop_replication` command at the source-HBase shell.

> Internal working, core and advanced concepts, and more updated information about replication can be obtained from the following links:
>
> - `http://hbase.apache.org/replication.html`
> - `http://blog.cloudera.com/blog/2012/07/hbase-replication-overview-2/`
> - `http://www.cloudera.com/content/cloudera-content/cloudera-docs/CDH4/4.3.0/CDH4-Installation-Guide/cdh4ig_topic_20_11.html`

Backup and restore using Export and Import commands

In this section, we will have a look at the `Export` and `Import` commands in detail.

Export

The Export utility is provided by the HBase JAR file, which writes the HBase table content to a sequence file on HDFS (on the same cluster or another cluster). This runs as a MapReduce job, and using HBase API, reads each row one by one and writes it to the HDFS location. Using this, we can take a full and incremental backup of a live cluster as it takes the start and end timestamps as parameters.

The syntax for this is as follows:

```
hbase org.apache.hadoop.hbase.mapreduce.Export <tablename>
<outputdir> [<versions> [<starttime> [<endtime>]]]
```

Here, `tablename` is the table that is to be exported; `outputdir` is the target where the output sequence file will be written, which can be an HDFS location on the same cluster or on different clusters; `versions` implies the number of version to be exported; `starttime` and `endtime` are the timestamp between which the data's timestamp should lie to be able to be exported.

Import

The import utility is used to read the exported sequence file—an output of the `Export` command—to be restored in an HBase table, a new table, or an existing table. If data already exists, it will be overwritten.

The syntax for this is as follows:

```
hbase org.apache.hadoop.hbase.mapreduce.Import <tablename>
<inputdir>
```

Here, `tablename` is the name of the table where data is to be imported/restored and `inputdir` is the path where the data exists or where it will be exported using the `Export` command.

The `Export` and `Import` commands work well with a live cluster and can also be run as Hadoop MapReduce using the following commands:

```
hadoop jar <full path of> hbase-*.jar export <tablename> <outputdir>
[<versions> [<starttime> [<endtime>]]]
hadoop jar <full path of> hbase-*.jar import <tablename> <inputdir>
```

We can pass the runtime parameter in these commands as `-D mapred.output. compress=true`, and other required parameters can be given after export operation.

If the export operation is done using HBase v0.94, and the same data has to be imported from a newer version, we can specify the runtime parameter as follows:

```
hbase -Dhbase.import.version=0.94
org.apache.hadoop.hbase.mapreduce.Import <tablename> <inputdir>
```

Miscellaneous utilities

ImportTsv is a utility that loads data from a **Tab-separated Value** (**TSV**) format into an HBase table. The syntax for the same is as follows:

```
hbase org.apache.hadoop.hbase.mapreduce.ImportTsv -
Dimporttsv.columns=a,b,c <tablename> <hdfs-inputdir>
```

> For more on this utility, visit the following links:
> - `http://hbase.apache.org/book/ops_mgt.html#importtsv`
> - `http://hbase.apache.org/book/ops_mgt.html#completebulkload`

CopyTable

The CopyTable tool can copy a part of the table, or the whole table, to the same cluster, or to another cluster. The target table should already be present with the same schema.

The following is the syntax to use this tool:

```
hbase org.apache.hadoop.hbase.mapreduce.
CopyTable [general options] [--starttime=X] [--endtime=Y]
[--new.name=NEW] [--peer.adr=ADR] <tablename>
```

The following are the options of the preceding syntax:

- `rs.class`: This is the `hbase.regionserver.class` of the peer cluster. It's specified if different from the current cluster.

- `rs.impl`: This is the `hbase.regionserver.impl` of the peer cluster.

- `startrow`: This is the start row.

- `stoprow`: This is the stop row.

- `starttime`: This is the beginning of the time range. If no `endtime` is specified, it means from `starttime` to forever.

- `endtime`: This is an end of the time range. This will be ignored if no `starttime` is specified.

- `versions`: This is the number of cell versions to copy.

- `new.name`: This is the name of a new table.

- `peer.adr`: This is the address of the peer cluster given in the `hbase.zookeeer.quorum:hbase.zookeeper.client.port:zookeeper.znode.parent` format.

- `families`: This is a comma-separated list of families to copy. To copy from `cf1` to `cf2`, give `sourceCfName:destCfName`. To keep the same name, just give `cfName`.

- `all.cells`: This copies deleted markers and deleted cells.

The only argument is `tablename`, which is the name of the table to copy.

Have a look at the following example:

```
hbase org.apache.hadoop.hbase.mapreduce.CopyTable --new.name=Copynew
table
```

Here, `new.name` is the name of the copied table, and `table` is the one to be copied.

HTable API

We can always write our own custom application that utilizes the public API (http://hbase.apache.org/apidocs/org/apache/hadoop/hbase/client/HTable.html) and queries the table directly. We can do this through MapReduce jobs in order to utilize the framework's distributed-batch-processing advantages, or through any other means of our design. However, this approach requires a deep understanding of Hadoop development and all the APIs and performance implications of using them in your production cluster.

Backup using a Mozilla tool

The in-depth explanation of backup using a Mozilla tool is out of the scope of this book, so visit the following links for more information on this:

- `https://github.com/mozilla-metrics/akela/blob/master/src/main/java/com/mozilla/hadoop/Backup.java`
- `http://blog.mozilla.org/data/2011/02/04/migrating-hbase-in-the-trenches/`

The following table shows the comparison between different backup processes:

Backup process	Effect on performance	Data size	Downtime requirement	If incremental backup is possible or not	Time for recovery
Snapshots	Minimal	Very small	On restore	No	Seconds
Replication	Minimal	Huge	None	Yes	Seconds
Export	High	Huge	None	Yes	High
CopyTable	High	Huge	None	Yes	High
API	Medium	Huge	None	Yes	High
Distcp	Downtime	Huge	Yes	No	Long

> We have another option of backup, and it is to increase the replication factor of an HBase cluster, which will be maintained on the Hadoop level and provide more availability and robustness. However, this will need more space, and if space is not a constraint, we can use this hassle-free backup method.

HBase on Windows

We already saw the configuration of Hadoop/HBase on Windows, so we will look at the distribution or service that Microsoft provides, HDinsight, which is a cloud-based Apache Hadoop service provided by Microsoft. It says:

- Scale to petabytes on demand
- Process unstructured and semistructured data
- Develop in Java, .NET and more
- No hardware to buy or maintain
- Pay only for what you use

- Spin up a Hadoop cluster in minutes
- Visualize your Hadoop data in Excel
- Easily integrate on-premises Hadoop clusters

It also provides the Hadoop Azure service for Hadoop.

 More can be studied at `http://azure.microsoft.com/en-us/documentation/services/hdinsight/`.

Scripting in HBase

We have seen how to do scripting in HBase. In this chapter, we will see some more scripting tips and tricks, which will enable an administrator to perform various tasks in HBase by automating. We can write scripts in Ruby, shell script, and a script that's a combination of HBase commands.

Now, let's consider a case where we need to create a table with two column families and two columns, and then insert some data. The script for the same is as follows:

 Here, we used a `vi` editor. Users can use any editor of his/her preference.

```
vi hbasescript.script
```

```
create 'table','data',
for i in '0'..'2' do
for j in '0'..'2' do
for k in '0'..'2' do
put 'table', "row-#{i}#{j}#{k}","data:column#{j}#{k}",
"name#{j}#{k}" end end end
```

After saving this script, we can run the following script:

```
hbase shell hbasescript.script
```

We can also do the same thing by going to HBase shell:

```
hbase > for i in '0'..'5' do \
hbase >* put "utable", "rowKey_#{i}", "address:address",
"address#{i}"\
hbase>* end
```

The preceding commands will insert five rows in the `utable`.

The preceding script will create a table and put 10 rows of data in the table. Likewise, we can write scripts to load data into the table and perform various operations such as inserting data from a text or CSV file.

We can run an HBase command to create an HBase table without going to the HBase shell, as follows:

```
echo "create 'tableToCreate', 'colFamily'" | hbase shell
```

Now, we will see a script to scan the table between two rows:

```
vi scanTable.sh
```

```bash
#!/bin/bash
 TableToScan=$1
RowStart=$2
RowEnd=$3
exec hbase shell <<EOF scan "${TableToScan}", {RowStart =>
"${RowStart}", RowEnd => "${RowEnd}"}
EOF
```

This code must be called `./scanTable.sh emptable row100 row1000`. This will display rows between `row100` and `row1000` (which are passed as parameters to the script) from the `emptable` table.

The .irbrc file

As we know, HBase uses Ruby shell, and this can be customized using the `.irbrc` file to perform commands such as clearing, maintaining history in HBase shell, and so on. If this file does not already exist in a user's `home` directory, we can create it and put the following content, which will enable us to use the `clear` command on HBase shell to clear the screen and maintain a command history for HBase shell:

1. From the `home` directory, issue the following command and add the following lines to the file:

   ```
   vi .irbrc
   ```

   ```
   #Clear HBase shell command
   def clear
     system('clear')
   end
   ```

```
hadoop_home="<your hadoop home path here>"


#Enable history(commands executed previously will be
preserved) in hbase shell
require "irb/ext/save-history"
#No. of commands to be saved. 50 here
IRB.conf[:SAVE_HISTORY] = 50
# The location to save the history file
IRB.conf[:HISTORY_FILE] = "#{ENV['HOME']}/.irb-save-history"


#List given HDFS path from hbase shell
def ls(path)
  directory="/"+path
  system("#{hadoop_home}/hadoop fs -ls #{directory}")
end
#<hadoop home path> is the full path of the hadoop directory


Kernel.at_exit do
  IRB.conf[:AT_EXIT].each do |i|
    i.call
  end


end
```

2. Save this file, and now we can execute the clear and directory commands from HBase shell as:

    ```
    hbase > clear
    hbase > ls <directory ls>
    ```

3. We can also assign variables to commands on HBase shell, and use it as follows:

    ```
    hbase > var = create 'table','colFam'
    ```

4. Now, we can use var to perform operations on the table, as follows:

    ```
    hbase > var.scan
    ```

    We will scan table, and likewise, we can use the put, get, and other commands of HBase with this variable.

5. If a table is already created, we can assign a variable for an HBase command, as follows:

```
hbase > var = get_table 'table'
```

6. Now, we can use the `var` variable on HBase shell to perform various operations on the given table, as follows:

```
hbase > var.scan
hbase . var.put 'row','colfam:name','shashwat'
hbase > var.disable
```

Likewise, we can use all the commands related to a table.

Getting the HBase timestamp from HBase shell

We can use HBase shell to get the date and time converted to the HBase timestamp, which is useful while specifying the timestamp in some commands in HBase, as follows:

```
hbase > import java.text.SimpleDateFormat
hbase > import java.text.ParsePosition
hbase > SimpleDateFormat.new("").
parse("", ParsePosition.new(0)).getTime()
```

The following is an example:

```
hbase > SimpleDateFormat.new("yy/MM/dd HH:mm:ss").
parse("14/07/01 09:00:00", ParsePosition.new(0)).getTime()
```

These three commands will give the specified date-time data in HBase timestamp, which we can use to scan or for some other commands.

For example, here we need a timestamp in the `get` command, as follows:

```
get 'tableToGetDataFrom', 'row1',
{COLUMN => 'colFam:Name', TIMESTAMP => 1317945301466}
```

We can get the date-time data from an HBase timestamp, as follows:

```
hbase > import java.util.Date
hbase > Date.new(1317945301466).toString()
```

This will show the equivalent date-time format of the specified timestamp.

Enabling debugging shell

We can execute the following command to enable more output on HBase shell about the commands we are executing:

```
hbase > debug
```

This will display more of the stack trace while being on HBase shell and executing commands.

Enabling the debug level in HBase shell

We can enable the debug level on HBase shell using the following command:

```
hbase shell -d
```

Enabling SQL in HBase

Let's see a separate project that enables us to fetch data from HBase using SQL commands, which we already know; consider the following taken from `http://phoenix.apache.org`:

> "*Apache Phoenix is a SQL skin over HBase delivered as a client-embedded JDBC driver targeting low latency queries over HBase data. Apache Phoenix takes your SQL query, compiles it into a series of HBase scans, and orchestrates the running of those scans to produce regular JDBC result sets.*"

We can configure to enable SQL facility in HBase using the following link, and play with SQL queries on HBase:

`http://phoenix.apache.org`

A good place to get a list of scripts is `https://github.com/search?q=hbase+script&ref=cmdform`.

Contributing to HBase

In this section, we will see how we can contribute to the HBase community and add our creativity and coding to HBase by fiddling with the HBase source code. The following links contain the lists of users who have contributed to the HBase project:

`https://hbase.apache.org/team-list.html`

The best way to contribute is to go through the source code of HBase, and then apply it as a committer if you think you can add something useful to the HBase source. Development can be started using any Java IDE, and the source where we can get the HBase source code is:

```
git clone git://git.apache.org/hbase.git
```

```
svn co http://svn.apache.org/repos/asf/hbase/trunk hbase-core-trunk
```

A step-by-step development process is listed at http://hbase.apache.org/book/developer.html.

Some leftovers and value-addition links

Automating Hadoop/HBase using Puppet can be learned at the following:

- https://github.com/viirya/puppet-hbase
- https://github.com/thattommyhall/cloudera-cdh3-puppet

Summary

In this chapter, we discussed various backup and restore techniques, namely offline and online backup, and their types. We also learned scripting tips and tricks in HBase. In the next chapter, we will start with the basic Java coding, and then move on to much more advanced Java coding.

8
Coding HBase in Java

In this chapter, we will start coding HBase using Java. First, we will see coding for the basic HBase APIs, and in the next chapter, we will discuss more advanced development. In this chapter, we will discuss the following topics:

- Data model operations using Java
- Setting up the development environment
- Data types
- Available clients
- Client APIs

We will also see some other miscellaneous coding styles.

First, we will look into setting the development environment for Java development in HBase, and then talk about IDEs, the required JAR files, and other aspects.

We can use any Java IDE to write HBase code such as Eclipse, NetBeans, IntelliJ, or others of your preference. We will consider Eclipse for development.

For HBase API coding, we just need an IDE that suits us or we are familiar with. We need Java, Maven, SVN, and IDE to play with, modify, and add new features into the HBase source code.

Here, we will concentrate on HBase development using HBase APIs and JAR files.

The following are the links to download IDEs:

- **Eclipse**: http://www.eclipse.org
- **NetBeans**: https://netbeans.org
- **IntelliJ**: http://www.jetbrains.com/idea/
- **JCreator**: http://www.jcreator.com

As per my preference, it is better to settle for Eclipse as it's free and widely available. We can find step-by-step instructions on how to set up Eclipse with optimized parameters at https://ist.berkeley.edu/as-ag/tools/howto/install-eclipse-win.html.

Setting up the environment for development

Start your IDE. From here, we will consider Eclipse as a development IDE. So, start Eclipse and create a new Java project. Once the project is created, add JAR files to the project needed for development. We will go through this process step by step.

Building a Java client to code in HBase

HBase provides HTable as a client that is responsible for finding RegionServers where a particular data is present. It is done by reading the HBase metadata, hbase:meta (called .META. in the older versions of HBase), which includes a key-value pair.

Let's discuss the format in short here:

- **Key**: It contains region key information about the table, region, and region ID in the following format:

  [table], [region start key], [region id]

- **Value**: This contains info:regioninfo (org.apache.hadoop.hbase.HRegionInfo with fields such as table name, start key, regionID, replicaID, encoded name, end key, split, and offline), info:server (the server port for RegionServer), and info:serverstartcode (the start time of RegionServer).

A more detailed layout and information about HRegionInfo can be found at http://hbase.apache.org/apidocs/org/apache/hadoop/hbase/HRegionInfo.html.

After getting the required RegionServer details, the client contacts the RegionServer serving the needed region, and the read/write operation can then happen without contacting the master.

This fetched information is stored at client side for further faster operation. If a region dies in between, the client queries the updated catalog table once again for RegionServer and region information, and the information stored at the client location is updated. A cluster might run without a master for some time; however, if the master is stopped, it must be restarted as soon as possible because it handles important tasks that we already discussed.

If we have a standalone HBase mode, we need not run any client configuration as everything runs on a single server, and the client can contact HBase from here itself. We need to specify the ZooKeeper address in the configuration for the client as there might be many masters; ZooKeeper keeps track of the masters' addresses. Usually, we maintain the ZooKeeper address in `HBase-site.xml`. For this, we need a ZooKeeper address and the port at which it is running. There might be more than one comma-separated ZooKeeper running for fully distributed clusters.

The first important thing is to make a client aware where our ZooKeeper, HMaster, and other components are running, for which we must include the `conf` directory of HBase. We need to include some library files (JARs) in the classpath of our ide Java project.

These required library files are shipped with HBase and Hadoop. The following are the JAR files found in the `HBase/hadoop` directory, which we can add to the class path in Eclipse, as follows:

- The following is the code for the HBase `lib` files:

```
hbase (hbase-<version>.jar)
log4j (log4j-<version>.jar)
slf4j-api (slf4j-api-<version>.jar)
slf4j-log4j (slf4j-log4j12-<version>.jar)
zookeeper (zookeeper-<version>.jar)
```

- The following is the code for the Hadoop `lib` files:

```
commons-configuration (commons-configuration-<version>.jar)
commons-lang (commons-lang-<version>.jar)
commons-logging (commons-logging-<version>.jar)
hadoop-core (hadoop-core-<version>.jar)
```

We can replace `<version>` with the version number we are using in the current Hadoop/HBase setup.

Let's start building the Java project:

1. Right-click on **Project** in Eclipse, and then click on **Build Path**, and **Configure Build Path...**. Go to the **Libraries** tab and add JARs, as shown in the following screenshot:

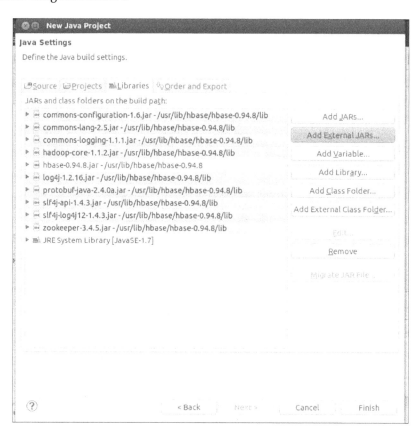

2. After adding the required resource files, move ahead with the coding. When this is done, the HBase client will look for the ZooKeeper address and port number from where it can connect to the active master and then to the required RegionServer. The client looks for the configuration property that lists the running ZooKeeper instances:

```
<property>
  <name>hbase.zookeeper.quorum</name>
  <value>zookeeper1,zookeeper2,zookeeper3</value>
</property>
```

3. To enable clients to communicate with HBase, we need to do either of the following:

    ° Include the `conf` directory in CLASSPATH

    ° Create a configuration for the client using the `HBaseConfiguration` class in the client code

    Here, we can specify the configuration explicitly, as shown in the following code snippet. If running in local standalone mode, use these settings:

```
Configuration conf = HBaseConfiguration.create();
conf.set("hbase.zookeeper.quorum", "localhost");
```

4. For fully distributed clusters where there are many instances of ZooKeeper running, we can specify all the ZooKeepers separated by commas, as follows:

```
Configuration conf = HBaseConfiguration.create();
conf.set("hbase.zookeeper.quorum",
"zookeeper1,zookeeper2,zookeeper3");
```

    We also have to specify the port if we are not using the default ZooKeeper port, that is, 2181. If we changed it in the configuration, we need to add the following line too:

```
conf.set("hbase.zookeeper.property.clientPort","2181");
```

5. Once this is done, try to run the code and check whether these three lines throw an exception or the connection is successful. We can use the following code to check the connectivity to ZooKeeper:

```
import java.io.IOException;
import org.apache.hadoop.hbase.client.Put;
import org.apache.hadoop.hbase.client.Result;
import org.apache.hadoop.hbase.client.ResultScanner;
import org.apache.hadoop.hbase.client.Scan;
import org.apache.hadoop.conf.Configuration;
import org.apache.hadoop.hbase.HBaseConfiguration;
import org.apache.hadoop.hbase.client.Get;
import org.apache.hadoop.hbase.client.HTable;
import org.apache.hadoop.hbase.util.Bytes;

public class HBaseClientExample throws MasterNotRunningException,
ZooKeeperConnectionException {

    {
        public static void main(String[] args) throws
          IOException {
```

```
        try {

            HBaseAdmin.checkHBaseAvailable(conf);
        } catch (Exception e) {
            System.err.println("Exception at " + e);
            System.exit(1);
        }
        Configuration conf = HBaseConfiguration.create();
        conf.set("hbase.zookeeper.quorum", "infinity");
        conf.set("hbase.zookeeper.property.clientPort",
          "2181");
        HTable table = new HTable(conf, "table");
        HBaseAdmin admin = new HBaseAdmin(conf);

        try {
            HBaseAdmin.checkHBaseAvailable(conf);
            System.out.println("connection made ! ");
        } catch (Exception error) {
            System.err.println("Error connecting HBase:
              " + error);
            System.exit(1);
        }
    }
}
```

This code will try to connect to HBase using the given configuration. If successful, it will print `connection made !`; otherwise, it will print the error message.

Data types

Let's have a look at the data types available in HBase. In HBase, everything is a byte. It is a byte in and a byte out, which means everything that has to be written in HBase needs to be converted/encoded to a byte array, and while reading, it can again be converted/decoded to an equivalent representation. This facility is provided by the `put` and `result` interfaces. So, no matter what the type of data is, as long as it can be converted to a byte array, it can be stored in an HBase table. The input data type might be an integer, image, or object, or a long or string. All of these can be converted to a byte array and stored in an HBase table.

Since we can store any type of data, it does not imply that we can convert and store huge amounts of data into an HBase cell as there is a practical limit; more than 20 MB is a big thing to ask for. So, it's better that we choose smaller data that can be converted and stored in an HBase cell, and for huge amounts of data, we can choose other options such as storing it on an HDFS file system, and storing the path in the HBase cell to avoid very prolonged read operations. Lengthy read operations might prevent client calls.

In the next section, we will look at various types of data, converting and storing it in HBase tables using `put`, or reading the data to equivalent representations using `get` and `scan`.

Data model Java operations

There are some operations that can be performed on HBase data; these are known as HBase data model operations. These operations might have tasks such as reading from, writing to, and modifying data into HBase. Now, we will see the following data model operations:

- Read operations using `Get()` and `Scan()`
- Write operations using `Put()`
- Modify operations using `Delete()`

Read

In this section, we will see the data models that are useful to read data from an HBase table.

Get()

`Get()` reads a row from a table. It can read a single or a set of rows based on the specified condition. It returns a result that contains data in key-value pairs or a map format. This method is provided by HTable classes and executed as `HTable.get` (condition). It returns a row specified as a row key or one that's based on a matching filter.

Constructors

Using the following constructors, we can create an object to access the HBase APIs to read the data:

```
Result get (byte [] RowKey) throws IOException
Result get (Get get) throws IOException
```

Supported methods

The following are the methods using which we can read different records from HBase. These methods consist of reading rows of data, locking rows for reading, setting filters for specific records, and others; these are listed as follows:

- `getRow()`: This method returns the row key when specified with `Get` object instances.

- `getRowLock()`: This method returns the row lock on a specified row.

- `getLockId()`: This method returns the lock ID for a locked row.

- `getTimeRange()`: This method sets a time range for a `Get` instance object.

- `setTimeStamp()`: This is used for setting the minimum and maximum values to the given timestamp.

- `setFilter()` and `getFilter()`: These are special filters that can be used to select specific columns or cells based on a variety of conditions about filters. We will discuss this in detail in the next section.

- `setCacheBlocks()` and `getCacheBlocks()`: These enable caching.

- `numFamilies()`: This retrieves the size of the family map containing the families using the `addFamily()` or `addColumn()` calls.

- `hasFamilies()`: This checks whether a family column is added to the current instance of the `Get` class.

> The most updated list of `Get` methods can be found at https://hbase.apache.org/apidocs/org/apache/hadoop/hbase/client/Get.html.

The following are the options that one has while using the `Get` class:

- Get everything of a row data for which we specify the row key

- Get column families from a row for which we add the `addFamily` filter for each column family to retrieve

- To get a specific column, we add an `addColumn` filter to `Get`

- To get columns written within a time range, we can add `setTimeRange` to the `Get` class

- For data written at a specific time, we can add `setTimeStamp`

- As we know, an HBase record maintains more than one version of data, so we can set the limit on the number of versions to return by setting `setMaxVersion`

- To add a string-related or any other filter, we can use `setFilter`
- The `Get` method can be called on a row key, a `get` object, or in batch modes using a specified list of `get` in the get list, `List<Get>`

Let's have a look at a few examples. Here is the basic code to use `Get`:

```
Configuration config =
HBaseConfiguration.create();
HtableObject tableObject = new HtableObject(config,
"tableObjectnametoreadfrom");
Get get = new Get(Bytes.toBytes("RowID"));
Result result = tableObject.get(get);
byte[] nameVal= result.getValue(Bytes.toBytes("details"),
Bytes.toBytes("name"));
System.out.println("Name : " + Bytes.toString(nameVal));
```

The preceding code will read a name column from the `Detail` column family of a table. To read data, we need to pass rows, column families, and columns as byte arrays using the `Bytes.toBytes()` method, which converts string parameters to byte arrays.

Now, let's see how we can use multiple gets:

```
Configuration config =
HBaseConfiguration.create();
HtableObject tableObject = new HtableObject(config,
"tableObjectnametoreadfrom");
List<Get> listOfGets = new ArrayList<Get>();
listOfGets.add(new Get(Bytes.toBytes("rowKey1")));
listOfGets.add(new Get(Bytes.toBytes("rowKey2")));
listOfGets.add(new Get(Bytes.toBytes("rowKey3")));
Result[] records = tableObject.get(listOfGets);
            for (Result r : records) {
                System.out.println("Row Key:" +r.getRow());
            }
```

This will iterate through the `result` object and display all the rows matched. This might return `map` or `result` that we will discuss in the `result` class after `scan()`. Likewise, we can use the preceding methods to utilize the power of `Get`.

A full code on `Get` is as follows:

```
import org.apache.hadoop.hbase.util.Bytes.*;
import java.io.IOException;
import org.apache.hadoop.hbase.client.Get;
import org.apache.hadoop.hbase.client.HTable;
```

```
import org.apache.hadoop.hbase.client.Result;
import org.apache.hadoop.hbase.util.Bytes;
import org.apache.hadoop.conf.Configuration;
import org.apache.hadoop.hbase.HBaseConfiguration;
public class GetExample {
        public static void main(String[] args) throws IOException
{
                Configuration config =
                  HBaseConfiguration.create();
                try { HTable tableObj = new HTable(config,
                  "logtable");
                Get getObject = new Get(toBytes("rowKey1"));
                Result getResult = tableObj.getObject(getObject);
                print(getResult);
                getObject.addColumn(toBytes("colFam"),
                  toBytes("col2"));
                getResult = tableObj.getObject(getObject);
                print(getResult);
}catch (Exception e)
{
System.out.println("error in reading data");
}
finally
{
tableObj.close();}

        }
        private static void print(Result getResult) {
                System.out.println("Row Key: " +
                  Bytes.toString(getResult.getRow()));
                byte [] value1 =
                  getResult.getValue(toBytes("colFam"),
                  toBytes("column1"));
                System.out.println("colFam1:colum1="+
                  Bytes.toString(value1));
                byte [] value2 =
                  getResult.getValue(toBytes("colFam"),
                  toBytes("column2"));
                System.out.println("colFam1:column2="+
                  Bytes.toString(value2));
        }
}
```

The following are miscellaneous data methods:

- `boolean exists(Get getobj) throws IOException`: Using this method, we can check whether the `get` operation we specify will return a result or the result will be null.

- `Result getRowOrBefore(byte[] rowkey, byte[] colFamily) throws IOException`: Using this method, we can get a row just before the specified row.

Scan()

Scan through the table for all data or sets of data based on filters. This is used like `get`, but to get more than one record based on the filter specified. In `Scan()`, we can specify the start row from where scanning will start and the stop row where scanning will stop. We can also specify the time range as a filter to get data between a given time range. To know more about scan optimization methods, visit `http://hbase.apache.org/book/perf.reading.html#perf.hbase.client.caching`.

Constructors

The following are the constructors that we can use:

- `Scan()`: This constructor is used to create scan operations that scan through all the rows

- `Scan(byte [] startRow)`: This constructor forces a lower bound on the row from where the scan will start

- `Scan(byte [] startRow, byte [] stopRow)`: This forces scanners to scan between the specified start and end rows only

- `Scan(byte [] startRow, Filter filter)`: This implements a start row and `Filter`, which we will discuss later in this chapter

- `Scan(Get get)`: Scan is done on the basis of conditions in the `get` object instance

- `Scan(Scan scan)`: Scan is done based on conditions in another scan object

These constructors can be used for various types of limiting, or filters can be applied in order to limit the scan to the required scope of data, avoiding the useless scanning of data in a table.

Methods

Here, we will learn about the methods used to read data using scan:

- `getStartRow()`: This is used to retrieve the start row of the scanning operation.

- `getStopRow()`: This is used to retrieve the stop row of the scanning operation.

- `setStartRow()`: This is used to set the start row of the scanning operation.

- `setStopRow()`: This is used to set the stop row of the scanning operation.

- `getTimeRange()`: This gets the associated timestamp or time range of the `Get` instance.

- `setTimeRange()`: This sets the associated timestamp or time range of the `Get` instance.

- `getMaxVersions()`: This gets the highest version of the configured record.

- `setMaxVersions()`: This sets the maximum version to return.

- `getFilter()`: We can get the currently assigned filter using this method. It might return null if no filter is set. We will discuss filters later in this chapter.

- `setCacheBlocks()`: This sets block caching for scans.

- `getCacheBlocks()`: This gets block caching for scans.

- `numFamilies()`: This is used to get the size of the family map.

- `hasFamilies()`: This checks whether column families have been added to the scan.

- `getFamilies()`: This retrieves the column families.

- `setFamilyMap()`: This sets the family map.

- `getFamilyMap()`: This retrieves the family map.

- `setFilter()`: This applies a filter to the scan query.

So, let's understand what we can do to customize scans to get the desired result:

- To scan the entire data, we can use the empty scan constructor as `Scan scanobj=new Scan()`

- To modify caching, we can use `setCaching()` or `HTable. setScannerCaching(int)`, or we can limit the result size by using `setMaxResultSize(int)`

- To get all the columns from a column family, we can add `addFamily` to scan objects

- To get single columns, we can add `addColumn` to scan objects
- To get columns only in a time range, we can specify `setTimeRange` in scan objects
- To get columns written in a specific timestamp, we can set `setTimeStamp`
- To get a specific number of versions for a column, we can set `setMaxVersions`
- To get the maximum number of values returned for each call in the result, we can set `setBath` for `next()` call
- To add a filter, we can set `setFilter`
- To enable/disable server-side block caching, we can set `setCacheBlock()` to `true`/`false`

Now, let's see some examples of `Scan`:

```
Configuration conf = HBaseConfiguration.create();
HTable table = new HTable(conf, "logtable");
Scan scan = new Scan();
scan.setMaxVersions(2);
ResultScanner result = table.getScanner(scan);
for (Result result: scanner) {
    System.out.println("Rows which were scanned : " +
        Bytes.toString(result.getRow()));
}
```

The preceding code will scan through `logtable` and print all the rows in the table. Now, we will see how to scan rows in between two rows, as follows. It will scan between `row100` and `row1000`:

```
Configuration conf = HBaseConfiguration.create();
HTable table = new HTable(conf, "logtable");
Scan scan = new Scan (Bytes.ToBytes ("row100"), Bytes.toBytes
("row1000");
scan.setMaxVersions(2);
ResultScanner result = table.getScanner(scan);
for (Result result: scanner) {
    System.out.println("Rows which were scanned : " +
        Bytes.toString(result.getRow()));
}
```

The following is the full-fledged code to display on scan:

```
import org.apache.hadoop.hbase.util.Bytes.toBytes;
import java.io.IOException;
import org.apache.hadoop.conf.Configuration;
import org.apache.hadoop.hbase.HBaseConfiguration;
```

```
import org.apache.hadoop.hbase.client.tableToScan;
import org.apache.hadoop.hbase.client.Result;
import org.apache.hadoop.hbase.client.ResultScanner;
import org.apache.hadoop.hbase.client.Scan;
import org.apache.hadoop.hbase.util.Bytes;
public class scanExampleFull {
  public static void main(String[] args) throws IOException {
    Configuration config = HBaseConfiguration.create();
    tableToScan tableToScan = new tableToScan
      (config, "HBaseSamples");
    scan(tableToScan, "row1000", "row10000");
    scan(tableToScan, "row0", "row200");
    tableToScan.close();}
  private static void scan(tableToScan tableToScan, String
    startingRowKey, String stoppingRowKey) throws IOException {

    Scan scan = new Scan(toBytes(startingRowKey),
      toBytes(stoppingRowKey));
    scan.addColumn(toBytes("detailColFam"),
      toBytes("Namecolumn"));
    ResultScanner scanner = tableToScan.getScanner(scan);
    for (Result result : scanner){
      byte [] value = result.getValue(
        toBytes("detailColFam"), toBytes("Namecolumn"));
        System.out.println("  " +
          Bytes.toString(result.getRow()) + " => " +
          Bytes.toString(value));
    }
    scanner.close();
  }
}
```

We can perform the scan in batches. The following code will display how to do this:

```
import org.apache.hadoop.conf.Configuration;
import org.apache.hadoop.hbase.HBaseConfiguration;
import org.apache.hadoop.hbase.KeyValue;
import org.apache.hadoop.hbase.client.HTable;
import org.apache.hadoop.hbase.client.Result;
import org.apache.hadoop.hbase.client.ResultScanner;
import org.apache.hadoop.hbase.util.Bytes.toBytes;
import org.apache.hadoop.hbase.client.Scan;
import org.apache.hadoop.hbase.util.Bytes;
import java.io.IOException;
public class scanInBatch {
```

```
public static void main(String[] args) throws IOException {
  Configuration config = HBaseConfiguration.create();
  HTable tableToScanObj = new HTable(config, "logTable");
  Scan scanObj = new Scan();
  scan.addFamily(toBytes("columns"));
  scanDisplayData(tableToScanObj, scanObj);
  scan.setBatch(2);
  scanDisplayData(tableToScanObj, scanObj);
  tableToScanObj.close();
}
private static void scanDisplayData(HTable tableToScanObj,
  Scan scanObj) throws IOException {
  System.out.println("Batch Number : " + scanObj.getBatch());
  ResultScanner resultScannerObj =
    tableToScanObj.getScanner(scanObj);
  for ( Result result : resultScannerObj){
    System.out.println("Data : ");
    for ( KeyValue keyValuePairObj : result.list()){
      System.out.println(Bytes.toString
        (keyValuePairObj.getValue()));
    }
  }
resultScannerObj.close();
  }
}
```

 The most updated list of constructors/methods can be found at
https://hbase.apache.org/apidocs/org/apache/hadoop/
hbase/client/Scan.html.

Optimization of scanners can be found at http://hbase.apache.org/
book/perf.reading.html.

Write

HBase provides the facility of writing data into HBase using the Put class. To write
the data into HBase, we use the Put() method.

Put()

The Put() method is available to write records and data into an HBase table. This
method takes parameter as row key and a put object. Using this we can write a row
or set of rows of data in an HBase table.

Constructors

The following are the constructors:

- `Put(byte[] rowKey)`

- `Put(byte[] rowKey, long timeStamp)`

- `Put(byte[] rowKey, RowLock rowLock)`

- `Put(byte[] rowKey, long timeStamp, RowLock rowLock)`

Methods

To perform writing, we instantiate the `put` object with the row ID that needs to be inserted. We can use the following methods to perform the `put (insert)` task:

- `add (byte[] columnFamName, byte[] columnName, byte[] cellValue)`: This adds the specified column and value for the column to the put operation

- `add (byte[] columnFamName, byte[] columnName, long timeStamp, byte[] cellValue)`: This adds the specified column and value for the column to the put operation, with the timestamp and cell value

- `add (byte[] columnFamName, ByteBuffer columnName, long timeStamp, ByteBuffer cellValue)`: This adds the specified column and value for the column to the put operation, with the given timestamp and its version to the put operation

- `add (Cell keyValue)`: This adds a key-value pair to the put operation.

The following is an example of a put operation:

```
import java.io.IOException;
import org.apache.hadoop.hbase.client.HTable;
import org.apache.hadoop.hbase.client.Put;
import org.apache.hadoop.hbase.util.Bytes.*;
import org.apache.hadoop.conf.Configuration;
import org.apache.hadoop.hbase.HBaseConfiguration;
public class ExampleofPutOperation {
  public static void main(String[] arguments) throws IOException {
    Configuration config = HBaseConfiguration.create();
    HTable toWriteDataInTable = new HTable(config, "logTable");
    Put putObj = new Put(toBytes("logdataKey1"));
    putObj.add(toBytes("colFamily"), toBytes("columnName1"),
      toBytes("internetexplorer"));
    putObj.add(toBytes("colFamily"), toBytes("columnName2"),
      toBytes("123456"));
```

```
        toWriteDataInTable.put(putObj);
        toWriteDataInTable.close();
    }
}
```

This code will put a row named `logdataKey1` in the `logTable` table with the `colFamily` column family, which will have two columns, `columnName1` and `columnName2`, which contain the `internetexplorer` and `123456` values, respectively.

> More updated information on the put APIs and list of methods can be found at `https://hbase.apache.org/apidocs/org/apache/hadoop/hbase/client/Put.html`.

Modify

HBase provides the `Delete` class and methods to delete and modify the columns in HBase tables.

Here, we will discuss methods such as deleting values from a table, using which we can modify table data.

Delete()

Using the `Delete` class and methods provided, we can delete a row or set of rows and a record or a set of records from an HBase table using specified parameters.

Constructors

The following are the constructors:

- `Delete(byte[] rowKey)`
- `Delete(byte[] rowKeyArray, int rowKeyOffset, int rowKeyLength)`
- `Delete(byte[] rowKeyArray, int rowKeyOffset, int rowKeyLength, long timestamp)`
- `Delete(byte[] rowKey, long timestamp)`
- `Delete(byte[] rowKey, long timestamp, rowKeyLock rowKeyLock)`
- `Delete(Delete delObj)`

Methods

The following methods are available with the `Delete` class to perform the deletion of columns, column families, or a record in the HBase table:

- `deleteColumn(byte[] family, byte[] qualifier)`: This is used to delete the latest version of a given column

- `deleteColumn(byte[] family, byte[] qualifier, long timestamp)`: This is used to delete the specified version of a given column

- `deleteColumns(byte[] family, byte[] qualifier)`: This is used to delete all versions of a given column

- `deleteColumns(byte[] family, byte[] qualifier, long timestamp)`: This is used to delete all versions of a given column with a timestamp that's less than or equal to the given timestamp

- `deleteFamily(byte[] family)`: This is used to delete all versions of all columns of a given column family

- `deleteFamily(byte[] family, long timestamp)`: This is used to delete all columns of a given family with a timestamp less than or equal to the given timestamp

- `deleteFamilyVersion(byte[] family, long timestamp)`: This is used to delete all column versions of a given family with a timestamp equal to the given timestamp

- `setTimestamp(long timestamp)`: This is used to set the timestamp of the delete operation

The following code is an example of `Delete()`:

```
import org.apache.hadoop.hbase.util.Bytes.toBytes;
import org.apache.hadoop.conf.Configuration;
import org.apache.hadoop.hbase.HBaseConfiguration;
import org.apache.hadoop.hbase.client.Delete;
import org.apache.hadoop.hbase.client.HTable;
import java.io.IOException;
public class DeleteOperationExample {
  public static void main(String[] arguments) throws IOException {
    Configuration config = HBaseConfiguration.create();
    HTable tableToDeleteDataFrom = new HTable(config, "logTable");
    Delete deleteobj1 = new Delete(toBytes("rowIDToDelete"));
    tableToDeleteDataFrom.delete(deleteobj1);
```

```
    Delete deleteobj2 = new Delete(toBytes("2ndRowIDToDelete"));
    delete1.deleteColumns(toBytes("columnFamily"),
      toBytes("columnName"));
    tableToDeleteDataFrom.delete(deleteobj2);
    tableToDeleteDataFrom.close();
  }
}
```

This code will delete two rows in first `delete`. It will delete the entire row, and in the second `delete` operation, it will delete the given column for a column family.

> More updated delete APIs and methods can be found at `https://hbase.apache.org/apidocs/org/apache/hadoop/hbase/client/Delete.html`.
>
> All the latest HBase APIs can be found at the following links:
>
> - `http://hbase.apache.org/apidocs/allclasses-noframe.html`
> - `http://hbase.apache.org/apidocs/index-all.html`

HBase filters

As the name suggests, filter means to extract or take out only required data and discard useless or excess data. HBase provides a good number of filters, which we can use in get and scan operations to extract or fetch only the needed data from HBase, preventing scanning-not-required data.

HBase filters are a powerful feature that can greatly enhance effectiveness while working with data stored in tables. The two read functions for HBase, `get()` and `scan()`, support direct access to data and the use of a start and end key, respectively. We can limit the data retrieved by adding limiting selectors to the HBase query. These include column families, column qualifiers, timestamps, ranges, and version numbers.

We can represent HBase filter uses as shown in the following diagram, where we specify filters in `get` or `scan`. It fetches data from different RegionServers where these filters are shipped using RPC calls and compared with the local data at RegionServers:

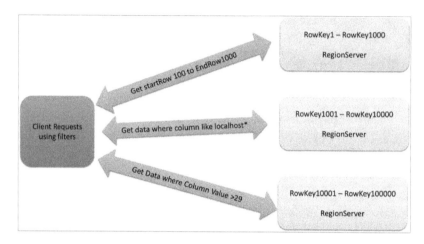

Types of filters

Now, let's see different types of filters and their uses. Before discussing this, we will see the operator on which filters depend for comparison:

Operator type	Description
`BitComparator.BitwiseOp`	This performs the bitwise comparison. The following are the enum constants: • AND (and) • OR (or) • XOR (xor) You can read more on this operator at `http://hbase.apache.org/apidocs/org/apache/hadoop/hbase/filter/BitComparator.BitwiseOp.html`.

Operator type	Description
CompareFilter.CompareOp	This is a generic type of filter that is to be used to compare. It can take operators such as equal, greater and not equal. This is also a byte [] comparator. The following are the enum constants: • EQUAL • GREATER • GREATER_OR_EQUAL • LESS • LESS_OR_EQUAL • NO_OP • NOT_EQUAL You can read more on this operator at http://hbase.apache.org/apidocs/org/apache/hadoop/hbase/filter/CompareFilter.CompareOp.html.
Filter.ReturnCode	These are the return code for the filter value. The following are the enum constants: • INCLUDE: This is used to include the cell • INCLUDE_AND_NEXT_COL: This is used to seek the next column by skipping and also include the cell • NEXT_COL: This is used to move to the next column by skipping • NEXT_ROW: This is used to move to the next row by skipping • SEEK_NEXT_USING_HINT: This is used to move to the next key that's given as a hint using a filter • SKIP: This is the skip cell You can read more on this operator at http://hbase.apache.org/apidocs/org/apache/hadoop/hbase/filter/Filter.ReturnCode.html.

Operator type	Description
FilterList.Operator	These are the conditions for more than one filter in a filter list. The following are the enum constants: • MUST_PASS_ALL • !AND • MUST_PASS_ONE • !OR You can read more on this operator at http://hbase.apache.org/apidocs/org/apache/hadoop/hbase/filter/FilterList.Operator.html.

We have seen the operators used in combination with filters. We will see the use of this in example code; now, let's understand the list of filters available:

Filter types	Description
BinaryComparator	This filter is used for binary comparison lexicographically. It compares against the given byte array, using Bytes.compareTo (byte[], byte[]). Have a look at the following example: ```SingleColumnValueFilter colValFilterbinary = new SingleColumnValueFilter(Bytes.toBytes("detail"), Bytes.toBytes("name"), CompareFilter.CompareOp.GREATER_OR_EQUAL, new BinaryComparator(Bytes.toBytes("shash")));```
BinaryPrefixComparator	This is a binary comparator filter that compares byte arrays at the prefix level.
BitComparator	This filter comparator performs the given bitwise operation on each of the bytes with the given byte array.
ByteArrayComparable	This is the base class for byte array comparators.

Filter types	Description
ColumnCountGetFilter	This is the filter that gives the first *N* number of columns on rows only.
ColumnPaginationFilter	This is based on the ColumnCountGetFilter; it takes two arguments, limit and offset, and is used for pagination.
ColumnPrefixFilter	This filter is used to get keys with columns that match a specified prefix.
ColumnRangeFilter	This filter is used to select columns between the min-column and max-column values.
CompareFilter	This is a generic filter used to filter by comparison.
DependentColumnFilter	This filter is used to add intercolumn timestamp matching cells with a corresponding timestamp.
FamilyFilter	This filter is based on column families.
Filter	This is the interface for row and column filters, which can be directly applied within RegionServer.
FilterList	Using this, we can implement a logical comparison. This is an ordered list or a set of other filters accompanied by comparison operators that must satisfy the conditions implied in the filter list while comparison. The following are the comparison operators: • FilterList.Operator. MUST_PASS_ALL (AND) • FilterList.Operator. MUST_PASS_ONE (OR)
FirstKeyOnlyFilter	This filter returns only the first KeyValue from each row.
FirstKeyValueMatchingQualifiersFilter	This filter checks for the specified columns in KeyValue.

Filter types	Description
FuzzyRowFilter	This filter is based on fuzzy row keys.
InclusiveStopFilter	This filter stops after the given row.
KeyOnlyFilter	This filter will only return the key component of each KeyValue.
MultipleColumnPrefixFilter	This is used to select keys with columns that match a given prefix.
NullComparator	This is a binary comparator; it lexicographically compares against the given byte array using Bytes. compareTo (byte[], byte[]).
PageFilter	This filter limits results to a specific page size.
ParseConstants	This holds a set of constants related to parsing filter strings used by ParseFilter.
ParseFilter	This allows users to specify a filter via a string.
PrefixFilter	This passes results that have same row prefixes.
QualifierFilter	This is a filter based on column qualifiers.
RandomRowFilter	This includes rows based on a chance.
RegexStringComparator	This is a regular expression-based filter.
RowFilter	This is used to filter based on the row key.
SingleColumnValueExcludeFilter	This checks a single column value, but does not return the tested column.
SingleColumnValueFilter	This is used to filter cells based on value.
SkipFilter	This is a filter that filters an entire row if any one of the row cell checks do not pass the comparison.
SubstringComparator	This is a filter based on substrings in a value.

Filter types	Description
TimestampsFilter	This is a filter based on timestamps of the data.
ValueFilter	This filter is based on column values.
WhileMatchFilter	This filter will continue till the match is found.

So, we have seen the list of filters that can be used in read methods; they are Get() and Scan(), which are used to filter out the unnecessary data and fetch only the required data. The following is a sample code that contains the use of filters in read methods:

```java
import java.io.IOException;
import org.apache.hadoop.hbase.client.Result;
import org.apache.hadoop.hbase.client.ResultScanner;
import org.apache.hadoop.hbase.client.Scan;
import org.apache.hadoop.hbase.filter.CompareFilter.CompareOp;
import org.apache.hadoop.hbase.filter.SubstringComparator;
import org.apache.hadoop.hbase.filter.ValueFilter;
import org.apache.hadoop.hbase.util.Bytes;
import org.apache.hadoop.conf.Configuration;
import org.apache.hadoop.hbase.HBaseConfiguration;
import org.apache.hadoop.hbase.client.HTable;
import org.apache.hadoop.hbase.util.Bytes.toBytes;

public class FilterExample {
  public static void main(String[] arguments) throws IOException {
    Configuration config = HBaseConfiguration.create();
    HTable hbaseTableObj = new HTable(config, "logTable");
    Scan scanObj = new Scan();
    scanObj.setFilter(new ValueFilter(CompareOp.EQUAL, new
      SubstringComparator("shash")));
    ResultScanner resultScannerObj =
      hbaseTableObj.getScanner(scanObj);
      for ( Result result : resultScannerObj){
        byte [] value = result.getValue(toBytes("ColFamily"),
          toBytes("columnName"));
          System.out.println(Bytes.toString(value));
      }
      resultScannerObj.close();
      hbaseTableObj.close();
  }
}
```

The following example shows how we can use a list of filters that is not a single filter but a combination of many, and this is done using a filter list:

```
import org.apache.hadoop.hbase.client.ResultScanner;
import org.apache.hadoop.hbase.client.Scan;
import org.apache.hadoop.hbase.filter.FilterList;
import org.apache.hadoop.hbase.filter.FilterList.Operator;
import org.apache.hadoop.hbase.filter.FirstKeyOnlyFilter;
import java.io.IOException;
import org.apache.hadoop.hbase.util.Bytes.toBytes;
import org.apache.hadoop.conf.Configuration;
import org.apache.hadoop.hbase.HBaseConfiguration;
import org.apache.hadoop.hbase.client.HTable;
import org.apache.hadoop.hbase.client.Result;
import org.apache.hadoop.hbase.filter.KeyOnlyFilter;
import org.apache.hadoop.hbase.util.Bytes;
public class ExampleOfFilterList {
  public static void main(String[] arguments) throws IOException {
    Configuration config = HBaseConfiguration.create();
    HTable hbaseTableObj = new HTable(config, "logTable");
    Scan scanObj = new Scan();
    FilterList filterListObj = new
      FilterList(Operator.MUST_PASS_ALL);
    filterListObj.addFilter(new KeyOnlyFilter());
    filterListObj.addFilter(new FirstKeyOnlyFilter());
    scanObj.setFilter(filterListObj);
    ResultScanner resultScannerObj =
      hbaseTableObj.getScanner(scanObj);
    for ( Result result : resultScannerObj){
      byte [] value = result.getValue(toBytes("colFamName"),
        toBytes("colName"));
      System.out.println("Value found :" +Bytes.toString(value));
    }
    resultScannerObj.close();
    hbaseTableObj.close();
  }
}
```

Client APIs

HBase provides a list of client APIs, classes, and interfaces to build clients for HBase. These clients can communicate with HBase to perform various operations such as administrating codes. The following is the list of all the interfaces, classes, and exceptions related to the client:

Interfaces	Classes	
• Admin	• AbstractClientScanner	• MultiResponse
• Attributes	• Action	• Mutation
• ClusterConnection	• Append	• Operation
• HConnection	• ClientScanner	• OperationWithAttributes
• HTableInterface	• ClientSideRegionScanner	• PerClientRandomNonceGenerator
• HTableInterface Factory	• ClientSmallReversedScanner	• Put
• MetaScanner.Meta ScannerVisitor	• ClientSmallScanner	• Query
• NonceGenerator	• ConnectionUtils	• RegionCoprocessorServiceExec
• ResultScanner	• DelegatingRetryingCallable	• RegionReplicaUtil
• RetryingCallable	• Delete	• RegionServerCallable
• Row	• Get	• Result
	• HBaseAdmin	• RetriesExhaustedException. ThrowableWithExtraContext
Enums	• HConnectable	• ReversedClientScanner
• Consistency	• HConnectionManager	• ReversedScannerCallable
• Durability	• HTable	• RowMutations
• IsolationLevel	• HTableFactory	• RpcRetryingCaller
	• HTableMultiplexer	• RpcRetryingCallerFactory
Exceptions	• HTableUtil	• RpcRetryingCallerWithReadReplicas
• NoServerForRegion Exception	• HTableWrapper	• Scan
• RegionOffline Exception	• Increment	• ScannerCallable
• RetriesExhausted Exception	• MetaCache	• TableSnapshotScanner
• RetriesExhaustedWith DetailsException	• MetaScanner	• UnmodifyableHTableDescriptor
• ScannerTimeout Exception	• MetaScanner.DefaultMeta ScannerVisitor	
• WrongRowIO Exception	• MetaScanner.MetaScanner VisitorBase	
	• MetaScanner.TableMeta ScannerVisitor	
	• MultiAction	

 Information on the classes, exceptions, and APIs with updated information can be found at http://hbase.apache.org/devapidocs/index.html.

Summary

In this chapter, we discussed the Java coding for HBase and various data model operations such as reading, writing, and modifying data in an HBase table. We also saw filters to read required-only data. The chapter also covers code for APIs. In the next chapter, we will see administrative programing; some advance coding concepts such as administrative code, available interfaces, classes, and exceptions in HBase; writing MapReduce for HBase; and details about rest and thrift API services.

9
Advance Coding in Java for HBase

In this chapter, we will learn about some more advance coding on topics such as administrative tasks; available interfaces, classes, and exceptions in HBase; writing a MapReduce for HBase; and operations on HDFS. We will also discuss details on REST and Thrift API services and other advance topics such as coprocessors, bloom filters, and available HBase tools for value addition.

In this chapter, we will cover the following topics:

- Interfaces, classes, and exceptions in HBase
- Java code for performing administrative tasks
- Data operation codes
- MapReduce in HBase
- REST/Thrift web service introduction
- Advance concepts in HBase
- Information about some add-on projects

Interfaces, classes, and exceptions

Interface is a set of abstract methods. A class in Java implements an interface and inherits the abstract methods of the interface. It is not a class. Writing an interface is the same as writing a class. A class tells us about the attributes and behaviors of an object. An interface contains behaviors that a class implements.

Class is a template/blueprint that describes the behavior that an object supports.

Exception is a problem that arises during the execution of a program.

Here is the list of some packages to be used in Java code:

- `org.apache.hadoop.hbase`: This package contains a base class for HBase
- `org.apache.hadoop.hbase.backup`: This package contains classes related to backup tasks
- `org.apache.hadoop.hbase.client`: This package contains a client-related class
- `org.apache.hadoop.hbase.codec`: This package contains the `Codec` interface
- `org.apache.hadoop.hbase.coprocessor`: This package is used to write coprocessors
- `org.apache.hadoop.hbase.exceptions`: This package contains the predefined exception in HBase
- `org.apache.hadoop.hbase.filter`: This package provides a list of filters
- `org.apache.hadoop.hbase.http`: This package contains HTTP functionalities
- `org.apache.hadoop.hbase.io`: This package contains I/O-related methods
- `org.apache.hadoop.hbase.ipc`: This package contains methods related to RPC connection
- `org.apache.hadoop.hbase.mapred`: This package contains MapReduce-related methods
- `org.apache.hadoop.hbase.mapreduce`: This is the newer MapReduce package, which provides HBase MapReduce I/O formats, a table indexing MapReduce job, and utility methods
- `org.apache.hadoop.hbase.master`: This package is used while interacting with the master
- `org.apache.hadoop.hbase.monitoring`: This package exports methods for monitoring
- `org.apache.hadoop.hbase.regionserver`: This package is used when interacting with RegionServers
- `org.apache.hadoop.hbase.rest`: This package provides REST API
- `org.apache.hadoop.hbase.security`: This package is used for tasks related to security
- `org.apache.hadoop.hbase.snapshot`: This package is used for backup and snapshot
- `org.apache.hadoop.hbase.thrift`: This package provides Thrift services

- `org.apache.hadoop.hbase.tool`: This package provides miscellaneous tools
- `org.apache.hadoop.hbase.types`: This package provides the definition and implementation of HBase's extensible data type API
- `org.apache.hadoop.hbase.util`: This package provides utilities
- `org.apache.hadoop.hbase.zookeeper`: This package is used for tasks related to ZooKeepers

 All the important packages, interfaces, and a list of the updated APIs can be found at `http://hbase.apache.org/devapidocs/index.html`.

Code related to administrative tasks

The following is the code for administrative tasks such as creating tables, deleting tables, enabling tables, and so on:

```
import java.io.IOException;
import java.util.Collection;
import org.apache.hadoop.hbase.MasterNotRunningException;
import org.apache.hadoop.hbase.ZooKeeperConnectionException;
import org.apache.hadoop.hbase.client.HBaseAdmin;
import org.apache.hadoop.hbase.client.HTable;
import org.apache.hadoop.hbase.util.Bytes;
import org.apache.hadoop.conf.Configuration;
import org.apache.hadoop.hbase.ClusterStatus;
import org.apache.hadoop.hbase.HBaseConfiguration;
import org.apache.hadoop.hbase.HColumnDescriptor;
import org.apache.hadoop.hbase.HServerInfo;
import org.apache.hadoop.hbase.HTableDescriptor;
public class hbaseAdminCodeExample {
  private Configuration conf = null;
  HBaseAdmin admin = null;
  public hbaseAdminCodeExample(){

  }
public static void main(String[] args) throws IOException {
  for(int i = 0; i < args.length; i++) {
    System.out.println("Argument Specified" + i + ":" + args[i]);
  }
  config.set("hbase.zookeeper.quorum", "infinity");
  config.set("hbase.zookeeper.property.clientPort", "2181");
```

```
hbaseAdminCodeExample adminObj = new hbaseAdminCodeExample();
adminObj.printClusterDetails(); /* this will print hbase cluster
details.*/
//rest of the methods also can be called as
adminObj.<method name with arguments>
}

static {
  config = HBaseConfiguration.create();
  admin=new HBaseAdmin(config);
}
public void addColumnToTable(String tableObj, String columnObj)
  throws IOException {
  config = HBaseConfiguration.create();
  HBaseAdmin adminObj = new HBaseAdmin(config);
  adminObj.addColumnToTable(tableObj, new
    HColumnDescriptor(columnObj));
  System.out.println("Added column : " + columnObj + "to table "
    + tableObj);
}
public void delColumnFromTable(String tableObj, String
  columnObj) throws IOException {
  config = HBaseConfiguration.create();
  HBaseAdmin adminObj = new HBaseAdmin(config);
  adminObj.deleteColumn(tableObj, columnObj);
  System.out.println("Deleted column : " + columnObj + "from
    table " + tableObj);
}
public void createTableInHbase(String tableObj, String
  ColFamName) throws IOException {
  config = HBaseConfiguration.create();
  HBaseAdmin adminObj = new HBaseAdmin(config);
  HTableDescriptor tabledescriptor = new
    HTableDescriptor(Bytes.toBytes(tableObj));
  tabledescriptor.addFamily(new HColumnDescriptor(ColFamName));
  adminObj.createTableInHbase(tabledescriptor);
}
public void performMajorCompact(String mytable) throws
  IOException {
  config = HBaseConfiguration.create();
  HTable table = new HTable(config, mytable);
  HBaseAdmin adminObj = new HBaseAdmin(config);
  String tableObj = table.toString();
  try {
```

```
      adminObj.majorCompact(tableObj);
      System.out.println("Compaction done!");
    } catch (Exception e) {
      System.out.println(e);
    }
  }
  public static void checkIfRunningFine() throws
    MasterNotRunningException, ZooKeeperConnectionException {
    config = HBaseConfiguration.create();
    try {
      HBaseAdmin.checkHBaseAvailable(config);
    } catch (Exception e) {
      System.err.println("Exception at " + e);
      System.exit(1);
    }
  }
  public void perfomrMinorcompact(String tabName) throws
    IOException, InterruptedException {
    config = HBaseConfiguration.create();
    HBaseAdmin adminObj = new HBaseAdmin(config);
    adminObj.compact(tabName);
  }
  public void deletetableFromHBase(String tableObj) throws
    IOException {
    config = HBaseConfiguration.create();
    HBaseAdmin adminObj = new HBaseAdmin(config);
    adminObj.deleteTable(tableObj);
  }
  public void disableHBaseTable(String tableObj) throws
    IOException {
    config = HBaseConfiguration.create();
    HBaseAdmin adminObj = new HBaseAdmin(config);
    adminObj.disableTable(tableObj);
  }
  public void enableHBaseTable(String tableObj) throws IOException
  {
    config = HBaseConfiguration.create();
    HBaseAdmin adminObj = new HBaseAdmin(config);
    adminObj.enableTable(tableObj);
  }
  public void flushTable(String tabName) throws IOException {
    config = HBaseConfiguration.create();
    HBaseAdmin adminObj = new HBaseAdmin(config);
    adminObj.disableTable(tabName);
  }
```

```
public ClusterStatus getHBaseclusterstatus() throws IOException
{
  config = HBaseConfiguration.create();
  HBaseAdmin adminObj = new HBaseAdmin(config);
  return adminObj.getClusterStatus();
}
public void printClusterDetails() throws IOException {
  ClusterStatus clusterStatus = getclusterstatus();
  clusterStatus.getServerInfo();
  Collection < HServerInfo > serverinfo =
    clusterStatus.getServerInfo();
  for (HServerInfo s: serverinfo) {
    System.out.println("Server name " + s.getServerName());
    System.out.println("Host name " + s.getHostname());
    System.out.println("Host name : Port " +
      s.getHostnamePort());
    System.out.println("Info port" + s.getInfoPort());
    System.out.println("Server load " + s.getLoad().toString());
    System.out.println();
  }
  String version = clusterStatus.getHBaseVersion();
  System.out.println("Version " + version);
  int regioncounts = clusterStatus.getRegionsCount();
  System.out.println("Region Counts :" + regioncounts);
  int servers = clusterStatus.getServers();
  System.out.println("Servers :" + servers);
  double averageload = clusterStatus.getAverageLoad();
  System.out.println("Average load: " + averageload);
  int deadservers = clusterStatus.getDeadServers();
  System.out.println("Deadservers : " + deadservers);
  Collection < String > Servernames =
    clusterStatus.getDeadServerNames();
  for (String s: Servernames) {
    System.out.println("Dead Servernames " + s);
  }
}
public void isHBaseTableAvailable(String tableObj) throws
  IOException {
  config = HBaseConfiguration.create();
  HBaseAdmin adminObj = new HBaseAdmin(config);
  boolean result = adminObj.isTableAvailable(tableObj);
  System.out.println("Table " + tableObj + " available ?" +
    result);
}
```

```
public void isHBaseTableEnabled(String tableObj) throws
  IOException {
  config = HBaseConfiguration.create();
  HBaseAdmin adminObj = new HBaseAdmin(config);
  boolean result = adminObj.isTableEnabled(tableObj);
  System.out.println("Table " + tableObj + " enabled ?" +
    result);
}
public void isHBaseTableDisabled(String tableObj) throws
  IOException {
  config = HBaseConfiguration.create();
  HBaseAdmin adminObj = new HBaseAdmin(config);
  boolean result = adminObj.isTableDisabled(tableObj);
  System.out.println("Table " + tableObj + " disabled ?" +
    result);
}
public void checkIfTableExists(String tableObj) throws
  IOException {
  config = HBaseConfiguration.create();
  HBaseAdmin adminObj = new HBaseAdmin(config);
  boolean result = adminObj.tableExists(tableObj);
  System.out.println("Table " + tableObj + " exists ?" +
    result);
}
public void shutdownCluster() throws IOException {
  config = HBaseConfiguration.create();
  HBaseAdmin adminObj = new HBaseAdmin(config);
  System.out.println("Shutting down..");
  adminObj.shutdown();
}
public void listAllTablesInHBase() throws IOException {
  config = HBaseConfiguration.create();
  HBaseAdmin adminObj = new HBaseAdmin(config);
  adminObj.listTables();
}
public void modifyTableColumn(String tableObj, String
  columnname, String descriptor) throws IOException {
  config = HBaseConfiguration.create();
  HBaseAdmin adminObj = new HBaseAdmin(config);
  adminObj.modifyColumn(tableObj, columnname, new
    HColumnDescriptor(descriptor));
}
public void modifyHBaseTable(String tableObj, String
  hbaseNewTableName) throws IOException {
  config = HBaseConfiguration.create();
```

```
    HBaseAdmin adminObj = new HBaseAdmin(config);
    adminObj.modifyTable(Bytes.toBytes(tableObj), new
      HTableDescriptor(hbaseNewTableName));
  }
  public void splitHBaseTable(String tableObj) throws IOException,
    InterruptedException {
    config = HBaseConfiguration.create();
    HBaseAdmin adminObj = new HBaseAdmin(config);
    adminObj.split(tableObj);
  }
  public void checkIfMasterRunning() throws
    MasterNotRunningException, ZooKeeperConnectionException {
    config = HBaseConfiguration.create();
    HBaseAdmin administer = new HBaseAdmin(config);
    System.out.println("Master running ? " +
      administer.isMasterRunning());
  }
}
```

The preceding code can perform all administration-related operations using the HBaseAdmin class. We need to pass the method name using < HBaseAdmin Object>.<method Name with arguments>.

Data operation code

Data operation code is all about adding a record, deleting a record, and getting a single record. It will also help in scanning the table and listing all records.

Let's see how we can build our own function to perform various tasks:

```
public void addOneRecordToTable(String tableObjName, String
  rowKey,
String colFamName, String columnName, String data) throws
  Exception
{
  try
  {
    HTable tableObj = new HTable(configurationObj, tableObjName);
    Put put = new Put(Bytes.toBytes(rowKey));
    put.add(Bytes.toBytes(colFamName), Bytes.toBytes(columnName),
      Bytes
    .toBytes(data));
    tableObj.put(put);
  }
  catch (IOException exception)
```

```
   {
      exception.printStackTrace();
   }
}
public  void delRecordFromTable(String tableObjName, String
   rowKey) throws IOException
{
   HTable tableObj = new HTable(configurationObj, tableObjName);
   List<Delete>list = new ArrayList<Delete>();
   Delete delObj = new Delete(rowKey.getBytes());
   list.add(delObj);
   tableObj.delete(list);
}
public  void getSingleRecordFromTable (String tableObjName, String
   rowKey) throws IOException
{
   HTable tableObj = new HTable(configurationObj, tableObjName);
   Get get = new Get(rowKey.getBytes());
   Result resultSet = tableObj.get(get);
   for(KeyValue keyVal : resultSet.raw())
   {
      System.out.println(new String(keyValue.getValue()));
   }
}
public void readAllRecordFromTable (String tableObjName)
{
   try
   {
      HTable tableObj = new HTable(configurationObj, tableObjName);
      Scan s = new Scan();
      ResultScanner resultScanerObj = tableObj.getScanner(s);
      for(Result resultObj:resultScanerObj)
      {
         for(KeyValue keyValue : resultObj.raw())
         {
            System.out.println(new String(keyValue.getQualifier()) +
               " "+keyValue.getFamily() + ":"+keyValue.getRow()+
               " :"+keyValue.getValue()+":"+keyValue.getTimestamp());
         }
      }
   }
   catch (IOException exception)
   {
      exception.printStackTrace();
   }
}
```

And we can call these methods in the main function as follows:

```
public static void main(String[] agrs) {
  try {
    String tablename = "logData";
    String[] familys = { "detail", "hostname" };
    hbaseDataOperationEg.getOneRecord(tablename, "zkb");
    hbaseDataOperationEg.getAllRecord(tablename);
  } catch (Exception e) {
    e.printStackTrace();
  }
}
```

The configuration parameter remains the same as we discussed earlier. We need to create configuration settings, and the other required parameters must be handled correctly.

MapReduce and HBase

HBase supports writing MapReduce jobs for processing data from the HBase table using the `org.apache.hadoop.hbase.mapreduce` package, which has lots of methods for the same. This also provides HBase MapReduce input and output formats that can be utilized in MapReduce jobs, a table indexing MapReduce job, and many other MapReduce utilities. It utilizes Hadoop MapReduce framework to do so.

The following is a list of MapReduce classes provided by HBase:

- `Import`: This utility is used to import sequence file from HDFS, which is exported by the `export` command.

- `ImportTsv`: This utility is used to import the **Tab-separated Value (TSV)** file using the MapReduce task.

- `CellCounter`: This counts the number of cells in the HBase table using the MapReduce job.

- `CopyTable`: This is used to copy table from one HBase cluster to another HBase cluster. The destination can be the same cluster or another cluster.

- `Driver`: This is the `Driver` class for MapReduce jobs in HBase.

- `Export`: This exports or writes data from an HBase table to a sequential file for backup on a HDFS location using the MapReduce job.

- `GroupingTableMapper`: This is used to extract grouping columns from the input record.

- `HFileOutputFormat2`: This is used to write HFiles.

- `HLogInputFormat`: This provides an input format for HLog files.

- `HRegionPartitioner<key, value>`: This partitions the output key to a group of keys.

- `IdentityTableMapper`: This passes the specified key and record to the Reduce phase.

- `IdentityTableReducer`: This is a convenience class that simply writes all values passed to the configured HBase table.

- `KeyValueSortReducer`: This emits sorted KeyValues.

- `LoadIncrementalHFiles`: This loads the output of `HFileOutputFormat` into an existing HBase table.

- `MultiTableInputFormat`: This converts HBase tabular data into a format that can be consumed by MapReduce.

- `MultiTableInputFormatBase`: This is a base class for `MultiTableInputFormats`.

- `MultiTableOutputFormat`: This is the Hadoop output format that writes into one or more HBase tables.

- `PutCombiner<K>`: This groups `Puts`.

- `PutSortReducer`: This emits a sorted list of `Puts`.

- `RowCounter`: This runs a MapReduce job to count rows in a specified HBase table.

- `SimpleTotalOrderPartitioner<value>`: This takes the start and end keys and uses this feature to figure out reduce key belongs to which partition.

- `TableInputFormat`: This converts the HBase tabular data into a format that can be consumed by MapReduce.

- `TableInputFormatBase`: This is the base class for `TableInputFormats`.

- `TableMapper<keyout, valueout>`: This extends the base `Mapper` class to add the required input key and value classes.

- `TableOutputFormat<KEY>`: This converts MapReduce output and writes it to an HBase table.

- `TableRecordReader`: This iterates over an HBase table data and key-value pairs of data.

- `TableReducer<keyin, valuein, keyout>`: This extends the basic `Reducer` class to add the required key and value I/O classes.

- `TableSnapshotInputFormat`: This is used to run a MapReduce over a table snapshot.
- `TableSplit`: This splits a table using the MapReduce job.
- `TextSortReducer`: This emits a sorted key-value pair.
- `TsvImporterMapper`: This writes content of an HBase table to files on HDFS.
- `TsvImporterTextMapper`: This writes table content to map output files.
- `WALPlayer`: This is used to replay WAL files using the MapReduce job.

> The updated and most recent MapReduce utilities can be found at `http://hbase.apache.org/apidocs/org/apache/hadoop/hbase/mapreduce/package-summary.html`.

We can run a MapReduce task using the following line of code:

```
hadoop jar ${HBASE_HOME}/hbase-0.90.0.jar
   <utility name from jar file > <list of parameters>
```

The utility names can be as follows:

- `completebulkload`: This is used for bulk loading data
- `copytable`: This is used to export a table from a cluster to peer cluster
- `export`: This exports a table on HDFS
- `import`: This imports exported data
- `importtsv`: This imports data that is in TSV format
- `rowcounter`: This counts the number of rows in an HBase table
- `verifyrep`: This is used to compare the data from tables in two different clusters

> More information about the Hadoop MapReduce framework can be found at `http://hadoop.apache.org/docs/r1.2.1/mapred_tutorial.html`.

Let's now look into a MapReduce code example for HBase. The following is the word count example that counts words in the HBase table:

```
import java.io.IOException;
import java.util.Iterator;
import java.util.StringTokenizer;
import org.apache.hadoop.conf.Configuration;
```

```java
import org.apache.hadoop.fs.Path;
import org.apache.hadoop.hbase.HBaseConfiguration;
import org.apache.hadoop.hbase.mapreduce.TableReducer;
import org.apache.hadoop.hbase.util.Bytes;
import org.apache.hadoop.io.IntWritable;
import org.apache.hadoop.io.LongWritable;
import org.apache.hadoop.io.Text;
import org.apache.hadoop.io.NullWritable;
import org.apache.hadoop.mapreduce.Job;
import org.apache.hadoop.mapreduce.Mapper;
import org.apache.hadoop.mapreduce.lib.input.FileInputFormat;
import org.apache.hadoop.mapreduce.lib.input.TextInputFormat;
import org.apache.hadoop.hbase.HColumnDescriptor;
import org.apache.hadoop.hbase.HTableDescriptor;
import org.apache.hadoop.hbase.client.HBaseAdmin;
import org.apache.hadoop.hbase.client.Put;
import org.apache.hadoop.hbase.mapreduce.TableOutputFormat;


public class hbaseMapRedExampleClaseeWorkCount {
  public static class Map extends Mapper<LongWritable, Text, Text,
    IntWritable> {
    private final static IntWritable count = new IntWritable(1);
    private Text textToEmit = new Text();
    public void map(LongWritable key, Text value, Context context)
      throws IOException, InterruptedException {
      StringTokenizer strTokenizerObj = new
        StringTokenizer(value.toString());
      while (strTokenizerObj.hasMoreTokens()) {
        textToEmit.set(strTokenizerObj.nextToken());
        context.write(textToEmit, count);
      }
    }
  }
  public static class Reduce extends TableReducer<Text,
    IntWritable, NullWritable> {
    public void reduce(Text key, Iterable<IntWritable> values,
      Context context) throws IOException, InterruptedException {
      int total = 0;
      Iterator<IntWritable> iterator = values.iterator();
      while (iterator.hasNext()) {
        total += iterator.next().get();
      }
      Put put = new Put(Bytes.toBytes(key.toString()));
      put.add(Bytes.toBytes("colFam"), Bytes.toBytes("count"),
        Bytes.toBytes(String.valueOf(total)));
```

```java
      context.write(NullWritable.get(), put);
      }
  }
  public static void createHBaseTable(String
    hbaseMapRedTestTableObj) throws IOException {
    HTableDescriptor tableDescriptorObj = new
      HTableDescriptor(hbaseMapRedTestTableObj);
    HColumnDescriptor column = new HColumnDescriptor("colFam");
    tableDescriptorObj.addFamily(column);
    Configuration configObj = HBaseConfiguration.create();
    configObj.set("hbase.zookeeper.quorum", "infinity");
    configObj.set("hbase.zookeeper.property.clientPort", "2222");
    HBaseAdmin hAdmin = new HBaseAdmin(configObj);
    if (hAdmin.tableExists(hbaseMapRedTestTableObj)) {
      System.out.println("Table exist !");
      hAdmin.disableTable(hbaseMapRedTestTableObj);
      hAdmin.deleteTable(hbaseMapRedTestTableObj);
    }
    System.out.println("Create Table" + hbaseMapRedTestTableObj);
    hAdmin.createTable(tableDescriptorObj);
  }
  public static void main(String[] args) throws Exception {
    String hbaseMapRedTestTableObj = "hbaseMapReduceTest";
    hbaseMapRedExampleClaseeWorkCount.createHBaseTable
      (hbaseMapRedTestTableObj);
    Configuration configObj = new Configuration();
    configObj.set("mapred.job.tracker", "infinity:9001");
    configObj.set("hbase.zookeeper.quorum", "infinity");
    configObj.set("hbase.zookeeper.property.clientPort", "2222");
    configObj.set(TableOutputFormat.OUTPUT_TABLE,
      hbaseMapRedTestTableObj);
    Job job = new Job(configObj, "HBase WordCount Map reduce");
    job.setJarByClass(hbaseMapRedExampleClaseeWorkCount.class);
    job.setMapperClass(Map.class);
    job.setReducerClass(Reduce.class);
    job.setMapOutputKeyClass(Text.class);
    job.setMapOutputValueClass(IntWritable.class);
    job.setInputFormatClass(TextInputFormat.class);
    job.setOutputFormatClass(TableOutputFormat.class);
    FileInputFormat.addInputPath(job, new
      Path("<hbasefilepath>"));
    System.exit(job.waitForCompletion(true) ? 0 : 1);
  }
}
```

We can write MapReduce code for HBase data for different scenarios, which will completely depend on the requirements. HBase stores data as a key-value pair, which is best for MapReduce.

 More on MapReduce in HBase and API uses can be found at the following links:

- `http://hbase.apache.org/book/mapreduce.example.html`
- `http://sujee.net/tech/articles/hadoop/hbase-map-reduce-freq-counter/`

RESTful services and Thrift services interface

These are the inbuilt interfaces provided by HBase so that clients can communicate using RESTful and Thrift calls.

REST service interfaces

Now, let's discuss the RESTful service and Thrift that HBase provides in order to contact HBase besides Java coding. Stargate is the server that provides RESTful service interface through Java package, `org.apache.hadoop.hbase.rest`. It internally runs an embedded Jetty servlet container to handle the request.

We can start it as follows:

```
hbase rest start -p <port to use>
```

The preceding command starts REStful services in the foreground. Alternatively, you can start it and send it to the background:

```
bin/hbase-daemon.sh start rest -p <port to use>
```

REStful services can be stopped with the following command:

```
bin/hbase-daemon.sh stop rest
```

HBase can handle all REST requests through `curl` or any computer languages that support web service such as PHP. The following is the `curl` request example:

```
curl -H "Accept: text/xml" http://localhost:8000/version
```

The preceding command will return the HBase version.

To delete a table, we can give a command as follows:

```
curl -v -X DELETE 'http://localhost:8080/test/schema' -H "Accept:
application/json"
```

The result can be fetched in XML or JSON and be parsed further.

> For more information, refer to the following links:
>
> - http://blog.cloudera.com/blog/2013/03/how-to-use-the-apache-hbase-rest-interface-part-1/
> - http://hbase.apache.org/apidocs/org/apache/hadoop/hbase/rest/package-summary.html

Thrift

The Thrift framework is provided by a Thrift server, which provides a way for scalable flexibility and interoperability across computer languages and services development. It builds an engine with the help of code generation, which works efficiently between HBase and C++, Java, Python, PHP, Ruby, Perl, and so on.

This service is provided by HBase using the `gthrough` package:

`org.apache.hadoop.hbase.thrift`

The Thrift service can be started like this:

`bin/hbase-daemon.sh start thrift`

And can be stopped like this:

`bin/hbase-daemon.sh stop thrift`

The following is the example for creating a table using Thrift in Python:

```python
from thrift.transport import TSocket
from thrift.protocol import TBinaryProtocol
from thrift.transport import TTransport
from hbase import Hbase
# Connects to HBase Thrift server
transport = TTransport.TBufferedTransport
(TSocket.TSocket(hostname, thriftport))
protocol = TBinaryProtocol.TBinaryProtocolAccelerated(transport)
# Create and open the client connection
client = Hbase.Client(protocol)
```

```
transport.open()
client.createTable
(tablename, [Hbase.ColumnDescriptor(name=cfname)])
transport.close()
```

The client can be built in Python or PHP or any language that supports Thrift.

Complete details of the Thrift service and updated APIs can be found at
the following links:

- http://nousefor.net/55/2011/12/php/hbase-and-
  hive-thrift-php-client/
- https://hbase.apache.org/apidocs/org/apache/
  hadoop/hbase/thrift/package-summary.html#package_
  description
- http://hbase.apache.org/book/thrift.html
- http://blog.cloudera.com/blog/2013/12/how-
  to-use-the-hbase-thrift-interface-part-2-
  insertinggetting-rows/
- http://blog.cloudera.com/blog/2013/09/how-to-use-
  the-hbase-thrift-interface-part-1/

Coding for HDFS operations

Let's now look at some code to perform operations on the HDFS file system and
interact with Hadoop, such as copying a file from the local to HDFS and vice versa,
deleting a file, and reading a file from HDFS:

```
import org.apache.hadoop.conf.Configuration;
import org.apache.hadoop.fs.BlockLocation;
import org.apache.hadoop.fs.FSDataInputStream;
import org.apache.hadoop.fs.FSDataOutputStream;
import org.apache.hadoop.fs.FileStatus;
import org.apache.hadoop.fs.FileSystem;
import org.apache.hadoop.fs.Path;
import org.apache.hadoop.hdfs.DistributedFileSystem;
import org.apache.hadoop.hdfs.protocol.DatanodeInfo;
import java.io.BufferedInputStream;
import java.io.BufferedOutputStream;
import java.io.File;
import java.io.FileInputStream;
import java.io.FileOutputStream;
import java.io.IOException;
```

```
import java.io.InputStream;
import java.io.OutputStream;

//To copy a file from local drive to hdfs
public void copyLocalFileToHDFS (String source, String dest)
  throws IOException {
  Configuration conf = new Configuration();
  conf.addResource(new Path
    ("<hadoop conf dir path>/core-site.xml"));
  conf.addResource(new Path
    ("<hadoop conf dir path>/hdfs-site.xml"));
  conf.addResource(new Path
    ("<hadoop conf dir path>/mapred-site.xml"));
  FileSystem fileSystem = FileSystem.get(conf);
  Path srcPath = new Path(source);
  Path dstPath = new Path(dest);
  if (!(fileSystem.exists(dstPath))) {
    System.out.println("No such destination " + dstPath);
    return;
  }
  String filename = source.substring(source.lastIndexOf('/') + 1,
    source.length());
  try{
    fileSystem.copyFromLocalFile(srcPath, dstPath);
    System.out.println("File " + filename + "copied to " + dest);
  }catch(Exception e){
    System.err.println("Exception caught! :" + e);
    System.exit(1);
  }finally{
  fileSystem.close();
  }
}

//copy a file from HDFS to local drive
public void copyHDFSFileToLocal (String source, String dest)
  throws IOException {
  Configuration conf = new Configuration();
  conf.addResource(new Path
    ("<hadoop conf dir path>/core-site.xml"));
  conf.addResource(new Path
    ("<hadoop conf dir path>/hdfs-site.xml"));
  conf.addResource(new Path
    ("<hadoop conf dir path>/mapred-site.xml"));
  FileSystem fileSystem = FileSystem.get(conf);
  Path srcPath = new Path(source);
```

```
    Path dstPath = new Path(dest);
    if (!(fileSystem.exists(dstPath))) {
      System.out.println("No such destination " + dstPath);
      return;
    }
    String filename = source.substring(source.lastIndexOf('/') + 1,
      source.length());
    try{
      fileSystem.copyToLocalFile(srcPath, dstPath)
      System.out.println("File " + filename + "copied to " + dest);
    }catch(Exception e){
      System.err.println("Exception caught! :" + e);
      System.exit(1);
    }finally{
      fileSystem.close();
    }
  }

  //delete a file from hdfs
  public void deleteAfileOnHDFS(String file) throws IOException {
    Configuration conf = new Configuration();
    conf.addResource(new Path
      ("<hadoop conf dir path>/core-site.xml"));
    conf.addResource(new Path
      ("<hadoop conf dir path>/hdfs-site.xml"));
    conf.addResource(new Path
      ("<hadoop conf dir path>/mapred-site.xml"));
    FileSystem fileSystem = FileSystem.get(conf);
    Path path = new Path(file);
    if (!fileSystem.exists(path)) {
      System.out.println("File " + file + " does not exists");
    return;
    }
    fileSystem.delete(new Path(file), true);
    fileSystem.close();
}

  //get block locations of a file on HDFS
  public void getBlockLocationsOfHDFSFile(String source) throws
    IOException{
    Configuration conf = new Configuration();
    conf.addResource(new Path
      ("<hadoop conf dir path>/core-site.xml"));
    conf.addResource(new Path
      ("<hadoop conf dir path>/hdfs-site.xml"));
```

```
    conf.addResource(new Path
      ("<hadoop conf dir path>/mapred-site.xml"));
    FileSystem fileSystem = FileSystem.get(conf);
    Path srcPath = new Path(source);
    if (!(ifExists(srcPath))) {
      System.out.println("No such destination " + srcPath);
      return;
    }
    String filename = source.substring(source.lastIndexOf('/') + 1,
      source.length());
    FileStatus fileStatus = fileSystem.getFileStatus(srcPath);
    BlockLocation[] blkLocations = fileSystem.getFileBlockLocations
      (fileStatus, 0, fileStatus.getLen());
    int blkCount = blkLocations.length;
    System.out.println("File :" + filename + "stored at:");
    for (int i=0; i < blkCount; i++) {
      String[] hosts = blkLocations[i].getHosts();
      System.out.format("Host %d: %s %n", i, hosts);
    }
  }


  //create a directory on HDFS
  public void createFileOnHDFS(String dir) throws IOException {
    Configuration conf = new Configuration();
    conf.addResource(new Path
      ("<hadoop conf dir path>/core-site.xml"));
    conf.addResource(new Path
      ("<hadoop conf dir path>/hdfs-site.xml"));
    conf.addResource(new Path
      ("<hadoop conf dir path>/mapred-site.xml"));
    FileSystem fileSystem = FileSystem.get(conf);
    Path path = new Path(dir);
    if (fileSystem.exists(path)) {
      System.out.println("Dir " + dir + " already exists!");
      return;
    }
    fileSystem.mkdirs(path);
    fileSystem.close();
  }
```

Likewise, we can create a function like this in our own HDFS client and perform similar operations. We can use all the APIs provided by Hadoop at https://hadoop.apache.org/docs/current/api/overview-summary.html.

Some advance topics in brief

In this section, we will discuss some advanced topics useful for developers that will enable them to interact with HBase more closely.

Coprocessors

Coprocessors are similar to Linux kernel modules. They provide a way to run server-level code against locally stored data. This provides a very powerful functionality. It runs in the process on each RegionServer. All the regions contain references to the coprocessor implementation classes associated. It can be loaded either from local JAR files on the RegionServer class path or through the HDFS class loader. These are not designed to be used by the users of HBase but by developers who add additional functionalities to HBase. These can be used for server-side operations such as region splits, major compactions, and client-side operations such as create, read, update, and delete operations, and also can be used to implement a custom use case such as user-defined functionalities.

Types of coprocessors

The following are the types of coprocessors:

- **Coprocessor**: This provides region life cycle management such as region open, close, split, flush, compact operations, and so on.

- **RegionObserver**: This provides a hook for monitoring table operations from the client side such as table get, put, scan, delete, and so on.

- **Endpoint**: This provides on-demand triggers for arbitrary functions to be executed at a region. For example, column aggregation at RegionServer.

For more information, we can refer to the following links:
- `https://hbase.apache.org/apidocs/org/apache/hadoop/hbase/coprocessor/package-summary.html`
- `http://hbase-coprocessor-experiments.blogspot.in`
- `http://www.slideshare.net/cloudera/3-h-base-coprocessors-hbase-con-may-2012`

Bloom filters

The bloom filters are a special kind of filter that are used when there is a lot of data to be avoided while scanning, and are also to skip internal data lookup to speed up the scanning process. This enables us to discard the data that we do not need. These are stored in the metadata of HFiles when it is written and then never needed to be updated as HFiles are immutable. These filters implement folding to keep the size down and combinatorial generation to speed up their creation. When an HFile is opened during deployment of regions to a RegionServer, the bloom filter is loaded into the memory.

> The full internal architecture and implementation can be found at https://issues.apache.org/jira/secure/ attachment/12444007/Bloom_Filters_in_HBase.pdf.

The Lily project

You can find the following definition at http://www.lilyproject.org/lily/ index.html:

> *"Lily is a data management platform combining planet-sized data storage, indexing and search with on-line, real-time usage tracking, audience analytics and content recommendations. It's a one-stop-platform for any organization confronted with Big Data challenges that seeks rapid implementation, rock-solid performance at scale, and efficiency at management."*

> *"Lily unifies Apache HBase, Hadoop, and Solr into a comprehensively integrated, interactive data platform with easy-to-use access APIs; a high-level data model and schema language; flexible, real-time indexing; and the expressive search power of Apache Solr. Best of all, Lily is open source, allowing anyone to explore and learn what Lily can do."*

Features

Lily provides the following features::

- Easy to use through a high-level schema supporting rich and mixed, structured and unstructured data sets

- It is developer-friendly, powerful, and expressive REST and Java API

- A flexible, configurable indexing system, supporting real-time indexing into Solr

 The documentation to configure, install, and get started with it can be found at `http://docs.ngdata.com/lily-docs-current/414-lily.html`.

Summary

In this chapter, we discussed various data operation coding using Java, different REST and Thrift services and how to use them, MapReduce in HBase, and a sample code. We learned a bit about coprocessors; bloom filters, interfaces, classes, and the exceptions provided by HBase in its packages. In the next chapter, we will discuss use cases using HBase in industry, and the architecture of these use cases.

10
HBase Use Cases

In this chapter, we will walk through some HBase user cases, zoom in the project layout and design to understand how to utilize HBase for different business usages, and provide some references to you for further development.

We will see the use case and architecture used at:

- Facebook
- Groupon
- Pinterest
- LongTail Video

This chapter will also show how these leading entities are using HBase for their project and the architecture of the project.

HBase in industry today

With the increase in demand for Big Data day by day in order to solve the problems comprising planet-size data, HBase is one of the players due to its characteristic of persistent read performance. Using these systems, one can store and analyze data in coordination with various other tools.

Also features such as HBase running on cloud and expanding and reducing on demand will enable even small-scale companies to use its services. With the increasing demand of data storage space, the need to process it and represent unstructured data into a structured format can be achieved by HBase.

The new sub and open projects that are being created, which enables HBase to support SQL queries (Phoenix), will surely boost and prepare conventional SQL developers to perform queries on HBase. This provides us with a facility to query faster than any other relational database system with the data of terabytes and petabytes' size.

The future of HBase against relational databases

It would be wrong to say that NoSQL, a column-based database, will replace the RDBMS. HBase is still evolving and it cannot be used for all the use cases. There will always be a need for different types of database to work in coordination with each other satisfying different use cases to build a complete production environment.

However, the new features of high availability, almost consistent reads, ability to store and retrieve petabytes of data, and support of various evolving open source tools to fill up the existing gaps will take HBase and other NoSQL databases very far for sure. We have just started looking at the power of these systems and are yet to understand and implement real-life use cases with enormous amount of data.

So, for sure, Hadoop plus HBase and other subprojects are the future of data warehousing and massive processing.

Some real-world project examples' use cases

In this section, we will list out use cases of HBase being used in the industry today. References and more details can be found at links provided in the *Useful links and references* section at the end of the chapter.

HBase at Facebook

Facebook, as you all know, is a social utility that connects people with friends and others who work, study, and live around them. Facebook uses HBase mainly to power their messages infrastructure. The following are the services where Facebook uses HBase:

- Messages between users
- Chats
- E-mails
- SMS

Choosing HBase

The following are the reasons why Facebook chooses HBase:

- Provides high write throughput
- Good random read performance compared to other DBs

- Horizontal scalability
- Automatic failover
- Strong consistency
- Benefits of HDFS such as fault tolerant, scalable, checksums, and MapReduce

HBase acts like a caching layer on top of Hadoop when bundled these two together, faster data process compare with other NoSQL + Hadoop.

Storing in HBase

Facebook uses HBase to store data. The following are the types of data that are stored in HBase:

- Small messages
- Message metadata (thread/message indices)
- Search index

Facebook also use Haystack (a software that runs on a single machine and stores data without replication; it only cares about local aggregated blob storage, concentrating upon reducing disk seeks, and speeding up file retrieval) to store attachments and large messages.

The architecture of a Facebook message

The following is a diagrammatical representation of how things work:

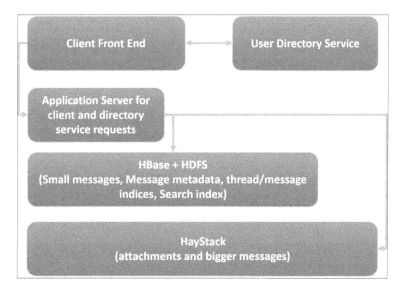

In this process flow, a client asks the user directory service for the user details, then after getting the detail of the user, the client sends the request to the application server, which may be a Tomcat machine, running a custom application.

The application server using a custom service HBase index is searched for the user-related cell from where a message can be written, appended, or retrieved, and for the attachments the Haystack is searched.

Facts and figures

Let's have a look at some of the eye-opening facts and figures:

- Talking about Facebook message statistics, number of messages sent and received per day is more than 6 billion
- Talking about traffic to HBase, have a look at the following points:
  - Almost 100 billion read/writes per day
  - At peak time, more or less 1.5 million operations per second
  - About 55 percent reads and 45 percent writes
  - More than 2 petabytes of data and with replication, it's more than 6 petabytes
  - Data is compressed using **Lempel-Ziv-Oberhumer (LZO)** compression
  - And the data is growing around 300 terabytes per month
- Schema changes during production
- Heavy use of bulk import

Let's now see some other use cases in the industry.

HBase at Pinterest

Pinterest is deployed on **Amazon Elastic Compute Cloud (EC2)**. Pinterest uses a follow model in which the user follows other users. It needs to update the feed data for every user as soon as a follower makes changes in a pin or updates a pin. This is the most classic social-media kind of application.

This happens for hundreds of millions of pins per month and about a billion writes per day. So the following are the specification of implementation:

- They choose a wide schema where each user's following feed is a single row in HBase
- This exploits the sorting order within columns as each user wants to see the latest in his/her feed

- They have increased the per region MemStore size to 512 MB MemStore which leads to 40 MB HFile instead of the smaller 8 MB file for default MemStore; this leads to less-frequent compactions

- Maintains **mean time to recovery** (**MTTR**) of less than 2 minutes by reducing various timeout settings such as socket, connect, and stale node.

The layout architecture

Let's now see the basic layout architecture. The following layout represents the follower and the followee relationship:

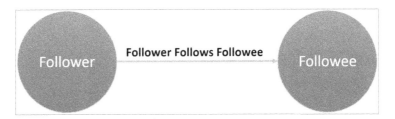

And according to this structure, it forms a kind of graph inside. As you can see in the following diagram, it shows the path or writes in the system. Internally, there is a single row for each user in HBase and all the followers' and followees' information is stored in it.

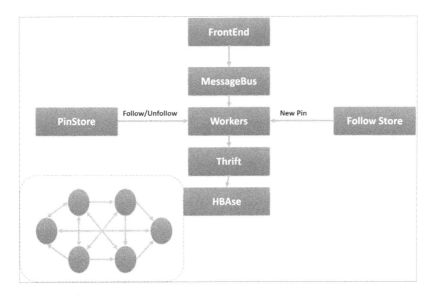

This is the HBase architecture that Pinterest uses to store hundreds and thousands of pins per month.

HBase at Groupon

Groupon is a deal-of-the-day website that features discounted gift certificates usable at local or national companies. Groupon was launched in November 2008. At Groupon, there are two requirements:

- Notify users about the deals via an e-mail
- Provide good user experience on the website

When they started off, they used Hadoop MapReduce jobs for e-mail deal delivery and used MySQL for their online application. Now, they have started relevance and a personalization system, both on HBase. They use a very wide schema in HBase as one column family for user history and profile and another for e-mail history.

The layout architecture

Now, let's see their read/write and architecture flow:

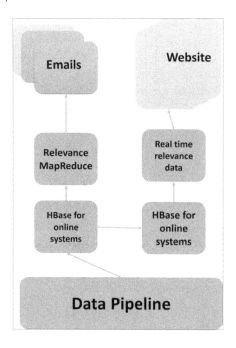

The data pipeline collects the data and keeps on writing to HBase, which is used for offline purposes such as sending e-mails from where the data is replicated to the HBase cluster, which is there for online relevance suggestions on the website.

The following are some of the optimization they performed:

- Presplit tables
- Increased lease timeout
- Increased scanner timeout
- Increased region size to 10 GB
- Keep less number of regions per region servers
- For heavy write jobs, they set the following values:

    ° `hbase.hregion.memstore.block.multiplier` to 4

    ° `hbase.hregion.memstore.flush.size` to `134217728`

    ° `hbase.hstore.blockingstorefiles` to `100`

    ° `hbase.zookeeper.useMulti` to `false` (for stable replication)

They performed all these changes in order to optimize and make HBase suit their requirement and this was done after evaluating the productivity and performance of the cluster.

HBase at LongTail Video

LongTail Video company provides JW Player, which is an online video player used by nearly 2 million websites. They are completely deployed on AWS and as such use HBase and EMR from Amazon.

Their requirements are:

- Very fast queries across datasets
- There should be a support for date-range queries
- Ability to store a huge amount of aggregated data
- There should be flexibility in dimensions used for rollup tables

HBase fits very well on these requirements. They use full-fledged Python shop so use HappyBase and have Thrift running on all the nodes of the HBase cluster for reading and writing.

Some statistics about them are as follows:

- 156 million unique viewers
- 1.04 billion video stream
- 3 TB compressed data per month and 12-15 TB uncompressed data per month

The layout architecture

This is a diagrammatical representation of the architecture:

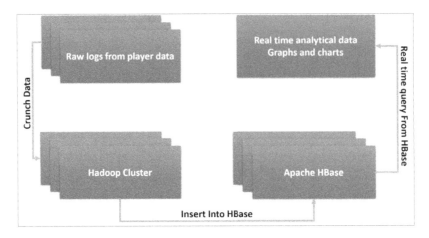

HBase at Aadhaar (UIDAI)

UIDAI is a government organization of India that provides unique identification to Indian nationals. At UIDAI, all the open source software such as Hadoop, HBase, and Hive are being used. HBase is used to store data about the residents.

The layout architecture

Let's see the architecture of the project that is available on the Internet:

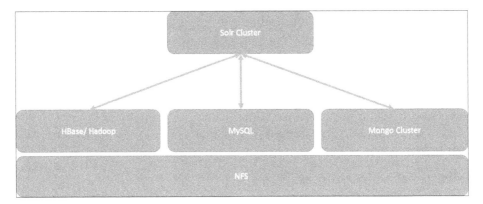

There are some use cases and the architecture flow of the use cases that are being used in different companies in the industry today. This trend is increasing day by day with more people coming and including this technology and implementing it in their project requirement.

Hadoop and HBase and other Big Data components today are providing a complete infrastructure for a production system with data migration tools, data mapping tools, and some add-on open source projects.

Likewise, according to our requirements, we can first design the architecture of our project based on the components and the type of functionalities required, and we can choose from a wide variety of Hadoop and its subproject components.

Useful links and references

You can always use these links for reference.

The following are the use-cases-related links:

- http://hbasecon.com/archive.html
- https://www.facebook.com/UsingHbase
- http://www.slideshare.net/brizzzdotcom/facebook-messages-hbase
- http://www.slideshare.net/cloudera/case-studies-session-3b
- http://www.slideshare.net/cloudera/long-tailvideo-hbasecon2013-24035928
- http://www.slideshare.net/cloudera/operations-session-1

These are some other references:

- https://github.com/larsgeorge/hbase-schema-manager/tree/master
- http://wiki.apache.org/hadoop/HelpContents
- http://www.jnbridge.com/jn/blog/tag/hbase/
- http://ianvarley.com/coding/HBaseSchema_HBaseCon2012.pdf
- http://www.slideshare.net/cloudera/5-h-base-schemahbasecon2012
- http://hbase.apache.org/book/schema.casestudies.html

The following links will be useful for schema designing:

- `http://www.slideshare.net/amansk/hbase-schema-design-big-data-techcon-boston`
- `http://0b4af6cdc2f0c5998459-c0245c5c937c5dedcca3f1764ecc9b2f.r43.cf2.rackcdn.com/9353-login1210_khurana.pdf`
- `http://www.slideshare.net/amansk/hbase-schema-design-big-data-techcon-boston`
- `http://hbase.apache.org/book/schema.casestudies.html`
- `http://www.slideshare.net/cloudera/5-h-base-schemahbasecon2012`
- `https://www.youtube.com/watch?v=_HLoH_PgrLk`
- `http://ianvarley.com/coding/HBaseSchema_HBaseCon2012.pdf`

The following are the links to HBase books and references:

- `http://hbase.apache.org/book.html`
- `https://www.youtube.com/results?search_query=hbase`
- `https://www.youtube.com/results?search_query=hadoop`

Summary

In this chapter, we discussed the future aspect of HBase and the different use cases being implemented in the industry using HBase, its process flow, and architecture.

Today, the need of HBase is growing rapidly and we can get the list of companies whose projects are powered by HBase at `http://wiki.apache.org/hadoop/Hbase/PoweredBy`.

After reading this book, you should be able to move forward and design the use cases, performing administrative tasks and writing codes for HBase. Furthermore, the reader can always visit HBase Wiki, the HBase Apache website, and HBase source site for more updated and recent information.

HBase use has grown a lot but it still has a long way to go.

Index

Thank you for buying
Learning HBase

About Packt Publishing

Packt, pronounced 'packed', published its first book "*Mastering phpMyAdmin for Effective MySQL Management*" in April 2004 and subsequently continued to specialize in publishing highly focused books on specific technologies and solutions.

Our books and publications share the experiences of your fellow IT professionals in adapting and customizing today's systems, applications, and frameworks. Our solution based books give you the knowledge and power to customize the software and technologies you're using to get the job done. Packt books are more specific and less general than the IT books you have seen in the past. Our unique business model allows us to bring you more focused information, giving you more of what you need to know, and less of what you don't.

Packt is a modern, yet unique publishing company, which focuses on producing quality, cutting-edge books for communities of developers, administrators, and newbies alike. For more information, please visit our website: www.packtpub.com.

About Packt Open Source

In 2010, Packt launched two new brands, Packt Open Source and Packt Enterprise, in order to continue its focus on specialization. This book is part of the Packt Open Source brand, home to books published on software built around Open Source licenses, and offering information to anybody from advanced developers to budding web designers. The Open Source brand also runs Packt's Open Source Royalty Scheme, by which Packt gives a royalty to each Open Source project about whose software a book is sold.

Writing for Packt

We welcome all inquiries from people who are interested in authoring. Book proposals should be sent to author@packtpub.com. If your book idea is still at an early stage and you would like to discuss it first before writing a formal book proposal, contact us; one of our commissioning editors will get in touch with you.

We're not just looking for published authors; if you have strong technical skills but no writing experience, our experienced editors can help you develop a writing career, or simply get some additional reward for your expertise.

Hadoop Cluster Deployment

ISBN: 978-1-78328-171-8   Paperback: 126 pages

Construct a modern Hadoop data platform effortlessly and gain insights into how to manage clusters efficiently

1. Choose the hardware and Hadoop distribution that best suits your needs.

2. Get more value out of your Hadoop cluster with Hive, Impala, and Sqoop.

3. Learn useful tips for performance optimization and security.

Big Data Analytics with R and Hadoop

ISBN: 978-1-78216-328-2   Paperback: 238 pages

Set up an integrated infrastructure of R and Hadoop to turn your data analytics into Big Data analytics

1. Write Hadoop MapReduce within R.

2. Learn data analytics with R and the Hadoop platform.

3. Handle HDFS data within R.

4. Understand Hadoop streaming with R.

5. Encode and enrich datasets into R.

Please check **www.PacktPub.com** for information on our titles

www.ingramcontent.com/pod-product-compliance
Lightning Source LLC
LaVergne TN
LVHW081333050326
832903LV00024B/1143